ANOTHER MARINE REPORTING, SIR!

Sea Stories: A memoir told anonymously

The Marines of TBS Class Alpha 1-80

Proceeds from ANOTHER MARINE REPORTING, SIR! will be donated to charitable organizations supporting Marine's and their families.

ADZ Press

San Diego, CA

Copyright © 2022 by TBS Class **Alpha 1-80**

All rights reserved. No part of this publication may not be reproduced, distributed, or transmitted in any form or by any means, without prior written permission.

Published in the United States by:
ADZ Press
3650 Third Avenue Suite 3
San Diego, CA 92103
www.JrStrayveJR.com

Cover Art: Chris Ryder of Witty Pics
Formatted I NOIR by Book Design

Another Marine Reporting, Sir! /TBS Class ALPHA 1-80 -- 1st ed.
ISBN 978-1-7371243-4-4 Paperback
ISBN 978-1-7371243-3-7 eBook

ANOTHER MARINE REPORTING, SIR!

WHAT READERS ARE SAYING ABOUT: ANOTHER MARINE REPORTING, SIR!

I thought this was a great read! Loved the fact that the stories were quick paced and not too long. I kept reading and reading, looking forward to the next one. - Tom C.

This memoir had me crying, laughing, and looking for a Marine to shake their hand. What a roller-coaster life. - RDF

These stories show why Marines are the toughest and the best. Smart, fast thinking, and acting. I wish I would have had a group of guys to bond with when I was in the military, Great book! I am planning on using it as a stocking stuffer. - TWY

...If I was going to go into the Marines, I would be nervous and excited. It seems like anything and everything good and bad happens with them. Just think, none of this was made up. Yikes! Thank you for your service gentlemen. - TM

This memoir has so many varied stories. I was pulled into so many of them. Easy to tell they came from the heart. It was interesting seeing the different writing styles, but it worked. I would recommend this book to anyone who doesn't have their head stuck in the sand and doesn't need a 'safe space' to read about real life. - JTW

Inspirational! I love these guys and their stories. Heroes! - HYO

In Honor of all Marine Corps Veterans

"There's no such thing as a former Marine."

– General James F. Amos

35th Commandant of the Marine Corps

Contents

FORWARD 1

Introduction 3

A Lesson in Marine Corps Philosophy 7

A Wedding Day Surprise 11

Adherence to Orders 15

Adventures as Officer of the Day 17

Ax Qualification 21

Bigger Than Our Paychecks 25

Bouncer 31

Brother I Never Knew 33

Butt Shot 37

Candidate Santa Ana 41

Captain DD 43

Cleaning the Series Office or Unintended Consequences 45

Condition One Alpha 49

Collective Let Down 53

Dead Sea 57

Desert Baptisms in Kuwait, Desert Storm, 1991 61

Disbursing Office 63

Does Anyone Have A Question?..69

Drop In Maui Weekends 73

Duck Soup 75

Dynamite 79

Earning the Title Marine.......................................83

Endurance Run 85

Everybody Needs A Story 89

Exotic Flame Dance 97

Field Day..99

Funerals for Two Friends 103

Gamma Goat Garage 109

Ground Round 115

Happy Birthday USMC..119

Health and Comfort... 123

Hot Dog Convincers 127

How Do You Spell Relief? 131

How I Got My Call Sign 135

Hungarian Good Luck Dance 139

Into the Dark... 143

Impractical Joke 145

It's a Dog's Life 151

Know Your Marines.. 155

Leinie Adventure 161

Lesson Learned 165

Life in the Fast Lane 169

Look a Cruise Missile between our toes! 173

LPA 175

Lt. Rock 179

Man in the Box 183

Marine Corps Career Ender? 187

Meeting General Gray 191

Micronesia Presidential Inauguration 193

Near Death Experiences in the F-4 Phantom 199

No Photos, Please 209

Nothing Lower 215

Olongapo Oil Wrestling 219

On the Blood of Aviators 221

Operation Bear Hunt '85 223

Over My Dead Body 227

Picking Up an ST1 231

PMO Revenge 235

Policing the BEQ 241

Power of Attorney 245

Propeller Head 249

Purrsonal Friends of Mine 253

Rib Buster, Career in the Crapper 261

Sea Bat 267

Skiing the Atlantic 273

Spring Butt Bingo 279

Stuck Tanks at MCCRES, Camp Ripley, MN 283

Support from "Tabasco Mac" 289

Tailhook '91 295

The Camera 297

The Cost of Doing Business 301

The Greatest of These is Loyalty 309

The Hole Story 315

The Immaculate Autorotation 319

The Pōhakuloa Tale 323

The Price For Peace 329

The Sands of Iwo Jima 333

The "Shell" Slides Downhill 335

The Streets of Beirut 339

The Voice of Peace 343

Turkish Prison 347

Track Guards Report 351

Two Weddings and a Funeral 357

Unarmed Peaceful Cubans 363

Unlucky Hog Board 369

Urgent Fury 375

Wrong Way Jose! 383

VIP Visit 387

Visual Aids 391

ABOUT THE AUTHORS 401

ADZ PRESS BOOKS 403

FORWARD

When we arrived in Quantico that October of 1979 as new 2nd Lieutenants, we were full of enthusiasm, pride, anticipation and many were nervous. While our nation was at peace during those six months at TBS, the world was tense as the Vietnam War was not far behind our rearview mirror. The Cold War raged on, and Iran was holding a number of Americans hostage, mostly U.S. Marines. We could not wait to get in the fight.

When we reunited in 2021, the world was engulfed in the COVID 19 pandemic, our country had been at war for nearly 20 years, and the Iraq and Afghanistan wars were no longer front page news. It was a different world.

As Marines have done for centuries, we remained constant. We instantly reconnected with each other, told old tales, and basically recounted the last 40 years of our lives. Many stories were distant memories, others we had never heard before. Time and our ages may have embellished these memories.

However, the stories were never the point. Being with each other, reminiscing with our old comrades, being around Marines whose warrior history was indelibly part of each of ours is why we travelled from across the country to meet in Virginia. While cheerfulness and camaraderie ruled the reunion, we remembered those who were unable to be with us, and those who were now in a better place.

Reality is that many of us will never see each other again. We were fortunate to have had this time together, but Father Time never rests. The news is not dire however, as long as there is a Marine Corps, Alpha 1-80 will live on. We can no longer pass the PFT, or fit in our Alphas. We have grayed. Our class picture depicting one hundred and sixty-two young, strong, and proud 2nd Lieutenants of Marines will never age, and will always hang in the halls of the Basic School.

I hope you enjoy the stories from the members of our Basic School Class, Alpha 1-80 (TBS A-180). The stories are personal memoirs and not an official history or reflection of Marine Corps policies, either from that period or currently. But they are ours. Enjoy.

Semper Fidelis

Juan G. Ayala
Major General (USMC Retired)

INTRODUCTION

In April of 1980, a bunch of Marine Corps officers graduated from The Basic School (TBS) in Quantico, Virginia. Our company's name was Alpha 1-80. We were an all-male class, with only three platoons compared to the normal four-platoon companies; about one hundred of us completed the training and graduated.

This all began as a reunion. I had met with Jerry Sneed and told him that our classmate, Jake Leinenkugel, had suggested that we "get the band back together." Jerry agreed. In early 2019 he called me and floated the idea of putting together a 40th reunion for our Basic School class (Alpha 1-80), to be held in conjunction with the graduation of Alpha Company 2020. We began searching for class members and quickly picked up Mark Haskett and Terry Hand along the way. With the help of our old Cruise Book – and the internet – the four of us found nearly everyone in the class and had the reunion set for April of 2020, but COVID shut everything down and our reunion got postponed. There was plenty of interest in getting together, but we figured that would wane as the months went by, so Terry decided to hold Zoom calls periodically to keep up momentum for the reunion and just for the fun of getting together, even if only virtually.

On these Zoom calls we began to share stories of our lives, particularly of our time in the Corps. Some were funny, some were poignant, and some were nostalgic. There were only twenty or so guys on the call, and, thinking the rest of the class would love to hear some of the tales, I began to ask that they write down their stories and email them to me. Initially, I planned to simply share some of them on our Facebook page for the others to see, but as they started to pile up, I thought maybe we could format them and, when we got enough, we could share them all as a book for the class.

Then someone had an idea: as a way to give back to the Marine Corps, which taught us everything and made us into leaders, we could give our book to a charitable organization that could use our stories to do some good for Marines.

Through the process of putting this book together, we have learned that our Marine Corps is unique to the times in which we lived. We are not the Marines of WWII, of Korea or Vietnam. We did not see long deployments in war zones. For the most part, we are not the Marines of Iraq or Afghanistan. We are mostly Cold War Marines, a few of whom saw action in Grenada or Beirut and, even fewer, in the Gulf War. They didn't make movies about our time in the Corps, but we trained feverishly and played even harder. We saw things and did things that leave our civilian friends agape. We were gentlemen and animals. We roamed the world, and it was our playground. We were young and invincible as are all Marines of every era, but our time was our time. We know the feeling of walking into a room and having everyone just stop measuring because they all know who "the man" is. We also stood and wept over the graves of those just as strong and just as invincible as we were, knowing it could easily have been us. We brought fear to our enemies, but we kept some for ourselves. We went to dangerous places and lived close to the edge. When we left the Corps, we all felt the lack of camaraderie, of belonging, in our civilian lives. No one ever has your six out in the real world.

We learned much, and in the following pages we hope that we can convey something of what it was like to be a United States Marine

Officer during our times. This compilation is a series of stories from our Marine Corps experiences. We're geezers now at the time of writing and our memories may not be crystal clear, but for the most part, all of these things happened – most of them surprised us at the time, and many of them shocked us. We hope you'll enjoy these stories and maybe even take some of our life experiences and make them useful or remembered in your own life and your own travels.

There are abbreviations, acronyms, and unfamiliar words that you'll no doubt encounter in these tales. However, most or all of them won't affect your understanding of the story as a whole, so don't get worried or frustrated with the author if you don't know what they mean.

A LESSON IN MARINE CORPS PHILOSOPHY

Land navigation courses: terrain maps, compasses, objectives, obstacles, navigation markers, wooded terrain, undulating terrain, open terrain, fingers, bodies of water, unmarked roads, intermittent streams; all a part of the "basics" of being a competent Marine officer – and, evidently, a good philosopher.

Marines are practical in their philosophical leanings – perhaps more like Aristotle if you really stretch the analogy. Preparing for war and destroying an enemy enforces a certain simplistic dualism: winning, good, losing, bad. The empirical and practical dominates. No time to ponder platonic abstractions and contemplate how to best articulate conceptual theories. Do something, even if it isn't perfect.

My first introduction to the practicality of Marine philosophy occurred in the beautiful woods surrounding The Basic School in Quantico, Virginia in the Fall of 1979, just as the trees changed colors in the crisp days of October and November. Classes on map reading, terrain identification, and compass orientation were followed by searches in the woods for brightly colored ammo boxes stuck on poles with numbers painted on them. Finding these prizes during the daytime was one thing, but it was the night navigation course that introduced me to one of my first and most profound Marine Corps philosophical tenets: "A Marine officer is never lost, only temporarily disoriented."

I would find myself repeating that phrase quite frequently until I convinced myself of its validity – despite the difficulty of distinguishing between "lost" and "disoriented" at times. Strangely enough, it worked. From that fall forward, in my Marine officer career and even afterward, I have never been lost – regardless of how disoriented I may have felt at times. Aristotle had nothing on the Marines!

1981 – I am due to rotate back to the States from Okinawa, Japan and have been contacting my assignment officer in Washington, DC to determine which billets stateside I might prefer. "Well, lieutenant, there is this billet open in 2nd Anglico, but you would need to go to jump school and perhaps aerial observation school," he said. My reply: "Sounds great!" I mean how many opportunities in my life will I have to take my artillery skills to the air and apply them? Jumping out of a plane? Can't be too hard. Gravity does most of the work – a profound philosophical insight of immense practicality!

In a few weeks, I find myself in Aerial Observation training under the excellent tutelage of a CWO4 Hunter. (Gunner Hunter would later be taken captive by the Iraqis under Saddam Hussein in the first Gulf War after having his OV-10 hit and forced to eject. I watched with a pit in my stomach on TV as I recognized him in the line-up of pilots and observers captured and, about a month later, felt a weight lifted when he was on TV again, being brought home.)

For a guy whose first trip on an airplane was from Little Rock, Arkansas to Washington, DC to enter OCS, finding myself in Aerial Observation training was a giant leap. How was I to know that I would have to prove I could swim in my clothes and boots in order to fly in a plane? The Marine Corps was full of surprises.

The transition from navigating terrain on foot and in trucks gave way to the speed of an aircraft at altitude. On one of my first navigation flights, as the day was losing its light after hours of exercises, CWO 4 Hunter directed my attention to a large body of water to the east and asked, "What major navigation feature do you see?" My reply: "The Atlantic Ocean." His response: "Why don't we try that as our orientation point of reference?" Well, yes, I thought. How practical that we have the entire Atlantic Ocean as a navigation point of reference!

Skills were mastered and CWO 4 Hunter left all of us new Aerial Observers with the most profound philosophical lesson we would probably learn – one that would have sent Plato and Aristotle into days of contemplation: "Wherever you go, there you are!"

The profundity of that insight remains with me to this day. Its corollary – "Carpe Diem." In some strange way, it relates to "Semper Fi."

A WEDDING DAY SURPRISE

Marines are known to do things in a big way and when you get a pack of them together, often the pack mentality overtakes common sense. Such was the case in a wedding that took place in the early 80's in Jacksonville, Florida.

The groom and a number of the groomsmen were stationed near each other at Camp Lejeune, New River, and Cherry Point. There were other friends of the groom who were coming in from California and the DC area, so he asked that we hold off having the bachelor party until all of us could be together the night before the wedding. This showed a decided lack of judgment on his part, because getting married the day after a Marine-inspired bachelor party is not a good idea. One should plan for two days of rest following such an event.

The best man was a genius and, weeks in advance, asked each of us to perform certain traditional tasks like buying lots of alcohol, cigars, hiring dancing girls, etc. He further asked us to come up with detailed plans on what we could do to an inebriated groom that would forever make him remember our party. We then met and shared our plans about ten days prior to the event. The plans were discussed and rated through A, B, C, D and E. If one of the higher rated plans didn't work, we would abort that mission and move on down the line. Plan A was BY FAR better than all the others and we hoped that we would have the chance to make it work.

We arrived in Jacksonville, Florida on Friday morning and took care of getting set up for the party. I made a couple of trips to the airport to pick up family and friends coming in from the west coast. We hung out on the beach for a little while and then went to church for the rehearsal and then to a restaurant for the rehearsal dinner.

There were traditional toasts and traditional speeches, and I remember thinking that these people thought of us as perfect gentlemen. We knew which fork to use, which glass was for what. We opened doors for ladies and pulled chairs out as well. If they only knew what we had planned, what would they think of us then?

At about 7:30 p.m. the groom kissed the bride and we all headed upstairs. She told him to be good. He said he would. We had seen perfectly good parties get ruined by brides or bridesmaids showing up unannounced just to say hello. For this reason, we did not hold our party in the place where we said we would be. Instead, we slipped out the back of our hotel and went down the street to another hotel where we had rented a suite.

Drinks were poured, backs were slapped, a dirty movie was put into the VCR and we began a traditional-looking bachelor party. The groom was being over-served by all of us. He was drinking triples all night. The dancing girls showed up at about 9:00 p.m. and put on quite a performance. They stayed for a couple of hours and had lots of pictures taken with all of us, particularly with the guest of honor. One sat on his lap, totally naked as the other who was behind him draped her substantial breasts over the top of his head.

The photos were, of course, tastefully done with incredible composition. We did not want this confused with hedonistic depravity. This was art. The ladies left at around 11:00 p.m. and we fell into drinking games. The groom was very drunk already, so it was not difficult to cheat as we cut cards, so that he lost and had to drink twice as often as the rest of us. He passed out the first time at around 1:00 a.m. He was out for a little while, but we jostled him awake and handed him another drink. At around 2:00 a.m. we moved him to the car and he briefly woke up, asked for something to drink and we kindly obliged.

We arrived at the airport at around 2:30, put him into a wheelchair and draped a blanket over his head so the bright lights wouldn't wake him. He was an extremely heavy sleeper. We had sent an advance man a couple of hours earlier to buy a ticket. Earlier in the evening we didn't know exactly where he would be going, but the advance man called us from the airport, and we told him the destination would be Houston. This was not an arbitrary decision but was made based entirely on departure times and return flights.

Had we flown him to LA, he would be late getting back; Houston was the limit. The best man took the groom-to-be to his gate and was allowed to push the wheelchair onto the plane and buckle him into his seat. He explained to the stewardess that he was heavily sedated, was very afraid of flying, and should not be bothered at all during the flight. They apparently complied and he arrived, still drunk, in Houston early on the morning he was to be wed in Jacksonville.

The ticket he had traveled on was a one-way ticket. We didn't want to make it too easy. We knew that as a Marine officer, he would soon make an assessment of his situation, his assets, and liabilities. He discovered he was in Houston and that he had no ticket back to Florida.

Of course, he reached for his wallet, but it was gone. He soon found that all he had was a dime, his Military ID card and a slip of paper with a phone number on it. Even drunk, he knew the dime was for a pay phone to call the number. We had a betting pool going as to how long it would take him to make the call. In less than 30 minutes after landing, we got the call. He told us later, the first thing he did was go to the restroom and stick his finger down his throat. Very sobering.

We instructed him to go to the Western Union office in the airport. We had wired him the money for the return ticket. He just had to show them his ID card. We told him there was 20 dollars extra so that he could get something to eat. He should go to the ticket counter and purchase a one-way ticket back and that we would pick him up at the airport.

Amazingly, he executed perfectly and arrived an hour and ten minutes before the wedding. He shaved in the car with an electric razor we had brought. He likewise brushed his teeth. We had his Dress Blues and he changed in the car as well. He looked horrible. We gave him food to feed the hangover and by the time we got to the church he looked almost normal. Once we entered the church and he realized he was going to make it, he began to laugh about his adventure. The bride found out about his trip at the reception and would not speak to any of us. Plans B, C, D and E have long been forgotten, but the flawless execution of Plan A lives forever!

ADHERENCE TO ORDERS

During the late 1970's, one of the avenues for those aspiring to obtain a commission as a second lieutenant in the Marine Corps was the PLC program, which required two six-week training periods, known as PLC Junior and PLC Senior. During Platoon Leaders Course Junior (PLC Jr) candidate training at Camp Upshur, Quantico, Virginia in July 1977, a candidate rigidly adhered to the last verbal orders of his platoon sergeant.

The platoon sergeant had been conducting close order drill with his platoon of candidates on the drill field at Camp Upshur in the late July afternoon heat and humidity. One of the candidates continually failed to properly execute the close order drill movements. The platoon sergeant became so frustrated that he ordered the candidate to get out of the platoon and to take a seat under the pine trees that surrounded the drill field. The platoon sergeant concluded his verbal orders with a final instruction that the candidate would not rejoin the platoon until instructed to do so by the platoon sergeant.

The platoon sergeant and his assistant continued to conduct close order drill with the platoon until it was time to march to evening chow at the dining facility. The candidate, who had been exiled from the platoon, remained seated cross-legged under the pine trees. After evening chow, the platoon returned to their barracks in the Quonset huts and conducted their standard evening routine until taps or lights out.

At taps, the assistant platoon sergeant took charge of the platoon. He had the candidates stand in front of their racks with their rifles and count off. Each candidate counted off in turn. After proceeding through the platoon, the assistant platoon sergeant realized that he was short one candidate and one rifle. He had the platoon count off a second time with the same result.

At this point, one of the candidates requested permission to speak. After the assistant platoon sergeant granted the candidate permission to speak, the candidate reminded the assistant platoon sergeant that the platoon sergeant had instructed one of the candidates to remain seated under the pine trees until the platoon sergeant ordered the candidate to rejoin the platoon. This candidate was not present in the Quonset hut and had not been with the platoon all evening.

The assistant platoon sergeant dispatched two candidates with flashlights to locate the missing candidate on the edge of the drill field. Once all of the candidates were in the Quonset hut, the assistant platoon sergeant had the platoon count off again and finally was able to account for all of the candidates and rifles. The candidate, who had been exiled from the platoon for being unable to conduct close order drill, had remained seated cross-legged under the pine trees for well over five hours.

ADVENTURES AS OFFICER OF THE DAY

Between the time I graduated from Officer Candidate School and my Basic School Class formed, many of my classmates took lots of leave to go home and visit family. I took a couple of days and returned to Quantico with little to do. I was selected for my superior intellect and problem-solving skills (ahem) to serve as the Junior Officer of the Day for Camp Barrett. The actual OOD was a captain who knew what he was doing. I made the standard rounds and called him if anything interesting happened. When I was in elementary school the local fire department chief came to talk to us about fire safety. He gave us all plastic fire helmets and made us "Junior Firemen," which was identical to my position as the Junior Officer of the Day.

On my first round that evening, I was walking by the H&S Company (rightfully nicknamed Homicide and Suicide due to their stellar disciplinary record) barracks, when I witnessed a flaming mattress fly over the third-floor railing onto the ground below. Several Marines surrounded it and attempted to stomp it out until a fire extinguisher was finally brought out and the fire was finally extinguished. I went upstairs and, using masterful deductive reasoning skills, I determined which rack was missing a mattress. I gathered everyone who knew anything of the incident and hauled them up to the duty hut where the OOD had them all write statements for the legal officer to prepare destruction of government property charges the next day. He told the Marine who set the fire to give his mattress to the man who now didn't have one, and to sleep without a mattress until he could get one from supply.

At around 0130 I was making another round. I was walking towards the armory when I saw the guard sitting in a folding chair with the front legs off the ground, leaning back. I noticed his head was leaning forward but since the streetlight illuminating the armory was behind him and his cover shadowed his face, I had no way of knowing if he was asleep.

I was about 20 yards away when I gave him a friendly, "Good evening!" Startled, he almost fell out of the chair, regained his balance, jumped to his feet, raised the shotgun, pointed it directly at me, pulled the pump and released it, shouting, "Halt! Who goes there?"

Not at all what I was expecting, but he had my undivided attention. I was so scared I could barely whimper, "Lt Wilcox, Junior Officer of the Day." I felt so small facing the big crazy man with the shotgun loaded with double-aught buck. At that point, he should have been awake enough to figure out that the Marine Corps officer in front of him, dressed in summer Charlies with butter bars on the collars, was indeed the JOOD, but I guess he thought, in for a penny, in for a pound, so he yelled, "On your face! Where's your ID?"

As I slowly (no quick moves around the crazy guy) went to my knees and finally on my face on the wet pavement, I said, "It's in my left breast pocket." He obviously began to realize I was who I said I was, because only a Marine would know that Marines ALWAYS have their ID card in their left breast pocket. No Russian infiltrator would ever know that because it is a closely held secret between Marines. The guard, however, requested that I roll to my right, so that he could check my ID. He retrieved it and asked me several questions to determine my true identity. He then allowed me to get up, and he apologized.

As soon as I got the shotgun away from him, I called the Corporal of the Guard and had the guard replaced. I took him to the OOD and wrote out a statement and had him do the same. At about 0300, I had a phone call from a very angry man from West Virginia. He wanted to speak to the CO of H&S Company. I told him that the CO had gone home some ten hours ago and would be in at around 0700. He wanted the CO's home number. I wouldn't give it to him.

From the irate voice on the other end of the phone, I was able to surmise that he had just found out his fourteen-year-old daughter was pregnant and that the future father was a young PFC stationed in our command. I told him I would get the message to the CO and that he could expect a call from someone in the command sometime the next day. I asked the OOD if this was what a normal night of standing duty was like. He said, "No," explaining that this was a Wednesday and twelve days since the last payday. He said, "You don't want to be here on a payday Friday night. It's like a madhouse all night long!"

The only other time I stood duty at TBS was almost uneventful in that we had no fights, drunk shenanigans, drug busts; nothing except one phone call at 0100. The call came from Baltimore, Maryland. The caller said that he was a police officer and wanted to know if we had all of our fire trucks. Thinking it was one of those "Is your refrigerator running?" prank calls, I said that I believed we had all of our trucks and hung up.

In a minute he called back and said maybe we should check just to be sure. I called the Camp Barrett Firehouse and asked their duty to please take a physical inventory of all of the fire trucks. He came back to the phone in about a minute and very excitedly reported that there was a fire truck missing.

Apparently, a young Marine had a girlfriend in New York who had broken up with him over the phone that night. He felt he MUST get to New York immediately. He began searching for a ride and, having no money, thought a fire truck would work. He stole one. He made it as far as Baltimore and began to run low on gas. He pulled into a station and, still having no money, attempted to exchange some of the hoses and fittings from the truck for some fuel. The attendant, recognizing this as unusual behavior, called the police but told our Marine he was checking out the hose and fitting barter with his boss.

The police arrived and took our boy into custody. The rest of my night was spent taking statements and preparing the case for the legal officer. I was always amazed at the creativity of young Marines, the lengths they would go to keep themselves entertained, and the ingenuity they displayed as they put themselves into all sorts of predicaments, especially those hopeless romantic ones.

AX QUALIFICATION

The Marine Corps requires that every Marine be qualified on his or her table of organization (TO) weapon annually. This makes sense. After all, shouldn't we be sure that each person knows how to shoot in the event that the shooting starts? This principle works well when you talk about weapons and the inevitability of war.

However, the Marine Corps carried the idea further and further until it reached the absurd. Service Record Books (SRBs) must reflect that each Marine is checked out on the most ridiculous gear before that Marine is allowed to use it. This caused us to wonder whether the absurdities would ever end. For example, at TBS we were unable to wear field jackets in Virginia in the snow because we had not yet been instructed on how to properly wear a field jacket. Without the training, we could have used the field jacket inadvertently to harm ourselves, light it on fire, place it under our personal vehicles to catch oil drips, but we could never know enough to wear it to stay warm in the freezing weather. So, the Marine Corps made sure we remained bitterly cold... to keep us safe from the dangers of improper field jacket use.

I once went to the field and stayed for several weeks. While there, several of my men got orders for schools to attend classes elsewhere; the rest of us stayed in the field. When it was time to leave, we discovered we didn't have enough licensed drivers to move our gear out of the field, so we had to make multiple trips. We had men who had been licensed, but their licenses weren't current, and they needed to take classes to get them renewed.

There never were enough "chasers"; those licensed to accompany Marines from the hands of civilian police, back to the base. So we had people in chaser school. Marines with ten years' experience safely driving in the civilian world had to be checked and rechecked on the M151 Jeep, because driving on civilian and base roads at thirty miles per hour was much more lethal than driving a car on civilian freeways at seventy miles per hour.

The licenses, certificates and qualifications to perform simple tasks made the following gag ridiculous, but believable. A new man checked into the unit and immediately the corporals and lance corporals began to work on the hazing that would welcome him aboard. They'd clue me in, and as long as no one was going to be hurt, I'd usually go along. The men reporting directly from communications school had often not been checked out on certain equipment, since there are lots of different types of gear and there is only so much time to train. Consequently, it was routine to go through a checklist to see what a new man was and was not checked out on.

One day my NCOs let me know that they would need a few minutes just before lunch break to perform an ax qualification. As we formed up to break for noon chow, one of my corporals spoke up from the formation: "Sir, it looks like Tarwater has come to us without his ax qualification." I went into a little tirade, saying, "How can they send us men so ill-equipped to function in the field?" And I finished with, "If we hustle, we can get this done before chow."

I explained to Tarwater, "The MRC 134 radios look and drive like jeeps, but they are actually radios on wheels. When driving them in the field you will, upon occasion, go off road and may get stuck in the mud. The best way out is to use the ax which comes with the jeep, cut down a small tree or branch and wedge it under the tires so that you can get some traction and get yourself unstuck. The shovel, another piece of the jeep equipment, may also come in handy, but today we need to make sure you're proficient in the use of the ax, particularly in dark places so that you can remain tactical while trying to extricate your MRC 134 from the mud."

With that intro, I turned the show over to Corporal Seals who executed flawlessly. "First, we will check you for daytime use of the ax. Have you ever used an ax before?"

Tarwater responded, "Yes."

"Excellent! So, you stand there and choke up on the ax for accuracy. I'm going to place this quarter on top of this two by four. You have to hit the quarter in order to qualify. Ready?"

"I think so." He raised the ax and let it fall. It hit the quarter, almost cutting it in half.

"Outstanding!" shouted the corporal. "Now you just have to do the same thing, only in the dark. To simulate nighttime use of the ax, we will blindfold you. Corporal James can you blindfold Tarwater, please?"

As James put the blindfold on Tarwater, he casually removed his cover (in the Corps, uniform hats are called covers). He placed the blindfold and made sure Tarwater could not see. He then handed the cover to Corporal Seals who continued the show: "Okay, I'm placing the ax on top of the quarter, which is on the two by four, just like before." In actuality he placed the ax on top of Tarwater's cover on the two by four. "All you have to do is lift the ax two to three feet and bring it down in the exact same spot. When you make a mark on the quarter, you'll be qualified."

Up went the ax, down it came, cutting the cover neatly, followed by loud moans from the crowd, and Corporal Seals: "Damn, that was close. You missed it by half an inch. I'll reset you. Okay, back up everybody." Up went the ax. Down it came again with loud moans from the crowd. A new slice was cut in the cover. This process was repeated a few more times until they finally had mercy, removed the blindfold, and showed Tarwater his cover, followed by lots of backslapping and laughing. He was one of them.

Later that afternoon I stopped by the battalion office to turn in some training paperwork for entry into SRBs. The CO saw me walk in and stuck his head out of his office and said, "Lieutenant, the Sergeant Major and I went by the chow hall for lunch today. Did you by chance conduct an ax qualification down in your area today?"

"Yes sir, we did."

"He looked well qualified. He can wear that one today, but make sure he has a serviceable cover tomorrow."

"Yes sir."

BIGGER THAN OUR PAYCHECKS

Over the many years since I was welcomed into the Marine Corps family, I have talked with countless Marines from at least four generations about how they happened to choose the Marine Corps. I personally joined because my dad was a Master Gunnery Sergeant and a veteran of WWII, Korea and Vietnam. We butted heads for years and a few months before I graduated from college, I passed a Marine Recruiter on my campus and thought, the old man hates lieutenants worse than anything in the world! In ninety days I could be the thing he hates worst AND will simultaneously hold a higher rank than he achieved in twenty-seven years! Where do I sign?

For many, there was someone they looked up to – an uncle, a friend, or their dad – who exemplified the man they wished they could be. Others knew little of the Corps but had always heard they were the biggest bad asses on the planet. One officer I met was told by his father that he could never make it as a Marine, so he did it to prove that his dad was wrong. Another WWII Marine dad told his two boys that the family had done very well and as a result, when they finished college, they could do whatever they wanted to do with their lives... as soon as they got out of the Marine Corps.

I always remember wanting to be a good man, to do the right thing, to defend the helpless and to help those who couldn't help themselves. I've heard this, along with some occasional mention of patriotism, as reason for choosing such an unusual profession.

Among the officer corps, the one reason I never heard was, "I needed the paycheck," or "for the money."

It seems to me that we all knew we could probably be making more money and not have to sleep out in the elements, leave our loved ones for a year at a time, or even get shot at, had we accepted jobs in the civilian sector. I believe that finding others who feel that way, who are willing to put up with all of the downside of the Corps for the opportunity it offers, is probably what makes the bond Marines share even stronger.

I remember going home and hanging out with my friends as a young lieutenant and knowing that I was in charge of 75 men and millions of dollars of equipment. I knew the names of the girlfriends, wives, dogs, hometowns and the last four digits of the social security numbers of about half of them. I knew when each man had last had a day off and whose girlfriend had just dumped him. I knew their proficiency and conduct marks, their PFT and rifle range scores.

My friends were the assistant managers at a branch bank, worked in their dad's stores or on their dad's farms. They spent Thanksgiving AND Christmas with their families. I'd get a letter from home and eat an MRE for Thanksgiving dinner (and it wasn't even Turkey Loaf), five thousand miles from my family. My friends were buying their first houses. I lived in a sandbag hootch and bathed in my helmet.

But when I came home on leave, the playing field always seemed to level out. I had seen much of Europe and the Middle East. I had sailed the Atlantic, the Caribbean and the Mediterranean. They went to Panama City for a five-day vacation. I had flown and jumped out of helicopters and C-130s, pulled mangled bodies from the rubble left from a bomb in Beirut.

I remember telling some of my civilian friends that I frequently drove over to Cherry Point on Friday to catch the hospital flight going south. It made several stops along the way, but they were always happy to have a couple of healthy Marines aboard to help with the heavy lifting. We just signed up for "Space Available," and later that night we would land in Key West.

We'd catch a ride over the BOQ at Boca Chica, where we would get a room for three dollars a night. There were bicycles outside the Q, so we would take a couple over to Sloppy Joe's and hang out. The next day we would try to get in a couple of dives. We had masks, snorkels, fins, and regulators, so all we needed was air. Because we were Marines, the dive boats would use us like deckhands and let us have air for cheap, if we helped the other tourists and then cleaned up the boat and gear before we left.

On Saturday night, we enjoyed the night life in Key West. On Sunday afternoon the plane that we flew in on would return us to Cherry Point and we'd drive home. The whole weekend didn't cost any more than if we'd stayed at home. My friends were amazed at the lifestyle.

A few times my Marine friends and I would catch a "space A" hop up to Wright Patterson AFB in Ohio or to Andrews AFB in DC. We packed a seabag with parkas and Bermuda shorts because we had no idea where we were going. We might end up in Norway or Puerto Rico. There were international flights from these bases, and we'd hop a plane and be off on an adventure.

We once landed in Stuttgart, Germany. In those days we seldom needed a passport; a military ID would do. We landed in bad weather with no idea of where to go, so we boarded a train and road it up and down Germany, talking to other passengers and making a plan for what to see next. By the time we got off, we knew where to go, what to eat and how we were going to get home.

We had taken two weeks' leave and we used almost all of it. We saw Munich, Zurich, Paris, Brussels, Amsterdam, Hamburg, and so much more. We dropped most of our gear in train station lockers during the day and returned to the station at night, riding the rail to the next town and sleeping on the train. These were incredible adventures, made possible because we carried the US Marine ID Card. People everywhere were so friendly to us.

I still always longed for home when I was far away, and when I'd come home and go hunting or fishing with my dad, it was always fun. It was also fun when I'd come home and go to a Christmas party or to church with my folks. I would look around the room and know that I was the only one there that had been to fifty different countries, had been shot at, and had greater responsibilities for human lives and equipment than men twice my age. I had seen and done more in a handful of years than most of them would do in their lifetimes. I knew I was the man and, what's more, I knew that they knew it too. I knew who they were and what they had seen, and it wasn't that it was bad, it just wasn't for me.

By the time my leave was up, and I returned to my life, I was ready. I often couldn't wait to get back to my brothers, to debate geopolitics with people who know what that means, to the boring day-to-day training and the excitement of another deployment and another adventure, and the toys. God, I loved the big boy toys!

No, we didn't sign up for the big paycheck, and the lifestyle certainly wasn't for everyone. But for those who wear the Eagle, Globe and Anchor, we lived much bigger lives than our paychecks indicated, and we have no regrets over a few lost dollars. We all saw the movie Patton, and whenever we're asked what did we do at this time of our lives, we won't have to say, "I shoveled shit in Louisiana."

BOUNCER

One night in early 1980, I was in Winston's in Georgetown having a beer with Jake Leinenkugel. We were approached by a very large man who asked if we were Marines. We confirmed his assessment as to the nature of our funny looking haircuts and continued with our conversation.

He asked if we might lend him a hand. He was Winston's bouncer and said that he had just received a call from Pall Mall, a bar just up the street, and that a "gang of underage punk rockers" had just left there and was coming to Winston's to try and crash the place. Since there were five or six of them, he asked if we wouldn't mind stepping outside with him as a show of strength. I asked if maybe we should be deputized, sworn in or ordained in case the show of strength turned to actual fisticuffs. He assured us that we were covered. That was obviously legal enough, so no contracts were signed.

As soon as we set foot out the door, we saw a half a dozen teenagers with greased back hair, black leather jackets with lots of studs, pins in their faces and some dangling dog chains, but no dogs. Before we had time to say, "You take the two on the left," they were upon us, moving aggressively among the three of us. Jake did not hesitate or wait for first contact. He grabbed the lead punk by his oversized jacket lapels and pushed him into a signpost. Punk number two had a chain in his hand and pulled his arm back to hit Jake. I grabbed his arm and pushed him into the wall. The Bouncer did nothing. At this moment the Police arrived and hauled the young ruffians away. The bouncer told the officers that we had assisted him, and he took us back into the bar where he told the bartender to look after us. So, we got free drinks and were heroes for the night, for five seconds' work turning away some kids, none of whom weighed more than 150 pounds.

A few weeks later, I was in my room, watching TV and they had a show on called the Games People Play. This particular night was the "World's Toughest Bouncer" competition. I was shocked to see our bouncer from Winston's was a semifinalist! I ran up the hall and got Jake and we watched the rest of the show, amazed that the guy who made no contribution to our little skirmish was one of the toughest.

We had a good laugh over the whole thing, but we watched intently because this was the night that America was introduced to Mr. T, who won the competition by running an "obstacle course" in a bar and finally crashing through a door, leaving no doubt that he was, by far, the baddest. Jake and I concluded that if Mr. T had been the bouncer at Winston's, we would never have been called for assistance and some of the punk rockers would have spent the night in the hospital. I pity the fool.

BROTHER I NEVER KNEW

I did not personally know Michael Warren, but to me he felt like a brother. Let me explain. I grew up in Moline, Illinois and attended church at First United Presbyterian Church where Michael's parents, Mr. and Mrs. Warren, also attended church. I knew nothing of Michael until a sunny Sunday afternoon in July 1976. After church service that morning, Mr. Warren approached me and asked if I had spent some time in the Marines. Apparently, my haircut gave me away, since I had just returned home from my first increment of Marine Corps OCS (PLC Jr.).

To Mr. Warren, my haircut style was quite obvious, and I was impressed that he noticed and would ask – after all, this was 1976. I explained to him where I had been and what I had done, and he in turn mentioned his son Michael who had done something very similar, eventually joining the Marines. After a little more conversation about the Marines and other things, I asked about Michael and what he was doing now. Mr. Warren told me he had died in Vietnam. I was speechless. After mumbling some condolences, I tried to get away as quickly as possible. Mr. Warren graciously sensed my discomfort and explained that it had happened a while ago and that I shouldn't feel bad about it. Still, it was so unexpected and profound to me that I was, in my own selfish way, uncomfortable with him telling me about it.

On the way home from church, I told my dad about the conversation I'd just had with Mr. Warren. As a father, he was able to give me some perspective and respect for the situation. For the remainder of the summer, I would see Mr. Warren occasionally at church and have short conversations about general topics. Michael and the Marines didn't come up, and I was fine with that. I was a student at Illinois State, so I was only in Moline during holidays and in the summer.

That following Christmas break, I saw Mr. Warren at church again and we struck up another conversation. He asked about my plans and if I intended to follow through with going into the Marine Corps after I finished college. I told him I wasn't sure yet and he encouraged me to keep him informed about my plans, regardless of what I ended up doing. He was very genuine in his interest and an easy person to talk to.

The summer before I graduated, Mr. Warren asked me again about my plans. By this time, I had completed all the Marine OCS requirements and I was determined to become a Marine 2nd Lieutenant when I graduated. I told Mr. Warren that. He took a good look at me and invited me to come to his house sometime soon. He told me that he wanted to give me all of Michael's uniforms that they still had and that my height and weight looked very similar to Michael's. Once again, I was speechless. After mumbling some thanks, I told him that I would give him a call.

A few days later I told my dad what Mr. Warren had offered me and that I wasn't sure what to think or do about it. Obviously, it was a genuine and gracious offer, but at the same time I was uncomfortable with it. I certainly didn't want to come between grieving parents and their son. Also, the thought of wearing a uniform of someone who had died was somewhat macabre to me at the time. My father didn't know what to say either. A few weeks passed and we talked about it again. My dad said he had given it some thought and that he believed it would be okay to accept the offer, but that it was totally up to me.

A few days later and still somewhat uncomfortable, I called Mr. Warren and arranged for a good time to come over. When I arrived, he showed me into the living room where there was a medium sized moving box full of uniforms in the middle of the floor. He opened the box and suggested I try one on. The one at the very top of the box was the classic Marine Dress Blue jacket – so I put it on. It fit like a glove. Sleeve lengths and everything else seemed perfect – very little alteration, if any, would be necessary. We looked at a few more things and talked. I could sense a feeling of release from Mr. Warren and that he was pleased with his offer to me. At the same time, I was becoming more comfortable as well. After a half hour or so, Mr. Warren suggested I take the box home and sort through it all at my leisure.

I did become a Marine officer and wore those uniforms with pride. I can honestly say that after that day in the Warren's living room, I never had a moment of discomfort wearing any of Michael's uniforms. Because of changing Marine Corps uniform regulations, I could only use about half of Michael's uniforms – but it was still a great honor to wear the ones that I could. In a way that is hard to explain, each time I wore one of his uniforms, I felt a bond developing between Michael and myself; a Marine-to-Marine bond for sure, but also something more.

In the late 1980's I had a chance to visit the Vietnam Memorial in Washington, D.C. for the first time. Naturally, I wanted to look up where Michael's name was on the wall. When I found his name in one of the reference books available at the Wall to help locate where names are on the panels, I became speechless once again. In those books each name is listed along with the other details about the person, such as home of record, branch of service, etc. One of the most important details listed is the date the person died. For Michael, that day was April 25, 1968. That day was also my tenth birthday.

Michael, God Bless you and your parents.

Semper Fi!

BUTT SHOT

I was in Beirut serving with the 22nd MAU (Marine Amphibious Unit) in early 1982. Communications were up and all of my collateral duties were caught up and a recon friend of mine was taking a patrol out into the city. I was always up for a trip outside the wire (the area around Beirut International Airport where the Marines were stationed) and had driven to the embassy and to the presidential palace a number of times, but I'd never gotten to slow down and walk it with a platoon of recon Marines. I got permission to go, lined up with my buddy and waited to step off at the designated time. The rules for patrols were very strict and the times were precisely followed. Every step of the way was timed and radio calls back to base occurred at designated checkpoints.

In order to hit the checkpoint meant we had to leave at the right time. We were a few minutes early and waiting when a sergeant ran up and said there was a message from headquarters that every weapon in the MAU required a Limited Technical Inspection (LTI). This meant the armorers had to punch each barrel and check each weapon for serviceability. An LTI takes only a few seconds by an armorer, but we had minutes before our departure time. As we ran to the LTI site, the lieutenant called headquarters to see if we could possibly do it four hours later, when we returned. The CO said he wanted it done before we left and that he could have it completed in the next hour or two.

We arrived and there was much pushing and shoving as we moved to the front of the line due to the urgency of the situation. The lieutenant pressured the armorers to hurry, asking them to hustle to get us on our way. They complied and pushed us through as fast as possible. There were two armorers punching barrels. It should be pointed out that mine was likely the first pistol they checked that day. There were no officers in the area, evidently holding back and letting enlisted personnel go first. This meant that only rifles had been checked up until then.

As they took a rifle, they could immediately see that there was no magazine in the well. They pulled the charging handle back, locking the bolt to the rear, stuck a little finger through the ejection port into the rear end of the barrel to ensure no rounds in the barrel, and then proceeded to punch the barrel, let the bolt go home and, aiming the weapon into a barrel of sand situated between the armorers, pulled the trigger, just to be sure, in case the other safety procedures had failed.

I handed my pistol to the Marine on the left and he went through the above-mentioned procedures effortlessly. I was gone and headed back to the departure area. Moments later, the Marine on the right took the pistol of the recon detachment commander. The rules of the MAU said that we were not to carry loaded weapons inside the wire. As soon as the patrols stepped outside the wire, they locked and loaded their weapons until they returned. However, the detachment commander, in anticipation of leaving on his patrol, had slipped a loaded magazine into his pistol but had not chambered a round. This is where things went awry.

The Marine checking the pistol had checked a couple of hundred rifles in a row and with a rifle it is obvious that there is a magazine in the well, because it sticks out below the weapon. You can put your hand in the magazine well, but you already know there's no magazine. So, when the pistol was handed to him following many rifles, he failed to put his fingers up in the magazine hold. Then he pulled the slide back, put his finger in the back of the barrel and visibly checked for a round. Then came his next mistake: he let the slide go home (remember he's moving fast, we're in a hurry). He obviously did not know he had just chambered a round. He then pointed the pistol toward, but not into, the sand barrel. His partner was moving, reaching for the next rifle, and got between the pistol and the sand-filled barrel. Right about that time his buddy shot him in the butt.

There was suddenly a flurry of activity and lots of people got a lesson in first aid. Our wounded Marine was medivacked and got his glute patched up. There was a big investigation. Dozens of witnesses made statements. There were lots of findings and statements of fact. A number of conclusions were drawn and procedures reevaluated, but the long and short of it was that I didn't get to go on patrol for quite a while.

CANDIDATE SANTA ANA

I was a nineteen-year-old Marine officer candidate going through my initial basic military training at Camp Upshur in the summer of 1976. My sergeant instructor was an older, crusty gunnery sergeant with Vietnam experience and an inability to pronounce candidates' last names, especially mine. After a short time there, he gave up on pronouncing mine – "Ayala." He assumed I was a Native American and started calling me "Chief." He had nicknames for other candidates too, such as my buddy, Candidate Serum, but I won't say what he called him.

So, I answered to "Chief" as I was too scared of the Gunny, and at that point, not about to correct him. One of the ways he "corrected" our mistakes was to have us dig holes with our entrenching tools which we carried with us everywhere. After about four weeks, I finally got the courage to let him know about the real me. After being granted permission to speak, I told him I was not an Indian. Noticeably upset (great acting) and using his best drill instructor voice for the duration of the conversation, the following exchange took place:

Gunny: What! You and your relatives did not kill General Custer like I thought, and you had led me to believe!?

Candidate Ayala: No Sergeant Instructor, the candidate did not! The candidate is not of Indian descent.

Gunny: You've gotta be shittin' me! You did not kill General Custer!!? You are not an Indian? I don't believe you! What are you Candidate Chief?!

Candidate Ayala: Sergeant Instructor, the candidate is Mexican.

Gunny: OOOOH, you gotta be f*cking kidding me! You are not a chief?!! You didn't kill Custer?!! You are Mexican??!! Oh my God, f*ck me to tears! I knew it. I knew it!

Candidate Ayala: Sergeant Instructor? What? You knew what?

Gunny: Start digging Chief! Now! Before I really get mad!

Candidate Ayala: Why Gunny? I am Mexican. My relatives did not kill General Custer!

Gunny: Dig! Soooo... please tell me, why the hell did you kill Davy Crockett and John Wayne at the Alamo, Candidate Santa Ana?!!

Candidate Ayala: [Silent. Begins digging...]

Author's Note: This occurred in the hot summer of 1976 in Quantico, Virginia, forty-six years ago. It was at Marine Corps OCS. I never felt offended or targeted due to my appearance. The Gunny picked on all of us equally, gave us nicknames, regardless of what we looked like. In hindsight, it has always been funny to me. The only memory I now have of PLC Junior.

CAPTAIN DD

The following story was relayed to me from a very reliable source while we were stationed together at MCAS Cherry Point in the mid 80's; the event occurred during a deployment in the early 1980's. The guilty/complicit parties shall remain unnamed to protect their privacy, and, in this era of "political correctness," to prevent any future repercussions.

The story began while a certain Marine squadron was in port in Kenya. The squadron commander decided that, in an effort to retain pilot proficiency, local flights around the area would be conducted. The pilots referred to them as "go up and burn gas for three hours" flights. It was during one of these flights that this "infamous" event occurred.

After boring holes in the air for the better part of their three-hour sortie, the crew noted a long line of indigenous people, in full tribal regalia, walking down a dusty dirt road. At this point, being curious, a young captain aircraft commander decided to quickly circle back around over the group. He then flew down the road, ahead of the group and landed on the road. Upon landing, the captain instructed his copilot to "take the controls." After the copilot had control of the aircraft, the young captain unbuckled himself, exited the aircraft and proceeded to walk toward the group of locals. After several minutes of animated conversations with the locals, the captain returned to the aircraft.

Another several minutes go by and then the young captain reappeared in front of the aircraft totally naked and proceeded to re-approach the tribesmen, accompanied by the crew chief armed with a camera. The intrepid captain then proceeded to roll around in the red dust at the side of the road, covering himself from head to toe. At this point, one of the tribal elders presented him with a shield and a spear. This is the point at which the crew chief snapped the "infamous photo." With mission accomplished, the young captain donned his flight suit, and the aircraft returned to base.

After getting the film developed, the picture in question made its rounds about the ready room to much laughter. The young captain, who stood well over six feet, seemed to tower over the local tribesmen and was quite striking looking, armed with shield and spear. Unfortunately or fortunately, depending on your sense of humor, a copy of the photo somehow got sent back to the states by a fellow squadron mate. Apparently, the photo caused quite a stir back home as it was passed around and viewed by many of the dependent wives during their gatherings.

The photo became a topic of discussion, not only because of the height of this "tribesman," but rather, "Oh my, look at the size of his big penis." The photo was shown round and round through different gatherings until at one of them, a suddenly red-faced wife exclaimed, "Holy Crap, that's my husband!" Needless to say, after the squadron returned, the humor factor of the photo only got bigger. The young captain began to be referred to as an anatomical part of a donkey and was referred to by his last name, always prefaced by DD.

CLEANING THE SERIES OFFICE OR UNINTENDED CONSEQUENCES

The Marine Corps has a tradition of having clean spaces for their barracks, and office spaces so spotless that you can eat off the floor. The basis of this tradition becomes engrained in those aspiring to earn the title, "Marine," during their basic training. During basic training, the recruits who clean the hut of their drill instructors (DI's) and the series office are known as the house mouse.

During the winter of 1982, two recruits within a series in the Third Recruit Training Battalion at Parris Island, South Carolina drew the task of being the house mouse to clean the series office. These two recruits would report to the series office each morning after their platoon had breakfast in the dining facility. They would clean the series office while their fellow recruits would clean their squad bay. The two recruits would report, carrying a broom, dustpan, and mop as their tools of the trade.

These two recruits were a young African American from the Deep South and an older Caucasian from New York City. The older recruit was 28 years old and had entered the Marines in the hope of finding a purpose in his life, as he had been homeless and living on the streets with minimal prospects for a bright future. At the time, 28 was the maximum age for enlisting in the Marine Corps.

Marine basic training consisted of three distinct phases spread over approximately ten weeks. A series consisted of four platoons of recruits with each platoon occupying a squad bay on separate floors (also known as decks, due to the connection between the Marine Corps and the Navy) of the three-story barracks. The second phase of basic training was two weeks at the rifle range learning to shoot and to qualify with the M-16 rifle.

During the first phase of basic training the two recruits had reported to the series office each morning and attacked their cleaning duties with elan. Saturday was the start of the second phase of basic training and the platoons physically moved from their squad bays in the Third Recruit Training Battalion area to similar squad bays at the rifle range area. This was a distance of less than two miles.

After breakfast on Sunday morning, the two intrepid recruits took their tools of the trade and departed their squad bay to clean the series office, while the remaining recruits cleaned the squad bay. As so often occurs in the military and in life, there are often unintended consequences to our actions.

When the two recruits departed their new squad bay, their DI's had not thought to instruct them on the location of the new series office, which was also at the rifle range. The two recruits with their tools of the trade as house mouse had marched all the way back to the series office at the Third Recruit Training Battalion area, pounded on the hatch, and reported for cleaning duty. Much to their chagrin, no one responded from within the series office and opened the hatch, but absent any additional instructions, the two recruits waited outside the series office.

When they had not reported back to their platoon after a reasonable period, their DI went to the new series office seeking his two recruits. The series commander informed the DI that the recruits had not reported to the series office for their cleaning duties. At this point, the series commander and DI realized that the recruits had gone to the old series office, since they had not been instructed on the new location. After contacting a second DI who was still in the Third Recruit Training Battalion area, the DI located the two recruits and had them return to the squad bay at the rifle range. The two recruits retraced their steps, carrying their cleaning gear. The DI showed the recruits the location of the new series office and ensured that the two recruits knew that this location would change after the series completed their time at the rifle range.

CONDITION ONE ALPHA

I spent seven months on the USS Guam as a Marine Corps helicopter pilot. Between November 1983 and February 1984, my typical day was an 0430 flight brief and 0700 launch to Beirut International Airport (BIA), specifically to a landing zone we lovingly called, LZ Shit Bird. After landing, the pilots would go into the ops bunker to go over that day's flight missions.

Compared to Marines in the 22nd Marine Amphibious Unit encamped around BIA, the aviation combat element (the helicopter squadron, HMM 261) of which I was a member (stationed onboard the Guam), were perfumed princesses and not just glorified bus drivers. We slept on ship mattresses out of the weather, had hot chow at least twice a day, normally had heat in cold weather, took one shower per day with hot and cold running water, could watch a nightly movie, and the best luxury of all was that we could privately relieve ourselves in toilet-paper-rich toilet stalls when necessary (unless the back pressure in the ship's waste-water system caused the toilet to explode its contents on the hapless deuce dropper). Because the privacy and abundance of toilet paper on the ship was the premier luxury, I always tried to do my business before flying off the ship and landing at BIA.

One rainy, cold, mid-November morning, I was Jeff Marshall's copilot. We briefed at 0430, after which I tried to force myself to get my morning constitutional business completed before leaving the ship. Sadly, I was not ready to utilize the luxurious ship facilities prior to take-off and, when the morning coffee finally kicked in, would have to use the Marine latrine located near the LZ at BIA.

The latrine was constructed of plywood. There were six seating areas across a long plywood bench, one-foot circular holes cut two feet apart from one another, with a cheap and poorly attached toilet seat over each hole. There were no doors on the latrine and the "privacy" wall in front of the line of toilet holes consisted of a piece of window screen, so that anyone passing by the latrine – and of course Marines passed by constantly – could watch a maximum of six butt cheeks akimbo trying to complete their constitutional tasks. Another feature of the latrine was that there was no toilet paper. The only toilet paper available was the tiny packet of ten squares of toilet paper in the daily-issued, and of course delicious, MRE (meal, ready to eat). No one ever spared a square because, well, they couldn't since there was not even enough for one person.

A few minutes after landing at the airport, it was morning constitutional time, and I headed for the latrine. The cold rain filled the plywood floor along with other liquids that leaked from the plywood latrine holding tank. The toilet-hole bench was too high above the latrine floor for the feet of a normal six-foot-tall person to reach the floor, so the toes extending to the floor added another dimension to the personal business. Positioning myself as best I could on the toilet seat, I tried to hold up my semi-removed flight suit in order to prevent any part of it from touching the witches brew on the latrine floor; all this while Marines glanced at us hapless "doers" in progress through the window screen privacy wall. I'm proud of the fact that no part of my flight suit ever touched the latrine floor.

I was about halfway finished with my constitutional and nowhere near able to leave my spot in the latrine when enemy mortars began to hit the airport. Perfect. The only other Marine in the latrine, three holes from me, finished quickly and headed for a bunker. I was the only one left and nature still had more business to perform. My pathetic attempts to scoot nature along had no effect.

Suddenly the screams of "CONDITION ONE ALPHA" were yelled all over the airport by Marines as they ran to bunkers for safety. A young Lance Corporal ran up to the screen, yelling at me to get into a bunker NOW because, "It's condition one alpha!!!" He stood for a second, incredulous that I didn't immediately spring to my feet in obedience, pull up my flight suit, zip it up and run from the latrine to the ops bunker where Jeff was located. He barked out another direct order, "Marine, get your ass into the ops bunker right now. It's Condition One Alpha, damn it!!"

Unable to move due to my ongoing natural process, I looked up at the Marine and said, "Lance Corporal, when the lieutenant is finished, the lieutenant will find his way to the ops bunker. You may leave now." Dejected, he left just as he was saying, "But sir, it's condition one alpha," while I envisioned a nightly news broadcast in America with the report of a Marine lieutenant who was killed in Beirut that day... in a latrine... during a mortar barrage. I said out loud to myself as I manipulated my ten squares and while mortars were landing a hundred yards or so away from me: "Yeah. That's about right."

COLLECTIVE LET DOWN

On another mission when returning from the Kahuku Training area, Tongo was itching for something more exciting to relieve the boredom of another flight home to K-Bay. He had an idea...

Background: The CH-46E had a 200" hydraulic accumulator which held hydraulic fluid used in starting the aircraft's auxiliary power unit (APU). The accumulator had a hand pump that allowed the aircraft to travel to a remote landing site and shutdown for the night and easily restart at any time. The system was connected to several other aircraft systems and could among other things power the ramp etc. However, in its normal configuration if you pumped the handle, the pump would merely circulate the hydraulic fluid in the accumulator from the bottom of the accumulator to the top of the accumulator. Essentially it did nothing as far as aircraft systems go in that configuration. Of course, no one except CH-46 crew and pilots really knew what this system did.

Execution of the Plan: In concert with the Crew Chief, while flying at about 1500', Tongo suddenly dropped the collective and pushed the nose of the helicopter towards the ground. The Crew Chief gets up and runs to the back of the aircraft and starts pumping the 200-inch hydraulic accumulator pump. Tongo can see what is happening in the cockpit rearview mirror and after a few seconds begins to pull in power and level the aircraft and start climbing back up to altitude. But just as the aircraft is providing this uplifting feeling, the Crew Chief walks away from the accumulator pump towards the cockpit (presumably to discuss the on-board emergency with the pilots). But before the Crew Chief can reach the cockpit, Tongo drops the collective again and the Crew Chief goes running to the back of the aircraft and starts pumping the accumulator pump again. Tongo once again pulls in power, levels the aircraft and start climbing up a second time. About this time the Crew Chief pretends to be getting a bit fatigued and he stops pumping for a second or so. With Tongo watching everything closely, he immediately drops the collective again just seconds after the Crew Chief has stopped pumping. I can only imagine what the passengers watching this activity must have been thinking. So now on the third pumping cycle, the Crew Chief is showing his fatigue (feigned) and he drops to his knee to pump and then falls onto the pump with only a weak one-handed effort to continue pumping. As this cycle goes down, Tongo is letting off on the collective and people are feeling the aircraft beginning to descend again. Right at this point the Crew Chief gives his last feeble effort at one last pump and then he proceeds to crawl off towards the front of the aircraft towards the cockpit. When the Crew Chief gets close to the cockpit, Tongo let's the aircraft drop hard. With the collective down, the aircraft nose once again dropping towards the ground, and the Crew Chief "exhausted" and on the floor in front of all the passengers.... You see 16 people unbuckle and line up to take turns pumping the accumulator which the Crew Chief has them do all the way back to Kaneohe. They are Marines, they can do anything and to save their lives and keep the aircraft flying that's all in a day's work. We heard tales of this event and how they helped save the aircraft for months afterwards. Tongo once again shaping Marine Corps legends!

DEAD SEA

While I was stationed onboard the USS Guam in 1983 and 1984 off the coast of Lebanon, and a member of HMM-261, I had an opportunity to meet up with a Huey pilot friend of mine, who was serving in, and on, an actual secret mission in Tel Aviv, Israel. He lived two doors down from me in Jacksonville, NC and we knew each other from flight school. I wasn't supposed to know he was in Israel, but being my squadron's classified material control officer, I saw the message, and he made a trip to the Guam for a test and demonstration-proof of concept and gave me his secret phone number in Israel.

If you've ever watched the Discovery Channel about MEA Airlines out of Beirut, you've seen his name flash by on the screen during the documentary. His name was spray painted along a concrete block wall by some Huey pilot pals of his before he went to Lebanon. It's not flattering; however, it is hilarious, but that's another story.

He had been a member of HML-167 in New River. Someone hated him and sent him on a temporary three-month assignment to work with the Israelis on a secret program while I was on the USS Guam. Because of his work in Israel, drones are now ubiquitous.

On one particular flight to Tel Aviv, I was supposed to stay for two days. I sort of rolled my eyes at the big, top-secret logic pretzel, called my pal when I got to Tel Aviv, and we got together for some tourist activities. Because my Huey pilot friend was working on a very secret project, helped by the US government and also helping Israel as well, he had some kind of super handshake, diplomatic get-out-of-jail-free card during his stay. It was quite impressive. And he used it.

He had a rental car, so the first evening he and I went to Joppa, found as many bars as humanly possible and proceeded to drink as many Maccabee beers as humanly possible, before getting back into the car and getting in a wreck on a major and busy street between Joppa and Tel Aviv. It was definitely my pal's fault. Fortunately, no one was hurt. The Israeli police arrived, saw how drunk we were, and began the arrest portion of our evening. However, my pal flashed some card at the officers, who immediately made a radio call to their headquarters. Instead of a night in jail, a brand new shiny rental car appeared, my pal got a hearty handshake from the cops, and we were on our way.

I have no idea how I got back to the hotel, but the next day my pal arrived at about 10:00 a.m. and after stopping by the US Embassy to pick up some beverages for the road, we were off to Jerusalem and beyond. Maccabee is not the finest beer in the world. So, we got some—well, lots— of Heinekens instead.

One of our stops was the lowest point on earth where the Jordan River empties into the Dead Sea. We had to quench our thirst to prepare for our next stop, En Gedi on the shores of the Dead Sea, where there was a nice beach and restaurant/resort. Our timing was almost perfect as we donned our swim trunks and headed for the most buoyant body of water in the world.

On the beach, a pair of young and very good-looking German female tourists were in the process of being scolded by the local gendarme who required them both to put on their bikini tops. Apparently, going topless was not kosher in Israel. Because my pal and I were both married, we, of course, looked away and were, of course, appalled that we hadn't gotten there later so as to miss the entire show. We did invite them both to go swimming with us to try to cheer them up, but sadly the police would not allow the young German girls to join us in our swim, since they were banned from the beach for the rest of the day.

My pal and I swam, well, sort of floated, with most of our bodies out of the water, and we paddled out several hundred yards. In our inebriated state, we challenged each other to make history and go commando for a minute or two, holding our swim trunks high in the air. The Heineken courage-inducers gave us all the bravery required and we accomplished our mission. It was very stupid but sometimes alcohol does that. We both could tell our grandkids that we skinny dipped in the Dead Sea; a rare feat of which we were so proud to someday share with our grandkids, when our wives were not in the same room.

DESERT BAPTISMS IN KUWAIT, DESERT STORM, 1991

During Desert Storm, among other jobs, I served as the battalion NBC (nuclear, biological, chemical) warfare officer for 8th Tank Battalion. I got picked for this exalted position due to my science-oriented educational background. In the battalion command track, I was linked into the NBC nets from higher up, and as LtCol Cavallaro, the battalion commander told me that he wasn't going to get too excited about NBC unless he saw me getting excited. In other words, I was his "canary in the coal mine."

As part of my job, I inherited the battalion's NBC decontamination gear and NBC specialist. The battalion's decontamination equipment can be reconfigured to provide hot showers in a "gang shower" environment as long as you have diesel for heating and a source of water. I had both and after the ground war was over, we established a battalion shower with a rigorous schedule and time limits to conserve water and fuel and to make access fair to everyone. I got regular deliveries of water to supply my decontamination shower system and always made sure to maintain a reserve in my water bladders in case it was needed.

That reserve of water came to the attention of Lt Tostenson, USNR, our battalion chaplain. He had been receiving many requests for baptisms by Marines who were excited to be so close to the Holy Land, but who also found that a little sprinkle of holy water on the forehead just didn't provide the proper experience! He asked if he could perform full immersion baptisms in one of my water bladders on the days of resupply so as not to compromise my showers or reserve water supply. A quick check up the chain of command produced a response of: "It's okay if it doesn't interfere with our showers!"

I set the chaplain up with a half-full bladder warmed by the sun, and he was in business! The end result was a happy chaplain, happy Marines, unique baptisms of a lifetime, and some great pictures!

DISBURSING OFFICE

We had just returned to the States following a six-month deployment in Beirut in 1982-83. We were in the process of returning all the gear to the units to which they rightfully belonged and that sort of thing takes a little time, so we were somewhat in limbo, knowing we were soon to rejoin our old units but still attached to a group that was slowly dissolving. We were in MSSG 22, which was in support of the 22nd MAU, commanded by General James Mead ("Large James" to his men, at some considerable distance from the man himself). We had staff meetings in the mornings and basically went over what had been done the day before and what we intended to do that day; then off to get it done.

Deployments to Beirut were extremely well-staffed. I was given 200 service record books of men who had volunteered and was told I could select 20 to staff my detachment. I had not selected poster boys who could run three miles in fifteen minutes or who had perfect proficiency and conduct marks. Honestly, I didn't even care so much about how they looked in a uniform. I tried to get men who didn't complain all the time, didn't mind being dirty, got along well with their peers, and had a good attitude toward their work and the Marine Corps in general.

The gear we took was adequate. All the loaning units were told to give us the best they had, but no one did. We got gear that mostly worked, most of the time. For perspective, if we had been borrowing chairs, they would have had an average of three legs. We were given priority ordering repair parts through maintenance when we returned, because we couldn't return gear that wasn't working. So, we actually returned most gear in better shape than when we got it.

An order had come down while we were in Beirut that we must wear American Flags sewn onto armbands. It would seem the short hair, distinctive camouflage outfits, highly polished boots and "USMC" iron-on patch on the left breast pocket would have given us away, but someone higher up the chain decided that American flags on our left arm would be just the thing we needed to distinguish us from the Italians, French and Lebanese soldiers, who wore plain green uniforms and berets; the Brits wore an entirely different camo than us. But, our flags were purchased locally and sewn onto armbands locally, so we were contributing to the Lebanese economy.

We had one problem (I mean besides the whole thing just being stupid) with the flag. It would get dirty and would need to be washed. We tried everything to keep them clean. They were too delicate, sewn with fine thread, and would begin to fray and still looked dirty no matter what. We had Navy ships parked in the waters nearby and we would send the flags to the ships with our other laundry to see if they could do better than we could by hand. That didn't work either – they came back all frayed and nasty looking. We would spend a great deal of time with nail clippers, cutting the loose threads off and trying to make them look respectable, but they still looked pretty shabby.

Things got much worse when we got home because our troops got into fights with the local (non-flag wearing) Marines concerning the raggedy flag comments. We were told that because the flags were part of our uniform, we were to continue to wear them until the unit disbanded. To help where he could, General Mead gave us a "note from home." He wrote a "To whom it may concern" letter to explain that the flag-wearers were doing the best with what they had and should not be blamed for the condition of the arm-band flags and that we would only have them for a few days more. We distributed the letters to all of our troops, and everyone was instructed to carry them at all times and to show them to interested parties.

Pay day arrived and it seemed that every officer at Camp Lejeune showed up for unofficial Officer's Call. Not the traditional trip to the O'Club, but rather to the disbursing office. The Marine Corps was coming, kicking and screaming, into the computer age and it seemed that about twenty percent of the paychecks were screwed up, typically awarding No Pay Due (NPD) to the unlucky service member. All the officers tried to find out who had pay problems as early as possible so we could get to the front of the line to plead our cases to the disbursing office. Harvey Williams was my good friend and supply officer for the MSSG. He and I drove over to mainside on payday to get our pay problems squared away. We got there early enough that there were only about twenty guys in front of us. We stood chatting until we finally wound our way to the front of the line.

The counter was much like that of an old bank, about five feet high with marble tops. There were several teller windows, but only the one at the far end was ever used. They waited on one customer at a time. Harvey and I had been waiting at the window for several minutes when he noticed that some officers behind us were being waited on by the staff. He commented how nice it was that they finally opened a second window just as we made it to the front.

A couple more minutes of waiting showed us that they were really still operating at one window, just not ours. Harvey called to several Marines walking through the office and was ignored. In frustration he called out a particular staff sergeant and said, "I need to see you at this window RIGHT NOW!" The staff sergeant walked to the window and told us that by order of his captain, we were not to be served until we took those flags off our arms.

I showed him General Mead's letter and said that I thought it would straighten things out. He took it to his captain who we could clearly see on the far side of the large room. We saw the captain shake his head and the staff sergeant returned to us and told us that (we'll call him) Captain Smith said he still could not serve us.

At this time Harvey came unglued. All decorum vanished. At the top of his lungs he screamed, "CAPTAIN SMITH!! YEAH YOU, THE PENCIL-NECKED GEEK IN THE BACK!! YOU HAVE TWO CHOICES. EITHER GET SOMEBODY OVER HERE TO TAKE CARE OF US, OR I'M GONNA JUMP THIS COUNTER AND GO BACK THERE AND BEAT YOUR ASS RIGHT IN FRONT OF YOUR TROOPS!!"

The room fell silent and soon a lance corporal arrived and took care of us. The next morning at our staff meeting we covered everything and were dismissed. Almost as an afterthought, General Mead asked, "Gentlemen, yesterday there was a bit of a ruckus over at the disbursing office. Anybody know anything about that?" No one responded. "Okay, you're dismissed. Harvey, could you and Ken hang back for just a minute."

I thought we were in for big trouble and, even though I was just a bystander, I didn't mind, because I felt honored just to have been in the presence of such unbridled courage and audacity. Whatever we were in for, I was ready to pay the price. Instead, General Mead began, "Harvey, I have no doubt that you can kick the ass of any pencil-necked geek that disbursing can throw at you. I admire the sheer gumption and your sense of fairness. However, there were at least twenty underling geeks in that office, and I don't think it's fair to ask Ken to have to beat all of their asses should they decide to defend their boss. Next time, have a little consideration and attack when you are certain you have superior fire power. Call in an air strike, mortars, additional men, whatever. Use the tools at your disposal to accomplish the mission. That's all, you're dismissed."

It's just so beautiful when the boss has your back.

DOES ANYONE HAVE A QUESTION?

I was a young First Lieutenant on my first WestPac (Western Pacific) cruise in the Fall of 1983. We were on LHA-5, the USS Peleliu. I was a young HAC (Helicopter Aircraft Commander) in training on the UH-1N Huey. I have no idea of how things are done now, but back in those days when the Earth was young and dirt was new, we would head westbound out of Hawaii and, at some point, we would connect with the eastbound ship we were replacing and the 31st MAU (Marine Amphibious Unit) staff would be cross decked to our ship. The MAU staff was a year plus tour while our cruise was seven and a half months long, give or take.

So, we cross decked the MAU staff, and shortly after that, we headed somewhere to do an exercise in which we would be doing a battalion-sized helicopter assault with the grunts. This would be our first meeting with the MAU C.O., Colonel Curd. It was going to be one of those "dawn launch, Sea of Japan, Zero Dark Thirty wake up" kind of events. Now, normally, these types of full squadron, all hands-on deck type of helicopter operations would entail a brief of all the pilot participants that might take forty-five minutes to maybe an hour, tops.

Not this time. No sir. The squadron Operations Officer, Major Dan Diviney, was standing at the podium at the front of the ready room as he ran the Brief. He was going to, by God, make sure EVERYTHING was briefed for the Colonel's benefit. This event had transitioned under his direction from an operational brief to a true dog-and-pony-show style brief. We were two hours (TWO HOURS!) into this thing before we got even close to the end. Major Diviney had made sure that they had briefed every contingency known to man short of nuclear holocaust, and we were all dying of sheer boredom.

On a slightly separate note, I should add here that Dan Diviney had been my original on-wing instructor in VT-2 at Whiting Field and had the singular distinction of giving me my only down (a failure grade) in Flight School; Fam (Familiarization Flight) 5 as I recall, for failure to trim the airplane. When I joined the squadron, we had an AOM (all officers meeting) at the O'Club bar. As I walked up to him to say hello, he looked at me with the puzzled look on his face (he obviously had not read the roster) and simply said, "Oh. Wow. So, I guess you made it through Flight School." A real rocket scientist, that guy.

Back to the brief: as it was winding down, Major Diviney asked the same question that every other guy who has ever run any kind of brief has asked in some shape or form. With a serious, in-control, I-am-the-Ops-O voice, he asked, "Does anyone have a question?" to which my roommate, Joel Phillips, raised his hand. Joel was also a first lieutenant and a junior guy, a HAC in training on the CH-53, on his first cruise as well. We were sitting next to each other in our standard last row right by the back door location.

Now I should add here that Joel did not take many things seriously, whether they be life itself or the Marine Corps. As an example, when Joel left the Marine Corps a few years later, he spent about a year riding his Harley across America sleeping on friends' couches before deciding to attend Law School. A great guy then and now, just the kind of guy a squadron needs, and a great guy to have as a roommate.

As Joel raised his hand, Major Diviney, in the same serious, almost imperious voice, said simply, "Stand up, Lieutenant Phillips," as he made an upward sweeping motion with his hand, much like a choir director would do when they want the choir to stand, if you can picture that. He then said, "What is your question, Lieutenant Phillips?" to which Joel stood up and said, "Yessir. Who played Lumpy on Leave it to Beaver?"

And don't waste your time googling it - Lumpy was played by Frank Bank.

DROP IN MAUI WEEKENDS

On another mission to the Kahuku Training area with Tongo, we got talking about things that had been done in the past. Apparently Tongo had a Recon acquaintance who was Hawaiian and whose family lived on Maui. Tongo and he had an arrangement that when Tongo had a mission to the Big Island and his Recon friend wanted to go home for a visit, the two would make the travel arrangements. Tongo would inspect the aircraft maintenance record, sign for the aircraft and head to the flight line. When the time was right, he'd signal to his Recon friend to ride his bike onto the flight line and into the aircraft. Once in the aircraft, the Recon jump qualified Marine set up his jump plan. With a chute apparently checked out from Para loft and drop-straps for his bike, he was set. At the appropriate time while flying over a dirt road in a remote portion of norther Maui, Tongo would lower the CH-46E ramp and the Recon stud would just ride off the back of the helicopter, pull his chute and the bike would drop 15' below him as he guided the chute to the edge of the remote dirt road. The guy would land, roll up his chute, pack it in his backpack and ride off to his parent's house. On Sunday when Tongo was back in Maui refueling, the guy would meet him at the airport and ride right back on the 46 for the ride home.

I don't know how many times this "drop in vacation" was repeated, but I understand that once discovered (sometime before I arrived at Kaneohe) that the gig was up and never to my knowledge repeated.

DUCK SOUP

It was the summer of 1976 and my brother-in-law had convinced me to go with him to Officers Candidate School and their ten-week Platoon Leaders Class (OCS, PLC) in Quantico, Virginia. Shortly after Company B was formed, I found myself in the presence of forty other wild-eyed, hard-charging, ten-week wonders ready to begin our adventure as Platoon 1235. We were introduced to our senior drill instructor, Staff Sergeant E. He was our teacher and, for many of us, the prototype Marine.

Day three, I found myself assigned as the guide. (As an aside, this is where your unreliable narrator kicks in; my apologies for not introducing myself. I'm Captain Tango Golf aka Chipper, TD, and Romeo. According to my field journal, we were reminiscing about day three of our adventure if you can call Marine Corps officer-training boot camp an adventure).

On day two, Senior Drill Instructor taught us several valuable life tools; for example, portable hotel. What we would learn was one of SSgt E's favorite phrases, and there were many. This entailed moving our entire squad bay into the courtyard at the exact dimensions as in the squad bay, except OUTSIDE!! And watching television!

This became a favorite pastime that summer and involved being in the prone/push-up position, balancing our chins on our fists. He would always ask, "What are you watching?" And based on our answer, he would gently ask us to change the channel, which led to a balance or crash option (there were mostly crashes in the early weeks, but like most things, Platoon 1235 got better at watching TV as time went by). But I digress as I am prone to do...

Anyway, Day 3 started out with the usual morning wake-up call: junior drill instructors tossing garbage cans down the Quonset hut aisle and encouraging us recruits to rise and shine to another glorious day in the Marine Corps (actually about this time I was questioning my judgment for ever volunteering for this summer camp field study). As we were about to fall out to muster, SSgt E casually whispered to me, "Golf, do you know what they are having for chow this morning?"

I said, "No, Senior Drill Instructor."

He replied, "Duck soup."

I quickly spread the word to my squad leaders and heard them pass it down through their fire team leaders: "Duck soup...soup...breakfast is duck soup...duck...soup." I was fairly sure the senior drill instructor was not a Marx Brothers Fan, and I was equally confident that any type of delicious soup was not on the Quantico breakfast menu.

As SSgt E marched us over to the chow hall, I started to understand (Had an epiphany?) that every minute counted in a training day; and a place that a crafty drill instructor could steal a few minutes for extra teaching (especially close arms drill—

which was an especially sacred subject to senior drill instructors) was the chow hall. Then I was given the cipher when we arrived at the chow hall and SSgt E said, "Get in and get out. We have things to do besides feed your pretty faces."

I got it. Duck in and duck out. I led my squads through a chaotic charge through the chow line, eating eggs with my hands, cramming biscuits and whatever else I could into my mouth. I remember sitting for what seemed like less than five minutes, before I saw SSgt E moving towards the hatch, which was my signal to get up and lead my squads out into the inviting Virginia sun and the promise of another day of training with the one and only SSgt E.

DYNAMITE

Graves Hall was—well—like a graveyard that Sunday afternoon. The afternoon began with the lieutenants studying for a big exam. It ended with me locked up in front of Captain "Dyn-o-mite" (who looked something like J.J. Walker from Good Times), wondering if I was about to set a record for the shortest Marine Corps career ever.

The story actually began weeks earlier in New York City. My fellow TBS lieutenant, Juan, had invited me to his home in Princeton, New Jersey. It's common for lieutenants to invite secluded comrades to their homes. Juan's family was great. I felt welcome. Princeton isn't too far from New York City, so Juan and his sister, Kiki, offered to take this West Coast lad to Manhattan.

Bright lights, an off-Broadway show, and graffiti – it was everything that this California-boy had imagined. The activity was memorable and quite harmless, until Juan insisted that we visit Chinatown. That subway stop would prove to be my qǐng jūn rù wèng (boiling vat).

Fast forward a couple of weeks to Graves Hall. Juan, our fellow TBS lieutenants, and I were deeply engrossed in the material that would be covered in our final TBS test. The quiet was depressing. We were nearing the end of our TBS journey. Graves Hall should have been a joyous place.

I remembered my Chinatown souvenir—a firecracker string. Pop! An idea. I realized that the firecracker string would be the ideal way to liven up Graves Hall. I walked into the deserted hallway. Perfect, I thought, except the floors, they're too perfect. We had recently waxed them. I didn't want to leave powder burns, so I stepped back into my room and grabbed a Crossroads weekly. I placed the newspaper in the center of the hallway, set the firecrackers on the paper, lit the fuse, and rushed back into my room.

Boom-boom-boom! Boom-boom-boom! The firecrackers popped in short bursts. I put on a baffled face and stepped back into the hallway. It was full of confetti. Lieutenants were running around, laughing and waving Mamelukes. Mission accomplished. The diversion brought a moment of cheer, but soon everyone returned to their books. The hallway was full of bits of paper. I grabbed a broom and began sweeping.

A young, uniformed second lieutenant marched down the hallway. He halted in front of me and inspected the floors. "Do you know who is responsible for this?" he asked. I looked at the white nametag on the uniform. Hotel Company—boot Louie, I thought.

"I'm the junior officer of the day," announced the boot.

"You can see that everything is fine here," I smiled. "No harm, no foul. You can return to your post."

"I've already reported the incident to the officer of the day. Come with me."

I followed the boot to the headquarters building. We entered the duty office and came to attention. Captain Dynomite was pissed. He excused the boot and laid into me. "You are supposed to set the example. Do you know how we handle enlisted Marines that behave like this? Major Shallcross is your C.O., isn't he?"

I'm ruined, I thought.

After chewing my arse for five minutes, Captain Dynomite asked, "Have you learned a lesson here?"

"Yes sir."

"Dismissed."

EARNING THE TITLE MARINE

During the late summer/early fall of 1981, a recruit from Tennessee attended basic training in the Third Recruit Training Battalion at Parris Island, South Carolina. This recruit's father was a famous singer/actor during the 1960's, who had several Top 40 hits and a modest role in a television show.

During the mandatory interview with the series officers, the recruit allowed that his father was this famous singer/actor and would likely attend the series graduation at the end of basic training. This was in response to the standard questions regarding whether a recruit had any famous relatives and, if so, the likelihood of their attendance at the series graduation.

The admission of his father's career and obvious wealth prompted questions regarding the reasons and motivations for the recruit to decide to enlist in the Marine Corps Reserve and to commit to serving in the reserves as a "weekend warrior" for a finite period. The recruit responded that while his father was indeed financially well off and would likely leave a significant inheritance to the recruit, the recruit wanted to achieve something on his own that his father could neither provide nor influence. That achievement would be to earn the title "Marine" by graduating from recruit training. "Marine" was a title that the recruit would be able to claim solely on his own and through his own efforts. He would be able to proudly carry that title, "Marine," throughout his life.

The recruit successfully completed basic training to earn the "Marine" title, and his father attended the series graduation.

ENDURANCE RUN

Officer Candidate School in the summer of 1979 was full of constant anxiety, fear, excitement, and psychological and physical challenges that I had never before experienced. I was in constant fear of falling off an obstacle and being "recycled," sent back to heal and then returned to pick up where I fell out, only to graduate with a bunch of candidates I didn't know. I was not much in fear of failing, though I watched nearly half of my platoon go home without bars. I had never before participated in anything with that kind of attrition rate. They were constantly telling us the next thing, the thing we were going to do tomorrow, was the worst and that many of us wouldn't pass.

I think the most challenging thing for me was knowing that at any moment, I could just walk away. I found that when you are gasping for air, which just doesn't exist in the muddy stream leading to the Quigley, or being sent back for a fourth time through the "O" course because you didn't shout out your platoon number when you touched the crossbar at the top of the twenty-foot rope, it all seems too easy to just quit. The Marines don't need people who quit, so they repeatedly tell you that you can quit any time. Before I left home, Dad told me that they would try to make me quit and that it was just to weed out the weak. I wasn't weak, so I had no intentions of quitting, but the temptation to do so raised its ugly head daily.

Perhaps the most physically challenging event we experienced was the endurance run. It was a timed event and was pass/fail. As long as it was completed within the prescribed time, you passed. We were told that we could not graduate without passing the endurance run. It began with the obstacle ("O") course, wearing boots and utilities. We had run the "O" course so many times we could almost do it in our sleep.

As we finished it, we ran to the field nearby to pick up our gear (rifles, cartridge belts, full canteens and suspenders). We then took off on a three-mile run through the woods. There were lots of hills and plenty of mud to slip in. Although speed was important, we could easily lose time by slipping. There was a rope climb up the side of a big hill; a climb up a cargo net; lots of logs to vault over; and barbed wire to crawl under. Then there were the rope bridges, a two- and a three-rope bridge and a one-rope hand over hand or crawl across the top. Everything was made more difficult because of the gear on our backs and the rifles in our hands. The equipment was bulky and if it got hung up on something it could eat up valuable time trying to get it free.

Finally, there were the water hazards: crawling through a very smelly ditch holding eight inches of water and crawling through a concrete culvert pipe. We came out and then began the "sprint" home. We were nearly exhausted by the time we got through the obstacles, but then had to run about a mile back to the parade deck where the stopwatches awaited. We were wet and tired and slow. I passed guys who were somehow moving slower than I was, but I was passed by many more.

When I finally cleared the tree line at the far end of the grinder, it was like someone turned on the oxygen supply. The stagnant air of the woods was replaced by the intense heat of the sun on the wide-open field. My pace picked up, but others seemed to be flying by me. I could see the finish line ahead and was happy to know I was going to finish, though I had no idea what my time would be or whether it would be good enough to pass.

I crossed the line and discovered that I had over a minute remaining on the pass/fail clock. Many candidates were already lined up near the finish line cheering on those who had not yet arrived. I joined them as more and more came pouring in from the woods. I saw Candidate Mike O'Brien when he was forty to fifty yards away, and I knew he and a few others were going to make it.

I didn't know Mike at the time but got to know him at The Basic School later. He was pretty wobbly coming in the last forty yards, weaving back and forth as the cheers grew louder. He fell across the finish line, going slow enough that he didn't skid far, but he lost consciousness. Several candidates and a corpsman grabbed him up, took him over to the medical tent, and dropped him into a plastic kiddy pool filed with ice. The ice and an ammonia ampoule jolted him awake and the corpsman held him down to try to get his body temperature down. He was on the edge between heat exhaustion and heat stroke, his body operating without enough liquids. He was all out of sweat and heating up fast. In a few minutes he came around and wanted out of the ice, but the corpsman kept him there and quizzed him to see if his brain was functioning.

"Candidate, how many fingers do I have up?" asked the Corpsman.

Mike, always aware that questions asked of candidates were usually tricky, answered cautiously, but in the OCS format: "Sir, the candidate SEES three fingers." His eyes were rolling around and he wasn't fully back from wherever he went.

"Fine, what is your name?" Nothing tricky here.

"Sir, the candidate's name is Michael J. O'Brien, sir."

Not certain that he could have told us what the "J" stood for, the corpsman tried again: "Candidate, where are you currently located?"

This one seemed to stump him for a moment. He opened his eyes for a few seconds and looked around as though he was trying to get his precise bearings before answering. He took enough time that under normal conditions he could have given him an eight-digit grid coordination. Instead, this measured response: "Sir, the candidate is currently located approximately... on the ground." The Corpsman decided he needed a little more cooling off.

EVERYBODY NEEDS A STORY

It was the early fall of 1988, and I was on my last tour while on active duty. I was an instructor pilot (IP) in the Navy flight training program at NAS Whiting Field, FL, and had been there almost two years. I had been a hard-working instructor, flying the T-34C, Turbo-Mentor aircraft; we instructors liked to call it the Turbo Tor-Mentor. I was teaching new student naval aviators in their initial phase of flight school, known as primary.

I worked hard as an instructor to get qualified in all areas of the curriculum and by the two-year mark, I was qualified in all phases. I was qualified as a familiarization instructor and was also qualified as an IP in formation, precision aerobatics, as well as basic and advanced instrument flight. I had even gotten to the point that I was giving the end of course check rides to the students before they completed the primary syllabus and moved onto more advanced training. However, I had made the decision to leave active duty.

As a parting gift as it were, the squadron traditionally gave an instructor access to an airplane for a day. We would select another IP and go fly anywhere we wanted to go in the southeast. It was referred to as "IP to IP training," with the goal of the flight to be "peer evaluation of your instructional techniques with the goal of improved instructional Abilities." What it boiled down to was, as you can surmise, a boondoggle, good deal last flight to thank you for all of your hard work.

I planned to fly over to MCAS Beaufort, SC from Pensacola to see a friend of mine, have lunch, and return to Pensacola as my last flight. As the day approached, though, I started to get vibes that things were changing. We had a new schedules officer come onboard. The schedules officer was the staff pilot responsible for setting each day's training schedule and thus massaging and improving or possibly hurting what was known as the Pilot Training Rate (PTR). This schedules officer was a Navy P-3 pilot. For simplicity's sake, I'll refer to him as Lieutenant Buzz Kill. Buzz made it clear that he was going to make the PTR the best the squadron had ever seen. So, my last, best good deal appeared to be on shaky ground as, in his eyes, it was not a productive use of the airplane. That type of flight simply served as a small token of thanks for hard work, and that did (seemingly) nothing to improve PTR. Therefore, it was deemed unnecessary by Lieutenant Buzz Kill.

I got a call late one afternoon and Buzz informed me that my last flight had been cancelled. My last flight fell victim to his view of how the aircraft assets should be utilized. I was quite unhappy with the denial of what just a week or two ago had been the normal goodbye for a hard-working IP, but what could I do about it? Not a darn thing, so I told him what I thought about his PTR and hung up the phone. I had flown my last flight for my squadron. Or so I thought.

Not being on the flight schedule meant I was going to spend the next day at home, and I did so. As I recall, it was a Friday. I was leaving the following Monday for my new job as an airline pilot. I was going to check out on Monday morning and hop in my car for the five-hour drive to Atlanta where I would start my next career. However, things did not quite work out that way.

I got a call around noon, and it came from Lieutenant Kill: "I need you to come in and fly, right now. See me when you get here. I don't have time to explain." Click. He had hung up. Now I wasn't much inclined to go fly when I had MY flight taken from me, but I decided to drive in and see what was such a big deal.

I got to the squadron and had barely gotten out of my car when Buzz came up to me and said, "I need you to fly with 2nd Lt Downs (not his real name). He failed his instrument check-ride, and he needs a recheck. He was scheduled to fly with an evaluator and that IP just called in sick. You are the only evaluator available and I need him to finish today. He needs to be complete in the syllabus by the close of business today. If not, our numbers will be off for this week's PTR." There it was – the real reason for the call. He was worried about his PTR and not really anything else. I started to tell him where he could stick his PTR but then I thought I needed to finish my tour as I had started it: strong and motivated. So, I headed to the briefing rooms to meet up with 2nd Lt Downs.

I was actually surprised to hear that he was the student. I had flown with this 2nd Lt on a couple of occasions and he had always been prepared and flew reasonably well. When I got to the briefing room, there I found Downs. He looked dejected, quiet, and nothing like the student I had flown with before. We went through our brief, and he seemed to get through my questions okay, but I could tell something was off.

As we were waiting for our aircraft assignment, we had a few moments of slack time, and I figuratively pointed to the elephant in the room, and simply asked, "Lieutenant, what are we doing here?" He initially said that it was because he had gotten a "Down" (flight school speak for an unsatisfactory flight) on his prior check ride. I told him that that made no sense to me, as I had flown with him before, and he had flown well. So, what was the real story?

He finally admitted to me that his goal had been to fly jets. He had eaten jets, breathed jets, slept jets, and crapped jets ever since he had decided to go to flight school. However, when the time came for him to be assigned advanced training, there had been no jet slots available. The jet "pipeline" was closed that week. So, due to the needs of the Marine Corps, he had been assigned to advanced helicopter training. He was going to be a helicopter pilot. He was simply a victim of timing. Had he finished training a week sooner or maybe a week later, there might have been a jet slot for him, just not this week—his week.

I told him that he had it all wrong. Helicopter flying was the most fun flying I had ever done. He was going to get more flight time as a helo pilot than he would as a jet pilot and he would see things down low he could never see from tens of thousands of feet high. I told him, "Jet pilots respect helicopter pilots when they are cold, wet, and on the end of a hoist." He smiled, and I told him that if he would allow himself to see the possibilities, he was going to have a great time flying helos. Instead of me being offended at his view of my career as a helo pilot, I helped him to see the possibilities. Things started to get better.

On an instructional instrument flight of any kind, the student sits in the rear cockpit and flies in simulated instrument conditions by pulling a large canvas covering, much like a tent, over himself. We called the canvas covering "the bag." While he was flying only on instruments and "under the bag," I would evaluate him while watching for other air traffic. The student did his preflight checks and made sure the bag was working correctly, while I sat in the front cockpit and taxied out.

I did the take off and as we were climbing out, I told him it was time for him to fly and he put the bag over his head and took control of the airplane. Within just a couple of minutes I could see his instrument skills were fine. His only issue had been attitude and motivation.

As we continued to climb out, I suddenly had a thought as I realized that this really was going to be my last flight as an instructor. So, I said to Lt Downs, "Downs, I have the aircraft. Pop the bag." That was, again, flight school speak telling him to put the bag away and stow it, which he promptly did. I asked him over the interphone, "Downs, do you REALLY want to redo your instrument check?" He paused, not really knowing what to say, and simply said, "If given the option, no sir."

I then told him, "Downs, I am getting ready to do a loop. Then you are going to do a loop. If yours is better than mine, you get an above." For those of you who never went to flight school, the rating system in flight school at that time was one of four grades - above, average, below, and unsat. An above grade was like getting on A on a particular maneuver.

Again, he paused and simply said, "Aye, aye, sir." And we did just that. A pair of loops was then followed by a pair of spins, a pair of barrel rolls, and a couple of other aerobatic maneuvers that he had learned in the syllabus. He had not flown aerobatics in several months but actually did reasonably well. So, for about an hour we did a series of aerobatic maneuvers that had absolutely nothing to do with instrument flying. As I recall, I gave him a couple of above grades. I gave him above grades, not because he had really performed a couple of maneuvers better than me, but because his attitude had changed.

I heard him laugh and crack a few jokes as we flew. It was a different guy. I gave him control of the aircraft and told him to take us back to base. The "check ride" was over and he had passed with a couple of above grades, no less!

As we headed back to base, I asked him a question: "Downs, do you know why we flew acro today instead of instruments?" He said that even though he had had a great time, he didn't really understand what had just taken place.

And I gave him a speech something like this: "Downs, you are getting ready to head to helicopter training and you are going to love it. And in eighteen months or so, you are going to find yourself at the O'Club in Japan, or Okinawa, or somewhere and everyone is going to be telling flying stories. You're going to be one of the new guys trying to find their place in the squadron. You're going to feel a bit left out of the group as one of the new guys, except for one reason. You now have a story to add to all of their flying stories, your own flying story. Everybody needs a story. You now HAVE a story about the time you thought you had to fly an instrument recheck that you had fouled up and instead you came home with two above grades because you flew a better loop than the instructor. You will tell that story several times in your career as you add other stories, but this is your first one. It is my gift to you. Now go get your ass in gear and kick ass in helos. You're going to love it."

I left the Marine Corps and truthfully never heard from 2nd Lt Downs again. But I do have a feeling that he went on to have a great career as a helicopter pilot. He just needed a little motivation when he was down.

Everybody needs a story.

EXOTIC FLAME DANCE

Naval Air Station Cubi Point in the Philippines is a legendary place, especially among Marine aviators. Many "famous" stories have been told which to the average person, seem unreal, but all are true without embellishment. The Exotic Flame Dance (which some know under a different name) that was performed at the Cubi Point Officers' Club by an unnamed Marine Corps captain is no exception. Similar kinds of well-known events seem to start as a dare, then a bet, and then onto the event and resultant famous story. The Exotic Flame Dance was not one of those. It was entirely one particular captain's own idea and doing.

Unbeknownst to the future event witnesses, he first gathered his costume needs and accessories which consisted of a rolled-up newspaper, sparklers, running shoes, mask and a jock strap. He then stripped, put on the shoes and jock strap. He rolled the sparklers in the newspaper, lit the sparklers, and placed the make-shift stage props between the cheeks of his ass.

After disguising himself with the mask, he ran through the Cubi Point O'Club restaurant screaming an exotic sounding chant. He danced through the club, butt cheeks akimbo, unscathed by shocked patrons, officers, spouses and their children and then to the exit, stage left. The looks of those patrons were much like those of the officers in the NAS Rota O'Club in Spain when the

Great Santini did his famous puking scene, performed by Robert Duvall in the movie of the same name. The dancing captain was never caught. Though, to my knowledge, the few of us who knew his identity never uttered his name and, thankfully, he left no forensic evidence of sparkler-singed butt hair!

FIELD DAY

One of the many traditions of the Corps is that Thursday night is Field Day night. After securing for the day, Marines return to their barracks and begin the weekly ritual of cleaning every inch of their living quarters to such a state that it positively shines. The floors are waxed and buffed such that they gleam. The fixtures in the head are polished so that you can see yourself. The place smells of floor wax, ammonia, Clorox and Comet, but it is beautiful to walk through such impeccable cleanliness.

Marines stand at attention by their racks as their CO walks through on his Friday morning inspection. Sometimes wall locker or footlocker inspections accompany the barracks inspections, but usually it is just a Friday morning walk through to be sure the troops know that the details are being inspected, so the sparkle is always maintained.

I was a platoon commander at 8th Comm Battalion in the French Creek area of Camp Lejeune, NC. Our CO was Lt Col Don Lynch. Since our work area was about a mile from the barracks, the CO usually let the troops go to work on Friday morning as he did his barracks inspection. I always came in early to do a quick inspection with the Marines present so I could point out and hopefully correct deficiencies before the Colonel saw them. Then I'd send them off to the work area and wait for the CO to come down from the Head Shed.

When the CO arrived, I followed him along with my note taker who jotted down each deficiency the CO pointed out. He seldom found much, but always pointed out things like the "US" on the wool blanket was not properly centered on the rack, there was some dryer lint behind a dryer, or a water spot on a faucet. The note taker would judiciously jot down everything the boss said, and I would pass it along to the men when I saw them later that morning.

On one such morning I met Col Lynch at the front hatch to the barracks, and we proceeded to do our dance. He would tell me a faucet was dripping and I would show him the work order that we had sent to maintenance two days ago. He found a fire extinguisher that hadn't been inspected in six months. There might be too much wax buildup in a corner of a room. The tiniest details were pointed out because that's the way of the Corps. Little things can become big problems, so take care of them when they are small.

As we passed through the individual rooms, I noticed that several of my men were milling around outside in the parking lot and had not yet left to go to our work area. I made a quick note to tell the Gunny about it later.

We were almost through the inspection when a clerk ran up from the office downstairs and told the CO that he had a call from General Winglass. He dashed quickly down to the company office to take the call and, in doing so, passed the lobby which was visible from the parking lot. The call from the general took about ten minutes and the colonel returned to me, and we went back upstairs to inspect a couple of more rooms as well as the head.

As we entered the head, I knew something was wrong. There was no antiseptic smell, but rather a putrid horrible stench that almost gagged me when I walked in. The CO turned to me: "What the hell is that, Lieutenant?"

"I don't know, sir... it wasn't like this a few minutes ago," was my lame response.

We rounded the corner and there, hanging in the shower, was a 140-pound doe. Her guts lay in a washtub below, her skin lay in a heap in the corner. She was strung up by a beam from above. I knew in an instant that one of my boys had hit a deer on the way to work this morning and they had waited until they saw the CO go to the company office, assuming the inspection was over. They then slipped the roadkill up the back stairs to dress her out. They heard us come back up the stairs and had to leave her and slip back down the back staircase.

The CO looked at me, knowing that I knew nothing of this. I had no idea what was coming next. He put his hand on my shoulder and said, "I don't even want to know how this happened. I just want a hind quarter on my desk within an hour and we will never speak of this again."

There was a hind quarter on his desk thirty minutes later, wrapped in newspaper. I heard the colonel tell this story many times in the years that followed, and it always got a laugh.

FUNERALS FOR TWO FRIENDS

These two memorial services happened while I was a Marine reservist flying in HMM-764 out of Marine Corps Air Station El Toro. Losing a fellow Marine is always brutally tragic but sometimes and somehow, those fallen brothers reach through the fabric of time and space and tell us to relax and keep on laughing.

Billy Anderson and Dudley Urbine were two amazing human beings, great pilots and beloved members of the squadron. I had been a member of 764 for about ten months and had flown with Billy a time or two. He was also one of the funniest people I've ever known; always smiling, always ready with a comment that bent you over with laughter. I knew Dud back at Marine Corps Air Station New River in North Carolina and flew with him a few times while I was on active duty. He was quiet, but also quite funny with gems of under-his-breath comments.

One evening Dud and Billy went out on a night vision goggle (NVG) training flight. Dud was an NVG instructor and it was Billy's first NVG flight. For whatever reason, they tragically flew into a mountain on their way to the training area, killing all four members of the crew.

Dud and the Whistling Boogers

I was a pall bearer at Dud's funeral along with five squadron mates: Bill Gaita, Mike Lewis, Ray Wersel, Dan Scandalito, and

John Comeau. The ceremony of course was very solemn, and it was so sad to see Dud's wife and the rest of his family weep so hard at losing him forever. It is during these kinds of occasions when a sudden burst of comedy is so unwelcome and yet somehow defies decorum by rearing its ugly head, sometimes staying during an entire memorial service.

As the memorial service started, the six of us were seated behind Dud's grieving relatives. I was seated sort of in the middle, Dan Scandalito (Scando) to my right and Billy Gaita to my left. Major Ray Wersel (we called him Gunny Ray, due to his crusty southern drawl) was seated next to the aisle and to the right of Scando. Just as the preacher started the eulogy, Ray's nose perfectly positioned an extremely loud whistling booger plugged into a Marshall amp. It whistled just like one of those clown whistles that goes up and down on a morning cartoon. And Ray... was completely oblivious to it, which of course made it that much funnier. Several minutes into the eulogy, I could feel Scando sort of bouncing in his seat, trying desperately like the rest of us not to laugh whatsoever, as Gunny Ray's Lonely Hearts Club Nose Boulder played along with the soft weeping.

Our only solution was pain. We all instinctively grabbed a part of our leg and started squeezing with all our might to conjure up as much self-inflicted pain as we could to keep from busting out laughing. After all we were Marines and no matter how hysterical each bar of booger ranch music came out of Ray's nose, we were not going to break out in laughter, and we didn't. We waited until we could get to the O'Club after the service to recount our glory in battle. When Ray walked into the club, the rest of us were already at the bar and went into a "cover band" rendition of Ray's greatest hits by whistling our version of the memorial service. Dud would have loved that but also would have wished we failed proper decorum and just broke out in a few minutes of belly laughter as an unknowing Major Ray Wersel and his Magical Mystery Nose Boulder Tour looked on with clueless horror, disgusted with his five disrespectful squadron mates.

Billy and the Electrolux

Billy's family wanted him to be cremated and his ashes spread into the Pacific Ocean by pouring out his ashes from one of our helicopters. Of course, we would oblige and were honored and privileged to do so. The plan for Billy's memorial service was put in action and one CH46E was to fly Billy's ashes just off Dana Point, California on a particular drill weekend Saturday. The family would all be just off the coast in a big white sailboat, waiting to watch as Billy's ashes poured out of the back of the helicopter and into the ocean. The time of the ceremony was noon.

I did not fly that mission, but I sat in on the flight brief in the back of the ready room along with the rest of the pilots in HMM-764. The mission was fairly straight forward. The pilots and aircrewmen were to take off about fifteen minutes before noon, make the ten-minute flight near the tip of Dana Point, find the sailboat, slow to around 30 knots, drop down to about 50 feet off the water, lower the ramp, raise the hatch, and the crew chief would pour Billy's ashes out of the rear of the helicopter in sight of Billy's family on the sailboat. Simple.

The amount of ashes of a cremated person the size of Billy is about a gallon or so in volume. It's a lot of ashes on the mantel at home but from a hundred feet away, it doesn't look like much.

During the brief, I suggested that perhaps a good idea would be to mix Billy's ashes with a large bag of Speedy Dry (kitty litter used to absorb oil and hydraulic fluid spills) and pour that from the aircraft. Before I could finish my sentence, the aircraft commander, an active duty major, stopped me and said my idea was ridiculous. He also stopped my suggestion just before I added, "And you might want to pour the ashes out of the right-side crew door since the airflow through the aircraft will be reversed at around 30 knots." Fortunately, the crew chief took my advice and had a few buddies put a big bag of speedy dry in the back of the helo just in case, unbeknownst to the good major.

Southern California weather is typically beautiful. Hundreds of thousands of Californians enjoy the outside activities, especially when the weather is nice. The day of Billy's memorial service was an exceptionally beautiful, clear day, especially just off Dana Point.

As chance would have it, when the pilots got to the ceremony area over the ocean, there were literally hundreds of white sailboats all around the point. What a surprise. The two pilots had to guess which sailboat was which and figured it was one of the bigger sailboats carrying lots of people. The aircraft slowed to around 30 knots and the crew chief raised the hatch and lowered the ramp, ready to proceed with the solemn memorial service. The crew chief positioned himself at the end of the ramp with the gallon container of Billy's ashes. At the right time, the major commanded him to pour out Billy into the blue Pacific. He did as ordered, and just as the last bit of ashes were gone, the major screamed, "STOP! Stop pouring out the ashes!" Too late. The cockpit, all the flight gauges, their flight suits, and windshield were covered with Billy's white-gray self. Both pilots frantically wiped Billy off the windshield just to see out to continue to safely fly.

Once the dust cleared (no pun intended), everyone on the helo realized that there were still people on some large sailboat waiting to see Billy come out of the aircraft and into the Pacific, but we were fresh out of Billy. Now what? The crew chief mentioned that someone forgot to remove a big bag of Speedy Dry from the back of the aircraft before they took off, and maybe they could use that to represent a ceremonial likeness of Billy. This time, however, they decided it would be best to pour Speedy Dry Billy from the right-side crew entrance door and hatch. And that's what they did. Billy's family witnessed fifty pounds of hydraulic fluid absorbent pour out of the right side of the aircraft thinking it was Billy instead of the Hollywood stunt version of Billy, consisting of dry, clay crystals so capable of absorbing cat urine and pesky oil spills.

GAMMA GOAT GARAGE

In 1981 I participated in an exercise called Solid Shield at Camp Lejeune, NC. I was the Platoon Commander for the Multichannel Platoon, which meant I was doing some long-distance microwave communication, bouncing signals off the troposphere whenever we could get it to work.

We had been in the field, out near Onslow Beach for nearly a month and morale was very low. The battalion had lost about a fourth of its rank while we were out there. Young Marines were sneaking around in the woods at night, drinking and smoking marijuana and getting caught. Each time it would cost them $500 in pay and the loss of a stripe. While we were out in the field and for the play of the exercise, the CO had commanded no alcohol, and this had been particularly hard on morale.

My platoon had been working very hard and I was looking for a little reward I could give them to thank them. There were no shower units, so we had all been bathing and shaving out of our helmets. Our helmets likewise served as a washing machine as no washers or driers were available. Thus it was, that we looked and smelled like we had been in the field for a while. Being young and foolish, I thought driving the whole lot of them back to main side, unlocking the barracks, and letting them get a quick shower and wash a uniform might be an apt reward.

First, I went to the CO, Col Whalen, and told him of my intentions. He said he'd rather not know about it, so I should be sure not to be caught by the duty back at the battalion. I told him we would lock the door, keep the lights off and hide the vehicles across the street in the woods, so no one would know we were there. He agreed that the troops would get a lot more satisfaction from sneaking back without permission than by doing it with his consent.

Nothing more was said and at around 1900 I had the gunny pull two gamma-goats down to the road, about 200 yards from our tents. At around 2200 he woke everyone up for a late-night formation. They assumed it was for a shakedown inspection, looking for booze and marijuana. We turned the formation into a classroom circle, and I told them of "Operation Shower Call." They were very excited. I told them they had five minutes to get their shower gear, an extra set of cammies and meet me at the vehicles. We loaded the whole lot in the trailers pulled by two gamma-goats.

A gamma-goat is a Vietnam era 6-wheel drive maintenance nightmare. Mine were usually rendered inoperable, but on this night, I had two that worked. My multichannel communications vans had come to the field in these trailers, but had been offloaded, so they were perfect for our mission. In twenty minutes we were in the woods across the street from our barracks. My Marines were instructed to toss their uniforms into the wash and head to the showers. When the clothes were washed and dried, they were to get dressed and meet me back at the vehicle in an hour and a half. I made sure they understood the time they should be back. At no time were they to turn on any lights. They were to maintain a watch at all times to make sure the battalion staff duty did not see them in the barracks. They followed the gunny. He unlocked the barracks, and they were on their way.

Everything went exactly as planned. The battalion duty personnel didn't come by. The clothes and the Marines were washed, dried and returned to me with several minutes to spare. They were happier than I had seen them in a long time. That is, most of them were.

Three of them were not with the others. These were some of my troublemakers. After questioning some of the others I learned that they didn't go to the laundry nor to the showers. Instead, they went to the phones and called their wives. The ladies, not expecting the call, took a while to get ready and then a while longer to drive to the barracks. They met their husbands in the tree line about 50 yards away from our vehicles. They then went deeper into the woods for a romantic encounter. Apparently, there is something that a Marine who has been in the field for three weeks wants more than a shower and clean clothes. They came dragging up seven minutes late with huge grins on their faces. I told them I would deal with them later. We loaded up and headed back to the field.

The next morning two of my corporals came to me and told me that the three, based on the sea-lawyering of the ringleader, Lance Corporal Bollinger, were not fearful of what would happen to them, because what we were all doing was illegal and I couldn't punish them without exposing my own wrongdoing. The corporals suggested that if it was going to get me in trouble, maybe I should just do nothing and they would organize a blanket party. I told them that I could handle it and I appreciated their concern for me.

Armed with this advance information I called the three in individually, no witnesses. I told them I intended to charge them with disobedience of a lawful order and unauthorized absence (UA). They would have a choice as to whether they would like to have a court martial or accept non-judicial punishment (NJP) administered by the CO.

The two followers folded immediately and requested NJP. The third, Bollinger, pushed back, saying, "Lieutenant, if you take me in front of the CO, he's going to know that you snuck us all back to the barracks, so you'll be getting yourself in trouble. And anyway, to prove disobedience, your order would have to be lawful, and you were doing something illegal at the time, so your order was not legal. And as far as UA, we were all UA from this LZ, so I wasn't any more or less UA than you or the rest of the platoon."

The fact is, I could have taken him to the colonel for NJP and the boss would have taken $500 and a stripe. Unfortunately, there would be witnesses who would learn what we had done, and the boss would not have liked that. Since I never told anyone that we were doing anything illegal or without permission (though everyone assumed it) the CO would have backed me and hammered him. After I told him I was more than willing to go to NJP or a Courts Martial, he softened. I told him I might consider a punishment that would not cost him $500 and bust him back to PFC. I called the other two in and offered them a chance to skip

NJP for some serious after-hours manual labor. We had two more weeks in the field and if they could dig me a gamma-goat garage, I would forgive the violations. I took them out to a sandy dune about 10 feet high.

"I want to be able to back a gamma-goat into the side of this dune and stretch a camo-net across the top so that it just clears the top of the vehicle. You can work after we secure each evening. If you're done by the time we go home, your debt to the platoon will be paid. If you choose NJP and lose, you can tell your wife how you lost $500 and will be getting less pay for a while. I will only do the garage deal if all of you choose that."

None of them were willing to risk the money and the stripe when hard labor would not cost anything but sweat, so they all chose that. It was all sand, so when they took a shovel full out, two more shifted into the hole. They filled sandbags and slowly the garage started to take shape. They were filthy and sweaty and had blisters on top of blisters, but they had it complete on the tenth night.

Three sandbag walls inclined from zero up to ten feet high. We ceremoniously backed in the gamma-goat and stretched the camo net across the top. I have never seen another such structure. There were lots of pictures taken. I announced at a platoon formation that the debt that these three owed had been paid in full and that further discipline would not be necessary. When you leave a training area, you are to leave it as you found it, so, though it pained me, I had them cut open all the sandbags and put the hill back as it was. My gamma-goat garage only lasted two days.

GROUND ROUND

We were seven TBS lieutenants looking for a good meal. Burgers would be fine as long as the beer was cold. We headed north on route one to the Ground Round in Woodbridge, Virginia. The parking lot was crowded. I parked the car in the boonies while the others went in to find a table. As I approached the table, I noted friendly banter between a lovely, young waitress and my comrades.

"We're Marine officers," boasted one.

"You're second lieutenants," she countered. "Someday you'll be Marine officers."

"You realize that we could be sent to war at any minute."

"I smell Quantico all over you. No one is sending you butter bars anywhere." Five of my buddies laughed. One sulked. I was now a couple feet from the table. The waitress turned to me and said, "I suppose that you're a second lieutenant too?"

Being a Marine intelligence officer, I sensed that I was walking into an ambush. Okay, who am I kidding? I was barely an officer and had yet to receive any intelligence training. Regardless, my perceptive skills were highly polished. Well, that's not true either, but my intuition was on high alert.

"No ma'am," I replied, "I am the colonel's driver. He asked me to drive these young men to dinner in recognition of their academic achievements this week."

The girl cocked her head and patted the empty seat and gestured for me sit down. She smiled at me and disappeared. A couple of minutes later she returned with a tall frosty mug full of amber. She sat the beer in front of me and said, "This one's on the house."

The friendly exchange between the waitress and the lieutenants continued throughout the meal. She took my order first. She served my meal first. She ensured that my mug was never empty. At some point she revealed that she was a Marine corporal in the Quantico band. I stuck with my charade.

The girl looked at me and whispered, "What would you like for dessert? My treat."

Bam! One of the lieutenants, I think it was the sulky one, pounded the table and barked, "That's enough, he's a second lieutenant too."

The girl cocked her head. Her eyes twinkled. She took our dessert orders. By the time we finished our desserts she had learned that we were heading to a local yuppie, night club. It was named Mysterious, Silky, Passion, or some other sultry word. We figured that we'd fit right in with our khaki trousers and polo shirts... and high and tights.

"I'd like to check out that club. Why don't you," she pointed at me, "wait at the bar until I get off shift and we'll meet the others at the club later. I'll drive."

Well, fraternization wasn't yet a buzzword, but I sensed that I was treading on thin infatuation. And I didn't want to miss the fun with my buds. Besides, if the girl was really interested, she'd show up at the club. It'd happened before.

"I think I'll stay with the boys. You can join us after you get off work."

Out of the blue one of my pals, it might have been the sulky one, announced, "I'll wait here with you!"

The girl smirked at me and said, "Sure."

And sure enough, my pal and the girl showed up at the sultry disco club a couple of hours later. I smiled. She sashayed passed me. Who cares? I had a new distraction—trying to keep us from getting thrown out of the club. But that's another story.

HAPPY BIRTHDAY USMC

When I left the active-duty Marine Corps, I was privileged to join Marine Medium Helicopter Squadron 764 and continue flying CH46E's, only this time on a part-time basis. Most of the annoying things about the active-duty Marine Corps were absent. Camaraderie and, well, the fun of flying was enjoyed by everyone most of the time. We got to support active duty and reserve Marines once or twice a month, privileged as always to be their glorified bus drivers. It was truly a blast and then they paid us.

Being the new guy in the squadron, the commanding officer, Tom Reid, assigned me to be a member of the ceremony at the upcoming Marine Corps Ball which would be attended by all the reserve Marine aviators and their spouses throughout Southern California. I was a captain at the time so would be part of the cake ceremony, and along with a handful of officers and enlisted Marines, stand in a line of two, one for officers and one for enlisted Marines in order of rank, to form an aisle: the "parade route" for the cake.

This particular ball occurred at the Anaheim Hilton, in their large main ball room. The room was divided in two with dining tables on either side of the cake ceremony aisle. Since the room was carpeted, the aisle floor was made up of a line of temporary hardwood parqueted panels to allow the cake platform wheels to roll easier. Part of the cake ceremony included the guest of honor's Marine Corps Birthday speech. During the ceremony, lights over the two large sections of dining tables were turned off, and only the cake ceremony aisle and guest speaker podium were illuminated. The rest of the large banquet hall was pitch dark.

Being a captain, I stood directly across from a lance corporal. Two Marines away from the lance corporal's left was the youngest Marine; a freshly graduated Marine private from boot camp, who stood directly abeam the giant cake. I could see him out the right corner of my eye and he was gleaming with pride to get to be part of the ceremony; a little overwhelmed but damn proud to be in his first Marine Corps Ball.

As the largest birthday cake known to man was rolled in, and the brave attempt was made to raise the cake cart three quarter inches onto the temporary wooden aisle floor, one of the stacked wine glasses fell onto the wood and shattered to pieces. As typical good fortune would have it, a piece of broken glass found its way into one of the cart's wheel axles. Unable to swivel in the proper direction of travel, the wheel broke the solemn silence with a loud and very annoying, broken-Walmart-shopping-cart squeal noise all the way down the aisle. Ahh, the comedy pyramid foundation was being laid.

Our speaker was a retired general who had been the assistant Commandant of the Marine Corps thousands of years ago. He began his speech by promising to keep it short. For some reason, I knew it was time to hunker down for a very long speech, probably fifteen or twenty minutes. At about twenty-five minutes into his speech, buttered rolls started flying out of the darkness from one dining area to the other: a Marine Corps Ball food fight, only with the etiquette of using buttered rolls instead of wet foods like green beans or salads. Proper decorum, no doubt. One of the rolls hit the major to my left. It stayed attached to his dress blues for a good two or three minutes before falling to the floor.

At the forty-five-minute mark of the general's speech and ongoing buttered roll mortar barrages, the brand new private started to forget about the unlocking-of-knees technique while at attention or parade rest, and courageously caught himself from swaying to much as the blood was leaving his head. Close call. Sadly, after fifty-three minutes into the general's speech, the private's "little knees that could" finally caused him to pass out. He fell forward, doing a Russian judge's ten-score face plant into the giant cake. His body made a splat sound on the temporary oak parquet, upper body and face akimbo with delicious icing and cake bits.

The MAG 46 CO and one of his staff ran over to the dazed Marine private and dragged his limp body in front of the speaker's podium and into the dining room darkness, then out one of the exit doors, sweet cream icing leaving a trail into the unknown. The general never skipped a beat. His speech lasted another ten or fifteen minutes and, of course, ended with Happy Birthday Marines.

HEALTH AND COMFORT

Young Marines have always been determined to push the boundaries of what is allowable. In the peacetime Corps of the early eighties, there was a growing permissiveness and a society that questioned all forms of authority. This spilled over into our beloved Corps and various forms of contraband began to appear during routine barracks inspections.

The main culprit was drugs and drug paraphernalia. They seemed to be everywhere, and leadership was at a loss for a way to curb or curtail the drug culture that had spilled over from the civilian world. There were questions being raised as to the legality of searches being conducted, and the term "reasonable expectation of privacy" reared its ugly head. If we couldn't sweep the barracks periodically, bringing serious consequences and putting the fear of the wrath of the CO to bear on the problem, all would be lost and we'd be in charge of a bunch of stoners. Who wants to go to war with that?

To the rescue: a great legal mind informed the commanders that they were responsible for the health and welfare of their men. They should have their junior officers check all the fire extinguishers periodically, to be sure they were functional. They should have the duty officer eat in the mess hall to be sure the food was fit for human consumption. Further, it was their DUTY to hold periodic "health and comfort" inspections to ensure that the living quarters were livable, that the men had an opportunity to bathe and wash their clothing, and that they had what they needed for reasonable comfort while not living in holes in the ground, eating MREs and bathing in their helmets.

These "health and comfort" visits allowed the inspectors to search rooms for items that might hurt the health of young Marines. Luckily pornography didn't seem to hurt them too badly or we would have had to shut down the Corps. Drugs and drug paraphernalia, particularly pipes, since marijuana seemed to be the drug of choice, were often found in these inspections.

While the command always referred to these as inspections, the troops throughout the Corps referred to them as shakedowns. It was an opportunity for the Marine Corps to circumvent normal search and seizure laws and protections that regular citizens enjoyed under the guise of protecting the health and welfare of the men. They were always unannounced and almost always caught a few violators, who lost lots of money and rank at the NJP (Non Judicial Punishment) which soon followed.

It was at one of these inspections that the team of searchers found a few ounces of marijuana, a couple of pipes and what at first appeared to be a clear plastic bong, used for smoking. All of the contraband items were identified as being illegal and then brought to the XO's office. Our XO was extremely zealous about throwing the book at every offense. Luckily, the CO asked for conclusive proof so that we would get a conviction. If a young Marine turned down NJP and opted for a court martial, there would be lawyers, a real defense and we could lose.

Losing at a court martial is an embarrassment to the unit and looks like the command was persecuting its men and overstepping its power. Several of the younger officers looked over the "bong" and no one could figure out how it could work. It was slightly curved at the top, which was odd, but the metal attachment at the bottom, where the weed would be placed and lit, seemed to be a fitting of some sort and did not appear to allow smoke to enter the 10-inch high plastic cylinder in any appreciable amounts. I knew the XO would push to charge the Marine, so I got the Marine's company commander to side with me in a quick meeting with the colonel.

We suggested that the prudent thing to do was to get an admission of guilt from the Marine in whose locker the item was found. We couldn't see how it could work as a bong, but if he said it was, then we could use his statement as evidence as to the nature of the item. The boss agreed and we reentered the XO's office where he was putting his nose into the metal fixture and the top of the dirty sticky device trying to see if he could detect the smell of cannabis. We told him that the CO had asked us to question the Marine and to see if we could extract a confession before charges were drafted. He said it was obvious and that we were wasting our time, but if that's what the colonel wants, he said go ahead. We sent for the Marine in question and I placed the item on my desk in plain sight.

He entered the room a terribly embarrassed young man. He saw the device on my desk and quickly averted his eyes. He looked at the floor. I informed him that he was not charged with anything and that we just had a few questions. I read him his rights and he agreed to talk with us.

"We found this device in your wall locker. Is it yours"?

"Yes sir," he said meekly.

"Do you use it?"

"Yes sir, sometimes."

"How often do you use it"?

"A couple of time a week, maybe."

"Can you tell us how you use it"?

"Well, sir, there's another piece that's in my car. It has a pump built into a tube. You snap the tube onto this fixture here on the side and then put your penis in this end and pump it up. It's supposed to make your penis larger."

Neither the captain nor I cracked a smile. After a long silence, I came up with: "Yes, of course, we understand that, but, as you know, the purpose of the inspection is for your health. This thing is filthy and we're afraid you may get an infection using it. Also, you should be very careful when using the pump, as you could injure yourself by putting too much pressure on your body. Now, you can take this back down to the barracks, clean it up, and you can keep it."

"Yes sir, thank you," and he left the office.

When word got out among the officers, they all recalled seeing the XO with his nose deep inside the device and uncontrollable laughter was the plan of the day. After the inspection of the unmentionable, when someone would voice a ridiculous idea in front of the CO, he would say, "That's as stupid as Major X sticking his nose down a penis pump!"

HOT DOG CONVINCERS

I was in a training area near "Combat Town" for about half the summer of 1981, in charge of a multichannel platoon doing some long distance communicating and, from time-to-time practicing line-of-sight over the very flat land with powerful microwave antennas. Bouncing signals off the troposphere was a difficult shot to work in and required precise calculation, detailed coordination, and a good deal of luck...mostly luck. We developed a whole array of excuses for why it wouldn't work; from too much iron in the soil, to sunspots, or weather interference. The fact is it just didn't always work.

My platoon had its share of characters and a few troublemakers. They worked hard when properly motivated and, like the big vans they worked in, often didn't work well. They adopted the slogan, "You can talk about us, but you can't talk without us."

On payday weekends, I cashed my check and stayed home, knowing I would be getting a call in the early morning hours from some young buck who needed bail money. I knew all the employees at the Jacksonville jail. I looked after my men because they looked after me. They were a fun lot.

One day they had procured some hot dogs, buns and condiments and set up a weenie roast. They managed to cut some long branches from some of the trees nearby without disturbing the rare pileated woodpeckers (they were endangered, and you could go to jail if you bothered them) and set up to cook the hot dogs. For experiment's sake, they speared four or five horizontally on the end of the stick and, standing behind the microwave antenna, held the stick of dogs in front of the antenna.

There were no OSHA inspectors around, but the Gunny and I thought that if we didn't curtail this, we were going to have somebody with a cooked body part. Those antennas were pretty powerful, and we had no idea how far out in front of them it might be safe to stand. So we got them to mount the hot dogs on a scaffold in front of the antenna, so that no Marines were near them. In the end the hot dogs did not cook, but we had long been told that they would and, not knowing the power of the microwave, we thought it better to be safe than sorry.

About this time several tanks pulled up and parked about 60 yards in front of our antennas. I asked one of our young communicators to let them know that we had reserved the training area for quite a few more days and would they mind moving up the road a ways? He ran down and came back in a few minutes, stating that the tank commander was a captain and that he said he's on the same exercise as us and wouldn't be moving until tomorrow.

Not the friendly, amicable response I had hoped to hear. The Gunny and I were just getting to the table to get some hot dogs that had been cooked in the traditional way over the fire we built. We developed a second message that had the Marines clamoring to be the one to deliver it. We picked our next communicator and a couple of his chums accompanied him as he walked back down to the tanks.

The captain stuck his head out again: "Tell the lieutenant, that we're staying here tonight, in defense of this sector! We're not going anywhere!"

"Oh no, sir, he understands that you're staying and wanted to welcome you to the LZ! He sent these hot dogs and wanted to let you know that we cooked them by placing them in front of those microwave antennas over there, the ones you're sitting right in front of. He also asked me to let you know that we aren't absolutely certain that your penis will look like this hot dog in the morning, but that should you happen to still be alive, you will most certainly be sterile with a good bit of brain damage. Anyway, welcome to the LZ!

Before the trio could get back to the picnic, the tanks were underway. They took the hot dogs with them.

HOW DO YOU SPELL RELIEF?

As the legal officer for 8th Comm Battalion, 2nd FSSG at Camp Lejeune in the early 80's, I had prepared the paperwork for an administrative discharge for a troubled young Marine who had already been busted from corporal all the way down to private due to previous incidents. The Corps had finally decided to send him home. I had met with him the previous afternoon and told him to be in my office the next morning to pick up all the paperwork and he could be on his way.

As usual, he was not on time and just as I was about to send for him, I received a phone call from the Jacksonville Police Department notifying me that my Marine was IHCA, that is In the Hands of Civilian Authorities; in other words, in the slammer, locked up in the Jacksonville jail. I was not surprised but inquired as to the charges. The police said they had him for possession of a controlled substance, specifically, marijuana.

I called the staff judge advocate office to ask if it would be okay for me to give him his discharge while he was in the hoosegow. They said I could. I then asked, since he would be a civilian at the moment when I'd hand him his papers, would it also be alright to give him a letter of persona non grata which would effectively not allow him back on the base. I got the OK for that as well, gathered up the papers and drove down to our barracks.

When I got to the barracks, I grabbed a couple of responsible young Marines. We got some packing boxes and headed to his room. Most of his things were already boxed up. There I instructed them to inventory his things and send them to his home of record since he would not be returning. This is a tedious and boring duty that happens from time to time, and everyone hates being assigned to inventory another Marine's gear. The corporal said, "But sir, his gear is mostly packed already. Can't we just ship it like it is? Besides, he's such an asshole!"

I explained that if we didn't do the inventory and something was missing when it arrived, he could file a claim against the government. But to soften the blow of having to conduct the inventory of the discharged asshole, I gave special instructions as to how they should be VERY detailed in conducting the inventory.

"What is this?" I asked.

"A tube of toothpaste," came the reply.

"Negative! This is a tube of toothpaste AND a toothpaste CAP! I want these two items inventoried separately. If some of that toothpaste happens to leak out on his disco outfit or his dancing shoes, that's not going to be our problem, is it?"

"No sir!" I could see the light bulb above both of their heads and big grins on their faces.

"Now, let's be sure we understand fully. What is this?"

"That is a bottle of aftershave AND a cap!" they replied in unison.

"Outstanding! Now, do the DETAILED inventory with special attention to all toiletries, take it all down to the Post Office and get it in the mail today."

I never saw two Marines so excited to do a gear inventory. As I drove away, I wondered how creative they might get. They might inventory the buttons separate from the shirts. The zippers might be inventoried separate from the trousers. I learned never to underestimate what a Marine might do.

I made my way to the Jacksonville Police Department, went in and asked for my boy. They brought him out and he was so happy to see me. He thought I was there to bail him out, or to at least appear as a character witness when he went before the judge later that morning. Instead, I opened my file folder and began showing him each document, informing him that he was no longer a United States Marine and these were his discharge papers. I showed him the monies that would be forwarded to his home of record the next payday and which would forever end his involvement with the Marines. Lastly, I gave him his letter of persona non grata.

"This means you are no longer welcome on Camp Lejeune. The Marines at the gate will not let you in," I said.

"But I have to go back and get my things."

"Your things are on their way to your home of record in Ohio."

"But I'm moving in with my girlfriend in Wilmington," he plaintively argued.

"Remember when you were told to ALWAYS keep your home of record up to date in case something happened? It just happened. Maybe your folks will ship it back to you in a couple of weeks."

"Lieutenant, I need to change clothes and clean up before I go to court. I only have two hours."

I stood up to leave. I looked at his t-shirt. Emblazoned on the front was a large cannabis leaf, and wrapped around it were the words: "HOW DO I SPELL RELIEF? M-A-R-I-J-U-A-N-A. This was a question asked in a catchy Rolaids commercial at the time.

"Sorry pal, but you are no longer in the comforting, protective arms of the brotherhood that is the Marine Corps. Welcome to the cold, unrelenting world of civilians. One last piece of advice, if I were you, I'd turn that t-shirt inside out before I approach the bench.

HOW I GOT MY CALL SIGN

In Navy and Marine Corps aviation, pilots are typically given nicknames or call signs by the leadership in the squadron. They are usually associated with a mistake; a screw up, committed by a pilot early on in his naval aviation career. It's the "Goose" and "Maverick" type names most people have heard from the movie Top Gun. The naval aviation rotary wing (helicopter) communities don't use call signs nor give them out nearly as much as the fixed-wing counterparts, but they're still common.

In the Marine Corps and Marine Corps Reserves, I was a CH-46E pilot. While serving on active duty with Marine Medium Helicopter Squadron 261 (HMM-261), I was involved in Operation Urgent Fury, the Grenada operation between 25 October and 9 November, 1983. On 26 October, one of the flights included rescuing American medical students from the Cubans at their Grand Anse Beach campus.

The CH-46's flew Army Rangers from a secure pick-up point to Grand Anse Beach, where they secured the beach head so that larger Marine CH-53 helicopters could load up the students and fly them to the secured landing area, then onto Barbados. After the rescue, the CH-46's were to go back to Grand Anse Beach, pick up the Rangers, and return them to the secured landing area. It was basic insertion, do something, extraction mission we'd trained for dozens of times.

The Cubans had surrounded the medical complex and were setting up gun emplacements with machine guns and shoulder-held missiles. After the first day of Urgent Fury, the Cubans were losing badly and figured they could hold hostage the American students and use them as bargaining chips. Our small operation prevented that from happening.

The 46's launched, picked up the Rangers, and under minimal small arms fire, landed four helicopters at a time, one behind the other, on the very thin strand of beach. Then, the first set of four CH-46's took off and went to a rendezvous point, while the second set of four, then third set of four, did the same thing. While the 46's rendezvoused, the 53's landed in front of the campus buildings, loaded up the students and took them to safety. The 46's went back to Grand Anse Beach to pick up the Rangers and get the hell out of Dodge, again landing three sets of four helicopters at a time.

Armed with two fifty-caliber machine guns, we had a crew of four; the crew chief, Corporal Dayhoff, a new guy who was the left-side gunner, and the two pilots. I was in the right pilot's seat in the lead aircraft in the second set of four aircraft. The aircraft commander, Major Dick Gallagher, asked me to fly in the right seat (normally the aircraft commander sits in the right seat in Marine Corps helicopter squadrons). The bad guys were on the right side of the aircraft and didn't want us to live. On this particular mission, in case anything happened, it would be easier to go to CoPilots 'R Us, where the shelves were full, to get a new copilot rather than try to replace an ops officer who possessed the necessary chops to run a squadron operations office. A sobering reality, especially for me, but that's part of smart utilization of limited resources.

Once the 53's departed with the medical students, AH-1 attack helicopters softened the medical school buildings so that the 46's could land along the beach and pick up the Rangers with minimum harassment. The first set of four helicopters landed seconds after our

Cobra close air support fire stopped. That kept the Cubans' heads down during the first Ranger extraction.

Being the lead aircraft in the second set of four 46's, we found the beach to be even thinner as the tides were higher by then. There was enough beach to get our right main mounts on dry sand but our nose gear and left main gear would definitely be in the water, which was not really that big a deal. Unfortunately, the Cubans had a chance to set up small arms positions between the last target softening by close air support and the landing of the second set of helicopters.

Our landing area of Grand Anse Beach was lined with beautiful palms, very close to the water, that sort of grew sideways and then turned vertical. The hurricane winds created by the downward rotor wash had the power to push the vertical part of the palm trees horizontal. Our rotor wash did that very thing but neither we, nor Corporal Dayhoff, realized it at the time. In addition, we could hear the Cubans' small arms rounds hitting the right side of our aircraft and we needed to land quickly to gain cover from taller palm trees while on the ground and loading our Rangers for their extraction.

Corporal Dayhoff cleared us to land rather forcefully since rounds were hitting the upper aft parts of the aircraft exposed to the Cubans' direct line of sight. Having the controls, I started to feel my way to the ground and water to avoid flipping over in case the shoreline dropped off too much, but Dick, my copilot, wasn't as worried about that as much as the small arms rounds hitting the aircraft, so he pushed down on the collective to get us on the ground.

As physics would have it, that made the downward hurricane wind from the rotor wash go away, which allowed one of the palm trees to stand vertically. That palm tree and our aft rotors went to battle. The palm tree won, breaking apart one of the three aft rotors, which chopped off the top half of the palm tree. Vibration hell broke loose, and an extremely violent break-up of the aircraft began due to the instant loss of balanced rotation.

The only thing I could think of was to shut down the engines to stop the violent shaking and that's what I did. There was no time to discuss anything. We were coming apart, both of us knew it and Dick would have done the same thing. Eventually, we got back to the ship, the USS Guam, and continued flying other missions on Grenada in the following days.

After our part of Operation Urgent Fury was complete, we headed toward our original destination, Beirut, Lebanon. In transient, I flew my day check ride and night check ride for aircraft commander and made HAC (Helicopter Aircraft Commander), a major milestone in one's flying career. On the day of my first HAC flight, or cherry flight, I went to the typical squadron ready room brief and immediately noticed something odd.

Everyone was calling me Larry. I wasn't Larry. Larry King, another squadron pilot was Larry. I was Ken. Confused, the overall brief began with the squadron commanding officer, LtCol Granville "Granny" Amos, giving the overall look at the days' several missions. He also mentioned my cherry ride to the squadron and called me Larry as he looked my way.

Okay, that was it; who is this Larry guy? I asked Granny, "Sir, why are you all calling me Larry?"

He said, "Well, that's what's on your name tag."

I looked down, and instead of my normal name tag which read, Ken Russell, someone had replaced it with one that said, Larry the Logger.

HUNGARIAN GOOD LUCK DANCE

One's Marine Corps experience is not limited to the times when one is wearing the uniform; often some of the memorable experiences are those shared with fellow Marines when off duty, and sometimes when sharing in a fellow Marine's experience reconnecting with their civilian past. For a Marine, tradition plays a large role in one's outlook and that love of tradition is often reflected in how we embrace civilian traditions. Case in point, the blessed union of man and wife in matrimony. When a man asks a woman for her hand in marriage and she accepts, the groom is aware the clock is ticking. That is, if he still has hopes of enjoying the full traditions and privileges associated with being single. The anticipated reduction in extracurricular activities is just around the corner.

One of the time-honored traditions shared by both the Marine Corps and civilian life is that of the bachelor party. However, the Marine tradition tends to be a little raunchier. One such event comes to mind: a fellow lieutenant was hosting such a bachelor party for a long-time civilian friend, and the initial venue was his parents' home in the Silver Springs, Maryland area. The invited guests included a few high and tight Marines and a few civilians, one of whom was recovering from a broken neck, wearing a Frankenstein halo designed to impress all by the shiny screws attached to the wearer's skull.

After formal greetings were exchanged, a competitive game of drinking hard liquor was undertaken which resulted in the man of the hour confessing that, should he be required to down his last drink, he would get sick. As mentioned, the venue of this gala event was the home of the parents of my fellow Marine, who spoke up and assured the man of the hour that he should not concern himself with the anticipated gastral explosion but rather concentrate on his obligation to drink his drink and the consequences of his actions would be dealt with.

As forecasted, none of the party goers were left wondering what the groom had recently eaten. And the worry regarding a potential mess was rendered moot as the host promptly kicked gastric discharge into a convenient closet, obviously underutilized by his parents, and we departed for the main event.

In the early 80's certain cities had allocated areas downtown for adult entertainment. New York had 42nd street, Boston, the combat zone, and Baltimore, the block. The prevailing feeling that almost anything in these areas was legal was accepted as fact. The challenge now was to provide the man of the hour an opportunity for him to never forget this night, and truth be known, had we failed in this mission the groom-to-be would very obviously be quite disappointed. While high and tight Marines may look somewhat law abiding, we nevertheless approached the delicate task of procuring a memorable event for groom-to-be. The veiled language of negotiation was unfamiliar to this group, so when these very friendly women suggested a Hungarian good luck dance for a mere $100 the deal was sold.

The groom-to-be, most likely standing at a position of attention south of the beltline, was provided sufficient funds to indeed partake in this Hungarian tradition. Sadly, the original Hungarian good luck dance is done fully clothed and this left our honored guest quite dispirited as he was shown the door. I felt an injustice had been dealt and that it was time to take this matter to the authorities. As a consequence of excessive alcohol consumption, I misinterpreted the city tolerance of vice in the neighborhood for a full-throated endorsement of the services on "the block." I approached one of Baltimore's finest to register my complaint regarding the overpriced, overdressed Hungarian good luck dance and inquired as to what consumer protection we might expect from the officer. Rather quickly, he dispensed with the idea of requiring a refund from the young ladies on our behalf.

In recognition of our service to the country as US Marines, our misunderstanding of what is legal would not result in our arrest.

INTO THE DARK

I was on my first WestPac Deployment and flying with the Squadron CO. We were aboard the USS Belleau Wood. It was a very dark and overcast night. I was doing my night qualifications as other lieutenants were also doing. I had completed several night landings, and all was going well I thought.

Then on my fourth or fifth landing, I was at the beam (180 degrees out from landing) and I was assigned Spot 6 which was going to be just in front of the CH-53D ahead of me in the pattern. Coming through the 90 I noticed that the ship was rolling a bit and the trainee was having a hard time getting the CH-53 onto the deck. We were on short final for Spot 6 when I heard the CH-53 call wave-off. The 53's rotors swelled up and it was looking like they were going to fly right into us. I called a wave-off as well and dipped away from the deck, pulling power as I went, waiting for the impact of the other aircraft's rotors into our rotors or fuselage. The deck screamed by and then darkness – total darkness. It was totally disorienting. You couldn't see the water below or the sky above. There was no horizon.

I continued ahead thinking that the 53 was still right behind us and could still impact us at any second. I was focusing on what was behind me. Then the real threat suddenly became apparent. While I was pulling what I thought was a significant amount of power to avoid the impending collision, I hadn't been – I was pulling only about 60% of my available power and we were settling. The radar altimeter showed less than 50' altitude. We were descending right into the black ocean, but we couldn't see it. My CO pulled the nose of the aircraft back and the power to 100% torque. It was like an express elevator upwards. We caught our breath passing 1500' for 2000' where we settled down and let our heart rate slow back down. We called for re-entry into the pattern and made an uneventful landing and called it a night. It had been a close one. At 50 feet with swells of 20'-30' in a descending flight path, we were probably only a second or two from impacting the water.

I learned from this. I hadn't been monitoring my instruments. The CO hadn't either. We were worried about an aircraft-to-aircraft mid-air collision. That is a real concern, but at night at sea there are many other things to worry about also. The CO being my co-pilot was to be tracking our instruments and secondaries – on take-off and landing, he was our inside scan. However, with the excitement of the emergency wave-off we had both been caught thinking behind and not ahead of the aircraft. I was lucky that night to survive and gain the experience that only this kind of event can so deeply impress upon one's conscience.

IMPRACTICAL JOKE

There have been hundreds of times when I have played jokes on friends, or they have played jokes on me, and we have enjoyed a good laugh, and maybe even continued on speaking terms afterward. This is not one of those times. This is about a time when just screwing with a guy got quickly out of hand, and I learned that if you're going to mess with someone, you better have a good handle on the situation.

I had been deployed for a while and was just returning to the states. I got chosen to run up to DC for a couple of days for a debrief on what was happening in Beirut. One great thing about the Marine Corps is that it's small enough that no matter what base you're on, if you've been in the Corps for more than fifteen minutes, you probably have a friend there. I had a good friend from a previous command, who was stationed at Headquarters Marine Corps. I stopped in to visit him while I was in town. He knew where all our old buddies were and was bringing me up to date on what everyone had been doing in my absence.

For the purposes of this telling, we will call my friend Captain Smith. I asked him about our mutual friend Marty Wasilewski, and he said Marty had made captain, was back from Okinawa, and was stationed with the Air Wing at Cherry Point.

"Hey, let's call him up and talk to him." It was around 0700 and in DC, in order to beat the traffic, you have to get in early. The rest of the east coast was just getting to work, and we were on our second cup of coffee. Smith looked up Marty's unit in the World Wide Locator and called to get a number for Marty's office.

A corporal answered the phone and gave Smith Marty's direct line but said that we would not be able to reach him for a half hour or so, because he was out at formation. I don't know what demon suddenly possessed Smith, but he pretended that he had just taken the phone away from the caller and slipped into a heavy Charlestonian accent: "This is Captain Jawnhnson and Ah'm cawlin' from Headquawtus Mawreen Coah in Wahshinton, Dee Cee. Cud yew pulees tell Captn Wasilewwski to cawl me back at his uhliest convenience. His name has been placed in consideration as an Aide de Caimp fo the Commahndant and we ahh cawlin to check on his interest in the position priah to fahnal selection." He then gave the kid the phone number and ended the call.

"What the hell was that all about?" I asked.

"Just screwin' with him. Can you imagine how quick he's gonna call back when he gets that message?"

What we didn't know was that Marty's unit had recently returned from a Caribbean cruise and apparently, he had performed admirably and was, along with some others, being awarded a Navy Achievement Medal that morning. It was a large formation, and the commanding general was handing out the awards for all who had been on the cruise. There were lots of Meritorious Masts, a few promotions, and then a handful of Navy Achievements and maybe a Navy Commendation Medal or two. In short, it was a very big deal.

Marty's wife and young child were present to see him get his award. The young corporal who took the phone call from Smith knew the importance of the call and did not want to risk Marty walking away after the ceremony and not getting his message, so he rushed it out to the rear of the formation where the award recipients were standing at attention. He handed the message to Marty whose eyes nearly popped out of his head.

His head was spinning when he heard, "Persons to receive awards, FRONT AND CENTERRR!"

He and the small contingent right faced and marched until they were centered on the podium. The awards were read by the adjutant and the CO and the CG moved from one to the next pinning on the awards. The general had noticed the messenger approach Marty at the back of the formation and, knowing that officers don't often break from the position of attention, thought maybe something was wrong. While his award was being read, he whispered to Marty, asking about the message. Still holding the paper in his cupped hand, he discreetly turned it so that the General could see it. Then HIS eyes almost popped out of his head. As he pinned on the Medal, he told Marty to come to his office immediately after the formation and he could return the call from there.

Following the formation there were the usual photos, congratulatory handshakes and finally things started to break up. Marty, his wife and child, the general, his aid, and perhaps one or two others headed for the general's office. The general was telling the Wasilewski's that they should not let the cost of living in DC concern them, and that Marty's ticket would be "punched" if he got such a prestigious position; and how he would meet not only Marine Corps contacts that would help his career in the future, but political contacts as well. After a few more words of advice and encouragement, the general and Mrs. Wasilewski went to the other side of the office and Marty nervously picked up the general's phone and dialed Captain Johnson.

I answered the phone. "Officer Selection Office, Headquarters Marine Corps, Corporal Wall speaking. How may I help you?" I don't know whether such an office exists, but I sounded official.

"This is Captain Wasilewski. May I speak with Captain Johnson, please?"

Smith turned on the speaker so we could both hear. "Hey Marty, you old horse's ass, it's Joe and Ken! How you been man? Ken stopped by to visit and we thought we'd give you a call. So, what have you been up to?"

There was a pause. He needed time to think. You could hear the tension in his voice: "Thanks for the call, Captain Johnson, and sorry for the delay in getting back to you. I was out at formation and the CG was giving me a Navy Achievement Medal when you called. As a matter of fact, my wife and I are in the general's office now."

"Damn Marty," I said. "Are you in the CG's office on his phone?" Marty had given us the whole story in a couple of sentences. We knew we had put him in a bind, and we also knew he would never forgive us if we didn't get him out.

"Yes, that's about it," he replied.

"Okay Marty, we understand. We'll get you out of this," I said. "Do you think he'll buy it if we tell him that we're only putting out feelers right now and that there are a dozen or so potential candidates? And we just don't want to bother pursuing anyone who's not interested. We should also say that the odds are long and that we'll be in touch, a kind of don't call us, we'll call you thing, so that no one calls checking on this. Do you think that will fly?"

"Well, sure, my wife and I have briefly spoken about it and we'd love the opportunity. Sure, I understand that you have lots of other candidates and you'll call us if there are any further developments. I know you have my records, but please let me know if you want any additional information. No, Captain Johnson, we'll wait to hear from you. I really do appreciate being considered and hope to talk to you again soon."

He hung up and we sat there dumbfounded, not knowing if he got out of the mess we put him in. I left and later Smith told me that Marty had called in and chewed him out, but they both laughed about it before he hung up. In the long term, he said it worked out great for him. It was good that the CG personally presented him with the medal, but to then find out that headquarters was considering him for the aide position proved to everyone he was a very hot commodity. He told me later he thought that the phone call had put a new light on him and that it was extremely helpful to his career. I never again played practical jokes from afar.

IT'S A DOG'S LIFE

I was the battalion legal officer for a 750-man battalion and was often called upon to perform duties that were not strictly within the exact specifications of what a legal officer should be doing. Sometimes the company commanders found themselves in situations they didn't want to handle and they'd kick it up to my office to handle. I believe this was the situation in the following case.

The CO told me to prepare to inform a young lance corporal that he was being evicted from Tawara Terrace housing. I wasn't sure why this honor should fall to me and not to his platoon commander or company commander or even the base housing people. Tarawa Terrace was somewhat below the standards of other housing the Corps had in other locations. In the 1950's, my father bought a trailer and moved us into that to avoid having his family living in Tarawa Terrace. This incident occurred in the 1980's, so you can imagine how substandard they were by then. I had to ask myself, "What would a man have to do to get himself thrown out of such a place?"

I dug further into the case, so that I could better understand and offer guidance. Our young Marine had graduated from communications school at Camp Pendleton, CA. Owning something that vaguely resembled an automobile, he began his cross-country drive to his first duty station, Camp Lejeune, NC. He had a week before he had to report in, so he stopped off in

Reno, met a hooker fifteen years his senior, married her in less than twenty-four hours and proceeded on his way to North Carolina.

A few days later, the two love birds arrived in Jacksonville. Since he was now married, he was assigned quarters in Tarawa Terrace. Obviously, these two were thinkers, off to a terrific start, working on a fool-proof plan, destined for great things.

Soon they were short on money and the young bride started entertaining male visitors while her husband was at work. While there was no firm evidence, it looked bad enough that the housing folks paid her a visit and suggested she should perhaps ply her trade in more suitable environs. She agreed to cease and desist, and they agreed to not pursue the matter any further; they didn't report it to the MP's or her husband. Everything was going well for a couple of months, and then, the neighbors started to complain. That was when I got the case.

After summoning the couple to my office, I started to read the message I was given by my superiors to communicate to them. I thought, If somebody said this to me, I would jump across the desk and beat the hell out of him. That is why I solicited the aid of two very large Marines to stand behind me and remove the young lance corporal if he came across the desk.

The two entered the room, holding hands and unaware of what was about to happen. They sat in front of my desk and waited to find out. I began, "Lance Corporal Jones, I'm sorry to have to inform you that you are being evicted from base housing and you will need to find housing elsewhere. Though the Marine Corps normally provides Marines with government-furnished housing, it has been determined through much investigation that, in your case, that right is being abused and should therefore be forfeited."

"But why?" he asked. "What did we do?"

"Lance Corporal Jones, your neighbors own a Doberman pinscher. They are no longer able to get their dog to return home, because each day, after you leave for work, your wife calls the dog over to your yard so that she and the dog can have sex. Here are pictures that they have taken which prove the accusation." There it was. I couldn't believe I had said the words, but it was done. He didn't come flying across the desk. He just shook his head and looked very disappointed. He didn't scream or curse or even raise his voice. He just turned to her and quietly, in his heavy Brooklyn accent, said, "Honey, I thought youse said you wuz gonna quit doin dat." That ended the counseling session.

KNOW YOUR MARINES

As Marine Officers, we learned the Eleven Leadership Principles, recited them at inspections, tested on them in the classroom, and tried to live them when we got to the fleet. One of the principles – "Know your Marines and look out for their welfare" – was, for me, the one upon which everything else depended. As a platoon commander, I tried to know all that I could about the men who were entrusted to me. I knew hometowns and the names of wives, girlfriends, and kids. I had a little box of index cards with information about each of my men. I would send birthday cards to their kids, and I'd try to keep up with what was going on in their lives. I knew who I could count on and who were the troublemakers.

While my friends from college were mostly working in corporate America, strapped to a desk and fetching coffee, I was taking care of seventy-five young Marines, was directly responsible for millions of dollars of equipment, smoked large cigars, and rolled around in the dirt for weeks at a time. With their cushy jobs, what were my friends thinking of me?

We were headed to the field for two weeks in 1981, ramping up for an upcoming exercise, when a brand-new Lance Corporal checked into my platoon. He had driven across country with his wife and baby and had burned up all the leave he had on the books. He was checking in a few days later than we had expected; we were seriously shorthanded and badly needed him. After checking into the battalion, our Gunny assigned a man to him, and they went to supply to check out all the gear he would need for two weeks in the woods. He was back in a few minutes and we loaded up our trucks and drove out to our training area.

A couple of hours later, one of my corporals reported to me that the new guy had told him that the movers were due to deliver his household goods and that his wife and baby were the only ones there at his new base quarters. I called back to the battalion office and asked the Officer of the Day to send someone to his house to check on his wife and let her know he wouldn't be home for the next couple of weeks. He radioed back to me a few hours later that they had checked on her and she was okay.

The chaplain went out with a couple of Marines to help her get unpacked. The chaplain must have brought a welcome basket and found that there was no money and no groceries in the house. He had the wife of one of my NCOs come by with a few things. They had a grocery shopping date set for the next morning with some money the chaplain had given her. I relayed the information to my young Marine and his whole attitude changed. He was a new man and did a great job the whole time we were in the field.

We returned on a Friday and as we offloaded and began to clean all of our gear, the Gunny handed out the LES slips. We mostly had direct deposits, so the Leave and Earnings Statement told us how much we got paid, how many days of leave we had on the books, allotments, deductions, etc. I was busy trying to get everything done before securing the platoon for the weekend, when the Gunny approached and said he needed to talk to me privately. He said our new guy had miraculously gotten an LES (the system was often fouled up for a while following a transfer, so we hardly ever got one for a new man) and that it showed NPD in the Pay Column. NPD is short for NO PAY

DUE, which was another common problem with the pay system; it often forgot how to pay after a transfer. It was my job to go to the disbursing office and get it straightened out, but it was after 1630 on a Friday, so we both knew I couldn't get it fixed until Monday morning. Unfortunately, so did our young Marine. The Gunny said he was sitting on the ground behind our building, crying his eyes out. I cleared the office and sent for him to report to me.

He was 19 years old with a wife and child. He had checked-in two weeks before having spent all his money bringing his family from the West Coast. He expected to return to his wife the day he checked-in, but we hauled him away to the woods for two weeks. Now he had to go home to her and let her know they had no money until Monday at the earliest. The world was crashing down around him, and I wouldn't have blamed him if he'd punched me right in the nose. Instead, he stood at attention in front of my desk, tears running down his face, and reported, "Lance Corporal Smith reporting as ordered, sir!"

"Smith, Gunny says you got an NPD."

"Yes sir! This is screwed up, sir!" (This is not precisely what he said, but close enough.)

"No doubt about it. I agree; totally screwed up. At ease, Smith. Sit down and let's talk about it."

The flood gate opened, and he poured out his frustrations about how he had car trouble crossing the country and spent all his money; how we shanghaied him and took him away from his family before he even moved into his house; how he had driven the car to check-in; and we left his wife without transportation for two weeks. He concluded by stating the obvious: that he was going to have to go home empty handed tonight, look like an idiot in front of his wife, and that he was screwed (again, edited for language).

"I'll have to agree with most of what you said, but I have a correction or two to make. First of all, knowing that you'd be in the field, the chaplain got your wife's keys, got PMO to locate your car, and had it delivered to her within a day or two of the time you arrived, so you'll need a ride home today. She probably knows her way around Jacksonville by now. Secondly, as Marines, we're taught to constantly evaluate out assets and our liabilities. It seems to me that you're only looking at your liabilities."

"What are my assets? I don't see any."

"Well," I said, "you've got a wife and daughter who, no doubt, love you and appreciate all that you do to try to provide for them. You've also got me. I'm the guy who's responsible to see to it that you get paid properly. That USMC club patch on our uniforms means that we are brothers, and we take care of each other. Just because they closed the disbursing office, doesn't mean my responsibility to you ends until Monday morning. The only thing better than getting paid is knowing that I got paid and I'm here to look after you. If you will go out there and help the men with the cleanup, when we secure, you and I will head over to the commissary and we'll get some groceries for the weekend and some milk for that baby. Then we'll stop off and I'll get some flowers for your wife, only you're going to present them to her. Then we're going to go to your house and I will finally get to meet your lovely bride and your baby. I'll loan you enough to get you through the weekend and we'll get this straightened out on Monday."

He looked like a kid on Christmas morning. I never saw an attitude change so quickly. We did all that I promised, and he was in my platoon for the next year. During that time, if I needed a volunteer to clean the head or jump-off the Empire State Building, his hand was the first to go up. He came by to see me when I transferred out and told me how much that had all meant to him and how his wife still talks about it. I didn't stay in the Corps for my career, but I took this lesson with me: If you are ever in a position to do someone some good, do it. I have had a few who bit the hand that was helping them and some that just borrowed my money and disappeared. But over many years I've learned that people are mostly good and if you can help someone who's down, they usually don't forget it.

LEINIE ADVENTURE

I have been fortunate in my life to always have friends around who kept me out of trouble. I have even had a few who, for some reason, always led or followed me to adventurous places. One of these was Jake Leinenkugel. I met him at OCS in 1979 and from then on, we always seemed to stumble upon some adventure – my kids grew up hearing "Uncle Jake" stories.

Jake was from Chippewa Falls, Wisconsin, where his family owned a small regional brewery named Leinenkugel's. It was a regional beer, sold only in the Upper Midwest. Being a southern boy, I had never had one until our OCS graduation, when his father, Bill, introduced me to his product. I fell instantly in love and asked Bill to marry me. He politely declined, so I started hanging out with Jake.

One night while we were in The Basic School, Jake and I ventured north to Georgetown to a bar called The Brickskeller, which advertised that it had 1200 different kinds of beer. We bellied up to the bar and Jake ordered a Leinie. He knew that Leinie's weren't sold that far east but was yanking the bartender's chain. Much to his surprise, the barkeep plops a cold can of Leinenkugel's in front of him. I had one as well and we were on our way to a fine evening.

Jake determined to find out where else we might find his family beer, called his dad from the Brickskeller, and Bill told him that there were twelve cases in the greater Baltimore/Washington area. There was a small distributor near Baltimore that had them, and Jake wrote down the address. We enjoyed our evening and went back to our hotel.

The next day we got up and drove to Baltimore and sought out the little distributor. It was in a nondescript, slightly shabby, aluminum warehouse. As we entered, we saw a single man driving a forklift around and moving beer from one stack to another. The man called out to us and told us he was closed. Jake said, "Could we just talk to you for a minute?"

"We're not open on Saturday and we don't sell to the public," replied the proprietor as he dismounted his conveyance to show us the exit.

"I understand. My name's Jake Leinenkugel and our company president tells me that you have some of our product here."

I thought the man would faint dead away. Let me stop here to let you know that the Leinenkugel can reads: "Brewed in Chippewa Falls, Wisconsin by Jacob Leinenkugel Breweries." Jake was named for his great-grandfather who started the brewery in 1867, but our distributor no doubt thought it was Jake's brewery and suddenly it was like Adolph Coors and Joseph Schlitz showed up at a ramshackle butler building in suburban Maryland.

The tone changed considerably. "What can I do for you today, Mr. Leinenkugel?"

"We're having a party with some of our friends down in Quantico and we wondered if we might be able to buy some of our beer back from you."

"Sure thing, how much do you need?"

The Leinies were in a single stack in an area with some other smaller breweries. He showed us there were twelve cases. That's twelve cases in the whole Baltimore/Washington area. "I think we'll need about six cases. Will that be okay?"

He sold us six cases at cost, which was fifty cents each. We loaded the beer in my trunk and headed for the Crystal City Marriott. The party Jake had mentioned took place in the Marriott and it was just the two of us, until we ran into some of our friends later in the afternoon.

That night we decided to go up to Georgetown to see what was happening. The Marriott connected to the Crystal City Underground, a mall of sorts with lots of small shops. The art of beer can collecting was at its peak and our empty Leinenkugels were very rare in the DC area. We had opened the cans from the bottom using a "church key," leaving the pop top untouched. We also left the plastic six pack holder attached, making them more attractive to collectors. The man in the Beer Can Collecting Store gave us seventy-five cents for each can we delivered. We drank the beer and made a fifty percent profit in a single day! I told Jake he was a financial genius and I had found my calling as a professional beer drinker!

LESSON LEARNED

I once heard, "You're a Marine, an Officer, and a pilot – handle it!" Sometimes that isn't enough. On this occasion, I was tasked with taking four CH-46's from MCAS Tustin to Yuma for night vision goggle training. As the old saying goes: "You never assume anything." I found this out the hard way.

My mission was to instruct two different students in night vision goggle training and navigation. The first student was pretty straightforward. We were to conduct a simple route to a landing zone (LZ) and conduct confined area landings. After refueling and a crew swap, the second student was to navigate a preplanned route with multiple landings along the way. This portion was to be conducted under low light levels, which increased the difficulty of the flight and required a higher level of situational awareness.

Upon completion of both events, we were to rejoin our four aircraft on the deck at Yuma and return to Tustin. This was a pretty routine evolution until operations decided to add the extra "fifteen pounds" to my five-pound sack. Ops decided that since the transit back and forth to Yuma was basically free time, I could add another mission. A third student was added, who would get a night vision familiarization flight on the way home. This was the point where the sack got full.

All went well with the first two students. We prepared for our return flight. My last student was a young lieutenant with a dubious reputation. He made no bones about informing anyone who would listen of his plans for using his Marine Corps experience as a resume footnote, for his pending career as an actor in Hollywood. He was well known for not possessing basic knowledge of the aircraft. He had a very cavalier attitude about pretty much everything related to being a Marine. Once airborne, I informed my wingman to assume position as the lead aircraft and to lead the flight back to Tustin.

As we moved into the last position of the flight, I started the lesson. While flying, I positioned our aircraft into different locations around the aircraft in front of us. I explained to the young lieutenant the importance of maintaining the proper position and distance in relationship to the lead aircraft. After repeatedly covering all the particulars, it was time for the student to take the controls. I moved our aircraft into position; one rotor diameter apart, forty-five degree bearing line, flying slightly higher. At this point I stated, "You have the controls."

Immediately, we started falling back behind the lead aircraft. I repeatedly kept advising the lieutenant to "close it up and get back in there," and the need for him to stay on the bearing line. Eventually, I took control of our aircraft. The lieutenant seemed clearly nervous and a little shaken. In an effort to calm him down, I repeated the demonstration of proper position and emphasized that while on NVG's you have to stay close or you lose perception. After he seemed to calm down a bit, I repositioned in the proper position with lead aircraft on his side. I gave the call, "You have the controls." We held tight position for a brief moment. Suddenly, our aircraft violently shuddered and almost simultaneously veered away from the lead aircraft. I immediately took the flight controls back and all but yelled over the intercom, "What the hell is wrong with you?" It was at this point, I glanced over at my copilot.

Almost afraid of what I observed, I inquired, "Are your goggles turned on?" It seems my student had never even turned on his NVG's. After turning his goggles on, the young pilot announced over the intercom, "WOW! I can see the other aircraft now. Sir, I think I can take the controls back." After glaring across at him in the cockpit, I calmly responded, "That will never happen as long as I'm in the same airspace."

I don't know why I would have assumed that a copilot would have his NVG's actually turned on, but I did. Lesson learned! Needless to say, I had a few choice words both with him and the operations officer about adding afterthoughts to the flight schedule.

This particular lieutenant went on to have a "star" career. He never made aircraft Commander; never obtained any flight qualifications beyond basic copilot; while on his first deployment, he was involved in a liberty incident in the first liberty port and was restricted to ship for duration of deployment; and finally, cashed his severance paycheck upon failing to get augmented and departed the Marine Corps to become a failed actor.

LIFE IN THE FAST LANE

I think everyone that met General Al Gray has a story or two to tell. He was quite a character. While working at the Development Center in Quantico, I made a habit of coming in very early before the crowd arrived and screwed with my concentration. I could get some good work done from 0600 to 0730; after that there were always distractions.

On one of these early morning sessions, General Gray came walking into my office and addressed me as he always did. "Lieutenant Wilcox, isn't it?" I was so proud that he had caught me working in my office before the sun came up and that he now knew what a fastidious and industrious young officer he had working in his office! Still, all I could muster in response was a sputtering: "Yessir."

"Are you going up to DC to reconcile your accounts today?"

Every two weeks I would drive up to Headquarters Marine Corps in DC and compare how much money they said were in our accounts to what we said we had. "No Sir, I'm going next Tuesday," I replied.

"No Lieutenant, you're going today. You're coming with me. Leave a note for Major Mutter. Grab your gear and meet me at my car out front in five minutes."

I did exactly as he requested and met him at his car. Easy to find, it was the one with two stars on the flags mounted on the front. The driver came around and opened the door. I hesitated, not knowing if I was to enter first or last. About this time another car adorned with similar two-star flags drove up behind us. General Bernard Trainer, Head of the Education Center at Quantico, exited and shook the hand of General Gray who introduced me. He shook my hand and General Gray told me that he and General Trainer would ride in the back and I could ride up front.

I had no idea what I was doing there, but I remember thinking how they must want to pick the brain of some hotshot lieutenant and see what I thought of the training I'd received at OCS and TBS. Maybe they had some assignment coming up and, noting what a great job I was doing, were taking me to DC to show me what it's all about.

As we left Quantico, I knew I couldn't reconcile accounts because I wasn't nearly ready to do so. I spread several notebooks across my lap and got to work, hoping to get enough done to at least make a partial reconciliation happen. As we hit I-95 North, though it was early, traffic was already starting to build. My head was buried in my books, and I felt the car move decidedly to the left and speed up. I looked up to see what had happened and it was then I found my purpose.

Hanging above the highway was a large black sign with a diamond drawn in the middle. Below the diamond, it said, "Four passengers minimum." It was the carpool lane and in order to ride in it, you had to have at least four people in the car. Few cars had that many, so it shortened the trip to DC by at least an hour. I did a quick headcount and discovered that I was exactly what these guys needed that morning: a human being!

Neither General Gray nor General Trainer spoke to me except to tell me where to meet them for the return trip that afternoon. I was not prepared to reconcile accounts, so I accomplished little. Still, I served my country faithfully. A blowup doll could have done what I did that day, but I got it done! Lieutenants at Quantico are a pretty cheap commodity.

LOOK A CRUISE MISSILE BETWEEN OUR TOES!

Just another day in the training command. I was flying a student on a tactics flight where he was doing a simulated Search pattern as part of a Search and Rescue curriculum. We were flying in the Escambia Bay Lower Training area below Route 10. Again, it was just another day. There were no flight notices (NOTAMS) and no South Whiting restrictions of any kind in any of the training areas that we would be using.

We were flying at about 500' AGL and doing a search coverage pattern to locate a target item (sunken boat) when all of a sudden a cruise missile flies right under us by no more than 20-30'. It blows past us as we are doing about 80 knots and it is doing better than 400 knots. We were shocked and barely had time to comment on the sighting when we suddenly saw two F-16's that were apparently in chase of the cruise missile swerving back in behind the cruise missile. It was likely that they were chase for Eglin AFB cruise missile and probably didn't see us until the last minute. The two F-16's also doing better than 400 knots were quickly off into the distance. If we were a few feet lower, we'd never have known what hit us.

It was just another day in the Training Command.

LPA

Back in the early 80's I was returning from noon chow at the O Club at Lejeune with my buddy Lt. Tim Learn. As we were cruising past officer housing on our way back to work, I remembered a message that I had seen on the read board that morning. It said that one of our fellow lieutenants, we'll call him Mike Smith, was being released from the naval hospital in Norfolk and would be returning to work the next day.

I had already had Mike's office cleaned in preparation for his return. He had spent several weeks in the hospital with testicular cancer; I don't remember what the treatment was at the time, other than him telling me it was long and arduous. As we passed lines of housing, I happened to think about the fact that his wife had been with him in Norfolk the entire time and that his house had been vacant. I asked Tim to turn and drive by Mike's house to be sure things looked presentable. I was more than sure that his neighbors would have pitched in to take care of things while he was gone but thought we should check, just to be sure.

We were shocked to find that the grass was nearly waist high with fallen limbs everywhere. The hedges were badly in need of trimming and garbage was scattered all over the property. We assessed the situation and went straight to Lt Col John Whalen's office. He was the battalion commander, and we respectfully requested the use of his lieutenants for the remainder of the afternoon for a working party. We explained the mission and he gave me the keys to his house and said his lawn mower, rake, shovel, and hedge trimmer were in the garage. We hopped on the phone and put the call out to all the lieutenants. About an hour later we met up at Mike's house and with about ten guys working, had the place looking great in short order.

We left the house feeling pretty proud of ourselves, dropped off the tools and headed for the club. We sat at a big table in the back of the bar, throwing back beers. The subject soon got around to a fellow lieutenant who had received a reprimand for failing to secure transportation to pull his platoon out of the field. He had taken them for training in the woods for a few days and had only requested trucks to take them to the training area. He thought transportation was a round trip sort of thing. He was a bit of a jerk, full of himself, overbearing, a know it all, and not liked by the staff NCOs. He did not run the request by his gunnery sergeant, signed it himself and sent it to Motor-T.

The gunny at Motor-T accepted the request, saw the error, and fulfilled it to the letter, not alerting his lieutenant as to the problem. When the platoon packed up and no ride home showed up, the lieutenant drove back to main side and started creating a ruckus. The Motor-T officer pulled the paperwork, showed him his error and the kid went off like a rocket.

Everybody ended up in front of the commanding officer's desk and, eventually, all but the young officer was sent from the room. The CO spent the next twenty minutes reaming a brand new, larger-size rectal orifice for the young man; informed him that if he didn't act like such an ass all the time, maybe the big boys wouldn't pick on him so much.

As we sat talking, the idea caught hold that we had several such lieutenants who were headed for the same kind of fall and maybe there was something we could do about it. That day we formed a pact. We all wrote down our home and work numbers, made copies and distributed them. The Lieutenant's Protective Association (LPA) was a mythological organization with few rules.

Rule One: If you are acting like an ass, full of your own importance, two or more of us will let you know and help you unscrew yourself. Listen and change accordingly.

Rule two: We should use our staff NCOs as we were taught to do. Learn all we can from them. Respect their knowledge and lean on them. Let them know we need their expertise.

Rule three: If you get in trouble, reach out any time day or night to the lieutenant that can most likely provide you what you need. Drop all the rank. If you need a truck, call Duke. If you need the keys to Supply, call Al. We'll fix the paperwork later. Just call.

Rule Four: If you get the call, drop everything and come running. We have to protect ourselves.

After this and a few more meetings the lieutenants began to police our own. There were a few holdouts who refused to comply, and they were allowed to twist slowly, slowly in the wind, unaided from below or above, standing alone against the elements. They usually found themselves ranked at the bottom come fitness report time. One or two had to sign twice. But those who used the LPA as a final protection against the unforgiving system learned to lead properly and use the tools they were given; life became easier and bonds became stronger. We had an officer's call at Quantico a couple of years ago and we were instantly, as we had been all those years ago, ready to help each other. There was not just a kinship but an easy comfort that some of us felt just being in a place where there could be no trouble; my brothers are here looking out for me.

LT. ROCK

I have no first-hand knowledge of the following tale. It was told to me as a news story as it happened while I was attending The Basic School in Quantico in 1979-80. Because it is a second-hand story, I cannot swear to its authenticity; as I have told it many times through the years, some of the edges may have worn off. However, I checked with my TBS classmates and several remember the events, but none exactly as I will lay them out. That being the case, please know that it happened, but the details may be fuzzy.

It begins with the Marine Corps' version of "Once upon a time" – only ours goes: "This is a November Sierra!" There was a company commander at The Basic School whose name was Major Rocky Ball. I know that sounds fictitious already, but that is absolutely true. He wanted his company to be the finest, so he added an unwritten "motivator" to the regular curriculum. He created Lieutenant Rock, a twenty-pound rock, which, having no legs, needed to be carried everywhere the other lieutenants went.

When they went for a company run, Lieutenant Rock needed to be carried. When they went for a hike, he was in an ALICE pack. He even had his own military ID card. Like standing duty, the rock was assigned to some lieutenant who was responsible for it each and every day. If he got dropped, there was hell to pay. During classes he was placed on a table beside his caregiver so that he could hear the instructions. Since he had no particular need for sleep, after working for hours, he stayed with the duty officer in the company office and was cared for by the Company Officer of the Day. As one might imagine, living day to day, fighting simulated wars, running through the woods carrying a twenty-pound rock on your back, and then being chewed out for placing it too deep in your pack – "He can't see what's happening on the battlefield!" – can get tedious.

The lieutenants of the company (I'll call them Charlie Company) began to grumble about this stupid rock. It was novel and cool for a few days, but as the program wore on, Lt. Rock was wearing on the nerves of the men. One night, in the Hawkins Room (the small bar positioned conveniently on TBS property, before officers and alcohol divorced and went their separate ways), some of the lieutenants of Charlie Company were complaining about the burdens of caring for their rock. Some lieutenants from Hotel Company overheard and couldn't believe that this kind of nonsense was happening. They determined to help out their comrades and a plan was hatched. I really wish I could track down the man or men who developed this plan, as it flies in the face of the axiom: "You can't fix stupid." Like fighting fire with fire, these men set about to fix stupid with stupider.

A few nights later, two men, a somewhat disguised Hotel Company lieutenant and a young male civilian, knocked on the Charlie Company office door. The duty lieutenant answered and the civilian asked if he could help him find Lt. Quincey. The duty officer's name was Barlow and there was little chance of him knowing if there was a Quincey because the Marine Corps arranges everyone alphabetically. The duty officer invited the two men in and while two of them searched the rosters for the imaginary Lt. Quincey, the third man quietly walked to the window and unlocked it. Both men saw Lt. Rock sitting on the duty desk.

Not being able to locate a Quincey, the duty officer directed the two to the Bravo Company office and bid them goodnight. Phase One was complete. About an hour later the Charlie Company office phone rang and the duty officer answered.

"This is Captain Bowhatch and I'm the TBS Officer of the Day! Are you standing duty for Charlie Company?" he shouted.

"Yessir."

"I was just down in your area and the entire parking lot is covered in trash! I'd suggest you get your butt down there and get it cleaned up ASAP! I'll be making rounds in about three hours and expect that I'll find it squared away! Goodnight lieutenant!" And with that, he hung up. The duty officer, fearing what might happen if he didn't get the lot cleaned up, ran out the door, locking it behind him, ran down the hall and down the stairs to see how bad it was. Phase Two was complete.

He did not know that his exit was being watched by a forward observer, who then signaled the fire team hidden in the tree line just behind the Charlie Company office. They sprang into action. Carrying an extension ladder they sprinted to the building, planted the ladder and raised it to the base of the Charlie Office window, in a reenactment of the Iwo Jima flag-raising. The chosen one scurried up the ladder, opened the window, entered the room, tossed out the rock and exited, all within seconds. He left an envelope addressed, "To the Lieutenants of Charlie Company." The letters, or words in some cases, were clipped from a newspaper and pasted on the envelope, kidnapper style. Inside, the ransom note read: "If you ever want to see Lt. Rock alive again, contribute one keg of beer to the Hotel Company Graduation Party." Signed, "A friend."

The ladder was put back from where it was taken. The rock was hidden and Phase Three was complete.

Slicker than the Raid on Entebbe, these conspirators should have been meritoriously graduated from The Basic School and promoted into Special Operations, but their identities remain unknown. The next morning Major Ball was informed of the kidnapping. Predictably, he went berserk.

For the next few days an investigation was conducted to try and track down the purloined stone, to no avail. In the wee hours of the morning, Polaroid pictures of Lt. Rock would appear on the Charlie Company bulletin Board. One day he was strapped to a chair with bright lights shining in his eyes and a shadowy figure swinging a rubber hose to show him being tortured. The next day he was holding a current Washington Post, to demonstrate proof of life. Finally, he was posed being held under the water at Beaver Dam Run, near Quantico. All of this designed to taunt Major Ball.

It is at this point when the stories diverge. Some say the ransom was paid by the grateful lieutenants of Charlie Company. Some say Major Ball was reported by some unknown lieutenants and was called on the carpet by the TBS Commanding Officer, Colonel E.T. Cook. You can pick any ending you like. As for me, I just love it when a plan comes together. My hat is off to the heroes who kidnapped Lt. Rock!

MAN IN THE BOX

The Marine Corps is steeped in traditions which separate it from the other branches of service. A Marine earns the Eagle, Globe and Anchor emblem upon completion of Recruit Training at Parris Island or San Diego, but when he finishes his MOS Training and reports to his first unit, he often needs to be initiated in order to be accepted by his fellow Marines.

The Sergeant Major for 8th Comm Bn at Camp Lejeune loved welcoming newbies into the fold. Admin corporals and lance corporals would swarm his desk to let him know that fresh meat had just arrived and would volunteer to be the "Man in the Locker." Soon a man was selected and the one-act play was set to begin. The young Marine, fresh from Communications School in California, marched briskly into the office, centered himself on the Sgt Maj's desk and reported, "Private First Class Shmuckatelli, reporting as ordered, Sgt Major!"

"Stand easy," said the Sgt Major as he studied the almost nonexistent Service Record Book of the new man. "It says here you're from Kenosha. Must be pretty cold up there this time of year. How did you enjoy the weather out in Calif—"

"PLEEEEASE, can I have some water?" came a voice from the metal locker directly behind Martinez.

Over his right shoulder the Sgt Major replied, "I just gave you water yesterday! This ain't the goddamned Ritz!" Facing the newbie again: "Says you finished second in your class at Comm School. Looks like you're on the right track."

"But Sgt Major, it's SOOO hot in here!" came the plaintive voice from the locker.

Martinez grabbed a night stick from his desktop and slammed it as hard as he could against the metal locker. The new kid was visibly shaken and had a slight tremble at the sight of this. "If I hear another word from you, I may have you drawn and quartered, Marine!" shouted the Sergeant Major.

The new man was now shaken and losing color fast. Martinez went nuts, framing on the locker with the night stick and shouting obscenities at the unseen Marine.

"Corporal Wallace get in here!" he shouted. In ran Wallace looking frightened.

"Get this worthless waste out of my office. Take him out back and hit him with the fire hoses again! What's today... Wednesday? Give him another piece of bread. Bring him back in here and put him back in the locker!"

"Yes, Sgt Major," said Wallace. He unlocked the padlock, opened the door, and out fell a young Lance Corporal soaked in "sweat." Martinez jumped, as if unable to control himself. He grabbed the fallen Marine by the ear and held his head up. "The next time you choose to come to my formation three minutes late, think of the consequences of your actions!" he shouted.

Wallace, aided by another Marine, drug the culprit out of the office. The Sgt Major settled back into his chair and continued studying the SRB. The kid was white as a sheet. "If you'll just finish getting checked in, we'll have somebody come up from the company office and take you down to your work area." Martinez added, as if nothing out of the ordinary had taken place, "You just keep your nose clean and I'm sure you'll do fine. Just remember what you learned at boot camp and comm school."

The kid snapped to attention, about faced and headed out the door. When he stepped outside, he was met with thunderous applause by everyone that worked in the battalion office. There were lots of handshakes and Welcome Aboards. He even got to meet the man in the box and got a handshake from the Sergeant Major as well. There were several variations to the play, but it always played to a packed house and always made the new guy feel like he belonged.

MARINE CORPS CAREER ENDER?

In 1981, I began my first tour as a Marine Officer. I served as a combat engineer officer with 8th Engineer Support Battalion at Camp Lejeune. I had spent a very enjoyable year and a half as a brigade platoon commander. Then I was afforded the opportunity to command Alpha Company.

I was still a first lieutenant with much to learn, but engineer captains were scarce at that time. The battalion commander, LtCol Luke Guthrie, had faith and confidence in my abilities so he placed me in command. It was a good year; we developed and executed good training plans. We participated in several projects in support of MCB Camp Lejeune: expeditionary building construction, recreation pavilions, and some of the running path to Hospital Point.

I got orders to the College Degree Completion Program at North Carolina State University and prepared to turn Alpha Company over. The preparations included throwing a troop appreciation event. It was an eight-mile company run from French Creek to Onslow Beach, followed by a picnic (burgers, dogs, chips, salads, soda, and beer) and activities at the beach.

We had a great run to the beach. No drops. Upon arrival, the company turned to the picnic, volleyball, and the beach. My platoon commanders and I enjoyed ourselves at the event and monitored for over-consumption of alcohol. The event went well, and the troops had a good time. I had arranged for truck transportation to return us to French Creek.

When the event was over, we loaded up into the five-tons and began the trip back. I put my senior platoon commander (didn't have an XO) in the lead HMMWV and I brought up the rear in the sweeper HMMWV. The last five-ton was crossing the bridge over the Intracoastal Waterway when it stopped suddenly.

A Marine named Griffin emerged from the rear of the truck. He looked wild and enraged. He began to run across the bridge, and other Marines spilled out of the five-ton carrying an inert Marine. They placed the Marine on the ground as I came upon the scene. He was unconscious and didn't appear to be breathing well. We got our corpsman on it and he stabilized the Marine.

I was told that, out of the blue, Griffin had gone berserk and pounded the Marine's head repeatedly on the five-ton's metal deck. My Marines intervened and Griffin jumped out of the truck and ran. We called the MPs and an ambulance. The MPs quickly located and subdued Griffin. They took him to MP shack for processing. The ambulance took the injured Marine to the hospital, where he recovered.

The MP directed me and my Marines in the relevant five-ton to the MP shack to provide statements. While my Marines provided their statements, I knew it was time to call my CO and report what was going on. I had been thinking about how to report that I and a bunch of my Marines were at the MP shack, and I was concerned about what LtCol Guthrie's reaction might be. I knew I had done things right that day. Griffin's psychotic break – or whatever it was – was not foreseeable. But the Marine Corps was in the grip of a "zero defect" mentality that had it "eating its young" in many cases. Junior officers were often featured in the menu. Under many COs, this could mean an early end of my chosen career.

I dialed LtCol Guthrie and made my report. He said, "Well Lieutenant Haskett, do you have the situation under control?" I responded in the affirmative. He followed with, "Well then, why the hell did you call me?" and hung up. I was absolutely relieved. I made my own statement to the MPs and got my Marines back to French Creek. I so appreciated how LtCol Guthrie handled the situation. I remembered it when I, in turn, had to deal with subordinate officers and SNCOs under similar circumstances.

MEETING GENERAL GRAY

In 1980, right after TBS, many of us were waiting to go to flight school in Pensacola, so we were farmed out all over Quantico as SLJO's (Shitty Little Jobs Officers). We were assigned to tasks for which we had no particular training, more or less to "mark time" until the pipeline cleared enough, and our orders came transferring to NAS Pensacola. I was assigned to the Development Center, working for Major Carol Mutter as a Financial Manager. She reported to Major General Al Gray, who ran the Dev Center.

My primary task was to keep track of where all the money was and to move it from one project to another as requested by the Project Managers. I was an English Major with a checkbook that hadn't been balanced in a while, so I was clearly the best qualified candidate for such menial tasks.

I had been working there for a week or so and noticed that none of the officers around me went to lunch, but rather went out to PT during the noon hour. I soon began to bring PT gear to work, as the pressure to do so mounted. I went out the first day, a hot day in May, and shot hoops with some of the other Marines from the dev center. At the end of the hour, we took our sweaty bodies back to the basement where the showers were located.

There must have been a hundred men waiting to get into the showers. I asked around and found there were only three or four shower heads. I determined that waiting inside was preferable, so I went to my air-conditioned office to wait for the line to shrink. While sitting there, I happened to remember that there was a small head right up the passageway from my office. I thought I even remembered there being a shower in there. I thought all those majors and colonels had not done a very good recon of the building and were standing in line while this perfectly good shower stood vacant.

I grabbed my uniform, walked up the passageway, hopped in the shower. I remember thinking that I would keep this shower a secret, so that I could take advantage of its convenience. As I finished my shower, I pulled open the curtain. There, naked, hands on hips, big frown on his face, stood General Gray.

I had only seen him once before, at our mess night at The Basic School. Then, of course, he was fully clothed. As he stood before me, his command presence told me that he was very much in charge and that I had violated some rule of which (as usual) I was unaware.

"Lieutenant Wilcox, isn't it?" he calmly inquired. (The man NEVER forgot a name!)

"Yes sir," I demurely replied.

"Lieutenant, you may not be aware that every General Officer in the Marine Corps has his own head, and this one is mine. I trust that I can rely on you to respect that in the future. Good day."

He entered the shower and yanked the curtain behind him. I dressed as quickly as possible and never returned. Not the recommended way to start a career.

MICRONESIA PRESIDENTIAL INAUGURATION

In 1999 I was stationed on Okinawa at Camp Courtney in the III MEF, G-3, where I performed duties as the Ulchi Focus Lens (UFL) exercise officer. The exercise section was a large wide-open space on the second floor of the headquarters building where there were several majors and lieutenant colonels who planned and coordinated various joint, combined, and/or bilateral military exercises with the Japanese Ground Self Defense Force, Republic of Korea Marines, and the Thailand and Australia military. This particular year, the father of one of our exercise officers had won the presidential election in Micronesia, and consequently, he was now the First Son of Micronesia. However, given his gregarious, boisterous, high-spirited, and flirtatious nature, combined with his proclivity as a party animal, he was definitely a liberty risk and we referred to him as the Prince of Micronesia.

Of course, there were inaugural events that were taking place in Micronesia for the prince's father that he was going to attend. Further, the prince invited a handful of us from the exercise shop to join him for this excursion. He also was accompanied by his girlfriend at the time, who was the former wife of one of our TBS classmates, as well as a social worker employed as a contractor for the Family Advocacy Program at Kadena Air Force Base. The prince also happened to be a C-130 pilot, and he invited the III MEF Deputy CG to come along, who was a C-130 pilot, too. Somehow, between the two of them, not only did they procure a C-130 aircraft, which they flew from Camp Futenma down to Micronesia and back for these inaugural affairs, but they additionally managed to get all of us permissive TAD orders for the trip without having to take any leave – not to mention there was no cargo and only about nine of us on the plane (Can you imagine trying to pull that off in today's environment?).

After our eight-hour rough and bumpy, no seat cushion C-130 ride, we finally arrived in Palikir on the northwest side of Pohnpei island, which is the capital city of the Federated States of Micronesia located in the western Pacific Ocean, just south of the equator. What most people don't know is the total population of this island nation is only 106,487. It consists of four states from west to east: Yap, Chuuk, Pohnpei and Kosrae. Together, the states comprise around 607 islands with a combined land area of approximately 271 square miles. Also, Micronesia has been associated with the United States since WWII, and we have had diplomatic relations with them since 1986 and have mutual Ambassadors to each other's country. Further, Micronesia has diplomatic relations with 88 other countries as well, including Japan, Australia, New Zealand, China, Thailand, Philippines, Singapore, South Korea, India, Mexico, Cambodia, Vietnam, Germany, France, Italy, and Spain. Many of these ambassadors were in attendance for the Inauguration and most of the related happenings.

The four or five inaugural events which occurred were spread out over a three-to-four-day period in mid-July, 1999. At this time of year in close proximity to the equator, it was blistering hot and humid, especially when having to wear a suit or a military dress uniform; very uncomfortable while profusely perspiring to say the least, even when standing or sitting in the shade. Before and following the inauguration itself, there were interrelated activities, including a church service and an inaugural breakfast. The inaugural breakfast was outside under a very large tent canopy which accommodated scores of people, and it was attended by numerous ambassadors and heads of state.

The morning I headed over to the inaugural breakfast I was dressed in a suit and was accompanied by a Navy lieutenant from our Okinawa contingent who wore his dress white uniform. Our going to the event at the same time was not planned and just pure happenstance, and I did not think anything of it. As I casually approached the tent canopy where the breakfast was hosted, I noticed that everyone was already there and seated. When I began to enter the area where everybody was gathered, I saw that all eyes were on me as they started to clap and give me a standing ovation. I was totally bewildered and had no clue what was going on. Then it quickly dawned on me they thought I was some important dignitary because I was being escorted by a military attaché in his dress uniform. As I continued to slowly proceed down the center aisle, diplomats and envoys were reaching out to shake my hand. In that same instant, I figured the best thing to do under the circumstances was to return the gesture so that I did not appear rude or snobbish. Consequently, I shook their hands as I strolled to the rear of the crowd while simultaneously greeting them with, "Nice to meet you," "Glad you could make it," or "Good to see you." Needless to say, I thought I was in an episode of the Twilight Zone, wondering what the hell just happened.

We finally reached our table and ended up with the Japanese ambassador and his wife who seemed alone and somewhat estranged since they barely spoke little to no English; most other attendees did. So, between my broken Japanese and their broken English we were able to muddle through very basic conversation, which at the very least made them feel welcomed and included.

In between the inaugural proceedings, we had a chance to do some site seeing which included a guided tour of the "Stone City," about a forty-five-minute boat ride from the main island of Pohnpei. It was a vast, several hundreds of years old city in the middle of the ocean that was built on sand bars by huge carved stones that weighed tons. To this day, it is still a mystery how these large rocks and boulders were transported to this site, let alone put in place to form these structures. Truly astounding. Additionally, some people in our group went scuba diving, and they reported that the coral reef around Pohnpei was absolutely spectacular.

Then, there was the night life which upheld the finest Marine Corps traditions of the past that are now only a distant memory, since the culture of today's Corps and other military services has shifted to a much less tolerant view of letting "boys be boys." Accordingly, it is best not to mention specific details about some of the alcohol-related, gregarious and carnal activities that occurred in order to protect the guilty, and especially because the "statute of limitations" has not run out on some of this behavior. That being said, good times were had by all who were at the local evening establishments where the attributes and qualities that formulate "living life to the fullest" were plentiful and in abundance. The ambiance, encounters, and experiences certainly did not disappoint.

The night before we departed Micronesia to return to Okinawa, our element attended a cocktail hour and social event at the U.S. ambassador's quarters. At one point, we were standing in a circle talking about how we did not want to go back since we were having such an incredible time. I then commented, "Wouldn't it be a shame if the C-130 developed sudden problems like some flat tires and was unable to fly." Not actually being serious, I nonchalantly said this purposely when I realized the III MEF Deputy CG was just an ear shot away to see how he would respond. Without hesitation he quickly turned around and firmly, but nervously, insisted that he had to be back to Okinawa tomorrow for a vitally important function. Not surprisingly, it could obviously be gleamed from the look in the eyes of those in the circle that some of us were secretly hoping the general would turn a blind eye. However, it was not meant to be, and as we embarked on the plane the next morning, we were grateful for having the experience of a lifetime.

NEAR DEATH EXPERIENCES IN THE F-4 PHANTOM

I flew the F-4 Phantom from December 1982 to December 1988 in three different squadrons: VMFAT-101, VMFA-212 and VMFA-235. I also flew the F/A-18 Hornet from January 1989 to February 1994, accumulating just under 3,000 flight hours on approximately 1,800 flights. During that time, I arrived at VMFAT-101 at MCAS El Toro, CA on August 2, 1990, to begin training to become a Hornet Instructor Pilot. This turned out to be a very infamous date in our history as it was the day Saddam Hussein first invaded Kuwait. I tell this with some regret of not ever really getting to do what I was trained to do: fly in combat. Even though I had just flown in a combat-ready squadron, I was now relegated to my new role as an IP and missed the entire Gulf War (Desert Storm) due to being in a non-deployable training squadron. However, in light of the above, the several days per week military training for Navy/Marine aviation is inherently unforgiving, and I'd like to share four occasions which nearly cost me my life – not too bad for 1,800 sorties!

On the first occasion (December 13, 1983), I was in VMFA-212 and still a "nugget" flying with my RIO, Chuck "Pedals" Pribyl, on a Trans-Pacific flight from MCAS Yuma, AZ to MCAS Kaneohe Bay, HI. We all carried mini tape recorders that were hooked into the comm cords on our oxygen masks. We used them to record the communication during our air combat training flights to help us reconstruct what had happened during the flight and to aid us in debriefing. However, on this 6.5-hour flight, the mini tape recorder's purpose was to simply entertain me with my pre-recorded music. We had just gone feet-wet off the coast of San Diego headed west prior to our first refuel point. Two KC-135 Air Force tankers and twelve F-4s were in a stacked formation with three F-4s on either side of each tanker.

I had my tunes running and decided I wanted to switch the tape to the other side. Keep in mind there's no autopilot on the F-4, so I was hand-flying it in formation. You know when you think you can get away with texting and driving and really you can't? Well, as I finished switching my tape to the other side, I looked up out the front windshield and noticed I was about twenty feet directly behind another Phantom doing 480 knots with about ten to fifteen knots of closure. All I could see were the "turkey feathers" (the exhaust nozzles) on the F-4 in front of me. I slammed the control stick full forward and we got about two negative Gs as we lost about 1,000 feet. "Pedals" started screaming on the intercom: "WTF are you doing?!" I responded to him, letting him know what I was trying to do with the tape recorder. Fortunately, we regained formation without incident and continued the remaining five hours to K-Bay.

The next near-death incident took place during my final Air Combat Tactics Instructor certification flight out of Kunsan Air Base on the western coast of South Korea. It was scheduled as two F-4s flying against an unknown number of F-16s that were based there in Kunsan. We launched July 19, 1984, on a very hazy, almost foggy day. I was flying with my RIO, Brian "Hollywood" Nicholas, and my wingman, MAWTS instructor Earl "The Pearl" Wederbrook, and his RIO, "Jaws" White.

We got to the training area about fifty miles off the west coast over the Yellow Sea. I first mentioned on the radio that due to the fact that there was no visible horizon, we would be "intercept only," meaning that there would be no "turning and burning" or three-dimensional maneuvering. A big emphasis to the certification program is the safety aspect, so I wanted to make everyone aware that it was not a safe day for aerial combat. My MAWT instructor quickly snapped back on the radio with "Noted!"

Everything sounded okay and we were all on the same page, so I thought, Let's rock and roll. We made our first intercept and, though I can't remember much of the details, on the second intercept we didn't have it suit-cased at all, so we decided to "bug-out" at about fifteen miles or 45 seconds from the merge. I then called, "Cross turn – I'm low," and we did a 6G nose low turn of 180 degrees. After completing the turn, we were "matching hands," meaning both hands full forward with the left hand shoving the throttles into full afterburner and the right hand pushing full forward on the control stick to achieve maximum speed and accelerate from the bad guys, the quickest way. This maneuver required us to do weaving turns and "checking six" (looking backwards) to try and acquire a visual on the bandits, or a smoke trail from a missile that may have been fired, in order for us to begin defensive countermeasures with chaff and flares.

On a normal day with a "visible horizon" there are visual cues to tell you when you are getting low, but on this day, having started out around 20,000 feet above sea level and extremely nose down, very shortly I heard "Hollywood" on the intercom yelling, "Pull up, pull up!" And shortly thereafter, the air combat maneuvering range safety officer saying, "Knock it off, knock it off!" (which means to stop the training immediately and see what is unsafe).

We carried "pods" on our aircraft, which record and show in real time what each aircraft is doing, revealing the airplane literally hitting the water at an airspeed of around 700 knots. Obviously, that didn't happen. I was so engrossed in rolling the wings upright and pulling maximum Gs that I had no recollection of what the radar altimeter actually showed. Whew, cheated death again.

Between West Pac deployments now flying out of NAS Barbers Pt. with VMFA-212 due to our runways being under repair at Kaneohe Bay, on July 31, 1985, I was leading a division (4-ship) of Phantoms flying with my RIO Maj. Bob "Zman" Zimmerman on 4 versus 4 air combat training mission against the Hawaii Air National Guard (HANG) F-15s. Our training area was 35 miles north of Oahu and extended 100 miles north.

We had just finished our first intercept to and engagement when we were all recalled to base due to deteriorating weather on the south side of Oahu. I got a quick fuel check from my flight as we joined up and headed back to base and, as usual, I, as lead, had the most fuel. This is simply due to the fact that as wingman they are moving the throttles more to maintain position and that uses more fuel. Talking to air traffic control I obtained an "individual clearance" for each aircraft in the formation as the weather was below section (two aircraft together) landing minimums. If we had higher weather, we could come in together and just get separation to land on short final or land together at the same time. But today it wasn't the case.

Since I had the most fuel, I was the last to start my HI-Tacan approach penetration to a teardrop (180deg reversal) entry to land. ATC gave me holding as they had to get enough separation for me since everyone else had gone first. I finally got my turn and started down. It was a long, steep descent to get down on the approach, which culminated with the teardrop turn to final.

During that long descent I noticed the radar scope flash, which Zman was using to ground map the coastline, but was too busy to investigate further as I was too busy with the workload of flying a non-precision approach. It's called non-precision not because I suck, but because there is no automation aiding the pilot or a controller talking you down. It's all on the pilot and flying the bearing needle of the TACAN navigation receiver. As I was leveling off to get the gear and flaps out for my final approach about six miles on straight-in to the runway the aircraft started rolling left.

From early flight school I was always taught to keep my hand on the flap handle in case they were split or asymmetric and then you would raise them back to the last or mid position. I instantly put the flap switch back to half, but now I was settling below my final approach fix level off altitude. I went into after burner to arrest the sink rate and it worked but not before leveling at about 500 feet above the water. At about the same time I picked up the coastline north of Barbers point and recognized the fuel storage tanks there. Also, at the same time I noticed the left engine generator light was on just outside of my right knee.

Hmmm, that is why the radar scope flashed, holy shit my left engine is out. I told myself, "That's why the radar scope flashed on descent." The engine quit and then the generator dropped off line which powered the radar. I told "Zman" this and he and I decided to try a relight of the engine with no luck. Now, we were in contact with the tower and they were saying the field was closed and that I would need to divert to Honolulu International.

With all the delaying I knew I don't have the fuel for that. I declared an emergency and requested a "contact approach." This is a procedure that can only be requested by the pilot and never offered up by the controller. It tells them that I have something on the ground in sight and am fully responsible for getting my own ass onto the runway safely. As I got closer to the coast, I knew I was a few miles west of the field. The bottom of the clouds was a ragged deck of around 300 feet, so I was forced to stay below that or lose sight of land.

I followed the coast east to the runway, but the only problem was that the coastline was perpendicular to the runway so as I flew over the end of the runway 90 degrees out, I made a right turn the reciprocal of the runway heading and punched the clock for one minute. At the end of that minute, I made a 180-degree turn back to line up with the runway. I no longer had the land in sight and was just skimming the top of the water at about 100 to 200 feet. As I picked up the land again, I was too far left to land, so I turned out to sea again, only this time Zman calls the squadron to have them turn the field lights on, as they were out because the field was "closed," and get the LSO or landing signal officer out at the end of the runway.

As I was heading away from the field this time, I made a wind correction to the east so I wouldn't end up too far left. It worked, as I came in this time toward the field, I picked up the lead in-lights and landed uneventfully and just in time as I only had about fifteen minutes of fuel left. Turns out, the left engine-driven fuel pump had failed during the descent and since I was at idle power, I didn't notice it until I attempted to level off for the approach. What a time for it to happen right?

Fast forward to my second West Pac deployment a few months later from October 1985 to April of 1986 at MCAS Iwakuni Japan. Still with VMFA-212 and tasked to support Operation Team Spirit, a joint exercise between us and South Korea, I was given a deep air strike (DAS) mission on 26 February to attack a target in a restricted training area on the South Korean side right along the DMZ. We did our tactical planning and decided a section of F-4s carrying four Mk-83 (1000 pounders) HE inert would do the job. John "Ping" Scanlon was my RIO and I had a MAG-15 augment pilot as my wingman.

We planned a high-low-high profile with the low part starting from the east coast of the Korean peninsula to the target area. We planned a pop-up attack to a 30-degree dive. There is no GPS in the F-4 so all navigation is just like Marines learned to do in "land nav 101" (i.e., time, distance, heading). The whole exercise that day was "comm out" so I can only communicate with my wingman via "combat section no comm" visual signals. Well, the signal for a wingman to leave our combat spread, one mile or so, abreast formation or trail, is for the lead aircraft to "porpoise" the aircraft (i.e., pitch the nose up and down with the control stick) and wing then joins up in tight "Blue Angel" formation, so he won't lose sight if we go into the clouds.

Just before we went "feet dry" on our ingress to the target, we dropped from 30,000 feet down to 300 feet, to the low-level ingress to the target. The weather was marginal and at times, the clouds were just about touching the ground. We made it for about ten minutes along our route dodging uncharted power lines that were above our altitude. Finally, up ahead it looked like the valley we were flying in became a mountain and the clouds were meeting it with no way around but to climb into the clouds and abort the mission.

I "porpoised" my aircraft but my wingman didn't respond. I didn't just want to climb and allow him to lose sight of me and either hit me or fly into the terrain ahead. I broke "comm out" procedures and told him to join up. At the last second, I could stand before we hit the terrain, he got aboard and I started the nose up with about 2 Gs so I wouldn't lose him and call "burners on now," meaning I'm going to push the throttles full forward into the after-burner range and the wingman should do the same on the word "now." The clouds were really thick so I could barely see him, but he was hanging in there and I was just praying I hadn't waited too late and we impacted the terrain. Well, we missed it obviously and ended up about 60-degrees nose high. As we popped out on top, I pulled it out of after-burner, so we didn't run out of gas and pointed the nose back toward home base and landed there uneventfully.

On a lighter note, at the end of my F-4 flying career and on the advice of my OCS and TBS buddy Ken Wilcox, I've got one last story. It is tradition on your last flight in a K-Bay fighter squadron that you get "bay qualed." It was December 11, 1988, and I was finishing up my stint with VMFA-235 Death Angels before transitioning to the F/A-18 Hornet during my second tour at MCAS Kaneohe Bay, HI. Not sure what the mission was on my last flight, but I had pre-planned carefully the post flight.

In K-bay our flight line is right on the bay and the tower is beside the runway with a big tree beside it on the flight line side. Before the flight I borrowed a one-piece, bright orange, swimsuit from my mother-in-law who was visiting and put it on under my flight suit. Once I landed, I detoured from the normal taxi route to the flight line where everyone awaited our arrival for the big festivities. When the tower asked where we were going, I told my RIO, Fred "LC" Greenwood, to tell them we had to troubleshoot something before parking in the line area.

We taxied behind the tree near the tower so we couldn't be seen. I set the parking brake and unstrapped from the ejection seat, stood up in my seat with the canopies open and stripped down to my boots and the suit and my helmet of course. We then taxied to the flight line with my family and everyone waiting where I shut down, hopped out and began trying to escape the troops in a valiant probably two-minute-long effort. To no avail, they then carried me down the WWII seaplane ramp and tossed me into the bay. They live for that shit and so do I. God Bless our troops.

I feel a great sense of pride when people say, "Thank you for your service," as I feel I was trained to the utmost during the waning years of the Cold War. Most people don't know how well the Russian military manufacturing machine was humming along (albeit at the expense of the rest of their economy), and that if I was ever engaged in air-to-air combat with them, I would be out-numbered four to one. Since the Russians got very little flight time and training compared to American military pilots, I still believe that we would have defeated them single handedly. I'm sure they knew this, and I assume it was a huge deterrent for them to investigate any hostilities toward the United States.

Yes, we who only fought the Cold War did serve well.

NO PHOTOS, PLEASE

A friend of a friend of mine was the recon platoon commander with the 22nd MAU in Beirut in 1982-83, and so I often hung out with the recon because they got to roll around in the dirt and play with the cool toys. He was assigned to help conduct some training for the Lebanese army and asked if I could help out. Unaware of what I'd be doing, I showed up as he and his staff sergeant were teaching a class in rappelling. I was by no means an expert, but as they concluded their presentation, I began to show each man how to rig himself. It was then that I noticed for the first time that these Lebanese soldiers appeared to be fifteen or sixteen years old. They had no facial hair and acted like schoolboys, joking and playing with each other, clearly with little interest in what we were teaching.

It is taught that there are only two certainties in life – death and taxes – but if you're a Marine, there's a third. It is the infamous: TRAINING SCHEDULE! Once the training schedule is published it cannot be changed. It must be executed, no matter what. I had not seen the training schedule, but soon learned that we were to take these youngsters to the roof of the BLT Headquarters Building and have them rappel off. This is a building that was blown up with a truck bomb a few months later. It was a four-story structure and I immediately thought that these kids weren't ready for such a jump. I located the recon staff sergeant and suggested maybe a little one-story building, like the MSSG building across the street, might be more appropriate for our young stalwarts. "Sorry, Sir, no can do. The BLT Barracks is on the TRAINING SCHEDULE," he responded.

Up to the roof we went, the ropes were tied off and the demonstrations began. The lieutenant and the staff sergeant hooked themselves up, stood on the edge of the roof, leaned back and pushed off, flying eight to ten feet away from the building and gliding down about two floors before they flew back to the building, hit it with their feet, squatted, pushed off again until they were five or six feet from the ground. They pulled up on the break and eased themselves down, walking off the end of the rope. It really is beautiful when done properly. A couple of more demonstrations and our Lebanese friends were deemed sufficiently trained.

It was very clear to me that they were not ready, but onward we went. When the first one went off, many things became instantly evident. He jumped and yanked the brake at the same instant, which gave him no rope to work with, and he slammed face first into the wall about six inches from where he started. He was still holding the brake but began to let it slide vigorously through his hand. He slid five or six feet at a time, his body grinding against the exterior wall, hitting and bouncing as he fell down the rope. It took quite some time for him to get to the bottom, but when he did, he was scraped up and his hand was a bit rope burned. At least he was still alive.

Then a funny thing happened. The half of his group that was still on the ground began to applaud loudly and cheered heartily, slapping him on the back with great congratulatory slaps, as though he had defeated some great foe. They were absolutely sincere. They had just seen this exercise executed perfectly, followed by their boy, who looked like he was wrestling the building and barely surviving, and they honestly could not see the difference. The others who followed him hardly fared better, but when the last one was safe on the ground and first aid had been administered, I comforted myself with the solace that at least we hadn't killed anyone.

As our honored guests sat on the ground before us, enjoying the tasty MREs we had provided them, I asked the recon commander, "When do we get to take these kids home to their mamas?"

"After they finish the next phase of training," he answered.

"What's that?" I asked, wincing in anticipation of the answer.

"THE TRAINING SCHEDULE calls for them to rappel out of helicopters this afternoon."

Most of these kids had never seen a helicopter and though rappelling is not particularly difficult, they had already proven they were really bad at it and going out of a helo is harder than going off a building. I just couldn't believe we were doing this.

When they finished lunch, we marched them over to the LZ, put them on the CH-46's and took off. I had a stick of ten or twelve men and we hovered near the main highway. The LZ was very sandy and we hovered 25 or 30 feet off the deck as they began to go out the rear. We were slinging a ton of sand towards the highway and traffic was stopping because drivers couldn't see for the dirt. A group of Marines would have been out and off the ropes in a minute or two, but these guys took forever. They went down sideways, nearly upside down and every kind of wrong way you could imagine, but God kept them alive, and gravity took them down.

My last guy had his heels off the ramp, leaning back on the rope, but after looking down, could not bring himself to jump. He looked back at me, his eyes were like saucers, large and full of fear. The pilot was screaming at the crew chief about the dirt and the traffic. The crew chief began to yell for me to get my "cargo" off the bird.

I had seen enough of them go out wrong and somehow land safely that I just wanted him out. I was wearing a cartridge belt with canteens ammo pouch and K-Bar attached. A K-Bar is a nasty looking Marine Corps fighting knife with a blade about a foot long. As I moved quickly to the back of the helo, I pulled my K-Bar and raised it high, coming toward the young soldier leaning back on the rope. As I got nearer to him, he jumped and yanked the break as most of his comrades had done. He had a rough trip down but walked off the end of the rope with only minor rope burns.

I sheathed my blade and walked back to the crew chief, sort of proud that we were done and that he was gone and not hurt badly. My relief was soon waylaid, for as I walked forward, I noticed the crew chief was pointing to the opposite side of the bird. There was a man with a camera sitting and though I had seen him earlier, there were so many journalists around all the time they had become almost invisible to me. But this one was special. I recognized him as David Hume Kennerly. He had won a Pulitzer Prize for his photos of Vietnam and had been the White House photographer for Gerald Ford. I had heard his name at a brief a few nights earlier but had not noticed him when we boarded. He was there, I believe, for Time Magazine. I knew immediately that he had pictures of me rushing toward the Lebanese kid wielding a very large knife. This would not play well back home and my superiors would not care to have a maniac on the payroll, so my momentary joy yielded to dejection. As soon as we landed, he stepped off the plane and was walking away.

"Mr. Kennerly!" I called sheepishly. I walked toward him like a whipped pup. "Could I have just a minute?"

He stopped, turned around, saw it was me and opened the back of the camera. He then pulled all of the film from the canister, exposing the entire roll and ruining it all. He handed it to me and said, "I guess you'll be needing this." I thanked him so much and took the exposed roll away in my pocket. He walked away and I saw him a couple of nights later and bought him a drink. I saved it for many years. Once my daughter found it in a drawer and asked me what it was, having never seen a roll of film. "That was my career," I told her.

NOTHING LOWER

I was born into a Marine family. I slept in a rack and made it tight each morning. It had a wool blanket with the letters "US" emblazoned on it. Walls were bulkheads, ceilings were overheads and floors were decks. We had room inspections and we had police call. My Dad was a Master Sergeant for nearly twenty years of his career. It was not a job or a role he played. He lived it, 24 hours a day.

He despised lieutenants because they didn't know anything yet and teaching them took up valuable time that he could have spent on other, more Marine-like duties. Often, they were full of themselves, thought they were in charge and didn't want to shut up, listen and learn. He hated stupid and they were too often stupid.

In 1963 I was in the third grade at Port Royal Elementary School near Parris Island. I was on the school safety patrol and got to roll out the life-size, tin policeman into the middle of the street notifying motorists that this was a school zone. We also raised and lowered the flag each day with great enthusiasm and ceremonious pomp. Our main function was to precede elementary kids, blocking traffic while standing at parade rest so that they could cross the street safely.

Mr. Forrester was the police chief, and, in fact, he was the entire police force of Port Royal. At the beginning of my third-grade year, he called us in and told us that he would be watching us closely this school year and that next year he was going to add rank structure to the program. Next year there would be a captain, a lieutenant and a sergeant who would handle the day-to-day operations, leaving him to keep the crime waves in check. He said the boy with the highest grades would be in charge, the second highest grades would be next and on down from there. We liked the sound of that!

I worked very hard all year and at the end of the school year I had all A's on my report card. My friend John had a single B, and he was my closest competition. After school that day, John and I ran immediately to the police station to report to the boss. We turned in our patrol belts and plain badges and asked if we could see our new badges.

Mr. Forrester studied the report cards, thought for a minute, and gave me the lieutenant badge. He then handed John the captain's badge. I was stunned and teared up a little.

He said we could take the badges home but to bring them back the next day. John and I left bewildered. Neither of us understood why he got the higher rank if I had the higher grades. We thought maybe we had the rank structure mixed up, so we ran to my house and asked my mom which one was higher. She laughed and suggested we wait and ask my dad when he got home. We sat on the steps waiting and a few minutes later he pulled up and boiled out of his car, steam coming from his ears. I could see that he was angry, and I knew it wasn't a good time, but I foolishly, tremulously, approached and blurted out, "Daddy, John and I were wondering which is higher, a captain or a lieutenant?"

There is no way that I could have known that he had spent the last hour getting his ass chewed out because his boneheaded lieutenant went behind his back and screwed up, cutting off the power to half of Parris Island. He was expected to teach the lad better and had failed to control him. Thus, his response to my inquiry was brief and to the point. I remember his index finger pointed directly at my nose as he replied, "Let me tell you something boy, THERE'S NOTHING IN THE WORLD LOWER THAN A LIEUTENANT!"

With that he stormed into the house. John ran home as fast as he could, and I stood crying in the front yard. I later learned that Mr. Forrester knew that my dad had orders for Okinawa and that I wouldn't be in Port Royal the following year. He couldn't not give me a reward for my good grades but wanted John to know that he would be the leader. He hoped my folks would explain it to me.

That was 1963. In 1979, I received my commission as a second lieutenant in the Marine Corps in Little Hall on Marine Corps Base, Quantico, VA. My Dad had seen our parade that morning and I saw him in civilian attire up in the stands. Later, we changed from camouflage utilities to our summer weight Alpha uniform for the commissioning ceremony.

When the ceremony was over, there were lots of young, enlisted Marines standing at the front door waiting for us to exit. Tradition holds that the first Marine who salutes a newly commissioned lieutenant is rewarded with a silver dollar, so they lined up for silver dollar payday. As I started out the door, a young Marine grabbed my arm and escorted me out a side door where I exited alone. Standing at attention, wearing the tropical weight Master Gunnery Sergeant uniform that he had retired in, stood my old man. He quickly popped a perfect, by-the-book salute and said, "Congratulations!" I returned the salute and reached to give him the silver dollar. He slowly lowered his arm and quietly said, "There's still nothing in the world lower than a lieutenant."

I didn't understand it the first time he said it, and I didn't understand the second time either, but he was right both times. When I got to the fleet, I found that those above me knew that I knew very little and those below me knew it as well. We lieutenants were the only ones who didn't know it. We had studied the book but had no experience at improvising and making it all work. Books don't teach that. Only years of experience in tight situations can teach that.

OLONGAPO OIL WRESTLING

Military people love the Philippines, especially Cubi Point and Olongapo. We were there in full force and ready for a good time after a long line period at sea. It was New Year's Eve and looking down over Olongapo from high up on the hill at the Cubi Point O Club, all you could see was a layer of smoke over the city. After a few frosty beverages and Cubi Specials, we headed into the "ville."

First stop and only stop that night was the Wagon Wheel Bar, where a boxing ring was set up in the middle with what had to be the largest waterbed in the world for a ring. A little person was the Ring Master. He began the bidding. We were not really sure what the bidding was for but joined in and learned the "why" later. Our bidding primarily was with the crew from a F-14 Squadron. It rose rapidly with our Commanding Officer cheering us on. We finally won the bid at $100. Our CO was in heaven that his boys beat out the Tomcats but little did he know, he would be the center of the bidding.

Four girls, scantily dressed, came over to him and escorted him to the back room. About five minutes later, he came out wearing a flimsy pair of shorts and was led to the oily ring. The Ring Masters announced the contestants with "Meester Skeeper" headlining the Main Event. The bell was rung and one of the girls jumped on the skipper. He threw her off and she got right back on him. Another girl joined the action. Their goal was to rip the flimsy shorts to shreds and then take them off.

They got him down and he sprung back. They sent in another girl. Meester Skeeper had one between his knees squeezing for all he's worth and was also holding one under each arm. The girls were screaming and conceding. The fourth girl ran away. The ring master was on the microphone screaming, "Meester Skeeper, let them go. Let them go! YOU are killing them." He would not let go until we interceded, and he emerged the victor. The girls took him to the back for his shower and other prizes while we collected seven cases of San Miguel beer which we shared with all the Tomcatters that lost! We were forever heroes to Meester Skeeper!

ON THE BLOOD OF AVIATORS

During World War II, pilots flew planes that were heavily loaded with fuel and ordinance. In order to get airborne, they would taxi to the head of the runway and apply and hold the brakes as hard as they could while running up the engines as much possible. When the brakes were released, the plane edged forward with the engine running at full throttle, and with a little luck, they would lift off before running out of runway. This procedure came to be known as "Take Off Power."

One of the senior aviators, who had served in World War II and had strong familiarity with this procedure, worked as a controller in the tower at Hill Air Force Base. The runway sits up on a plateau. From the tower, the controller can monitor an approaching aircraft for direction, distance, speed, and elevation.

On one occasion, while an aircraft was attempting to land, the visibility was not ideal, and avionics was not as developed then as it is today. As the young pilot approached the runway, he was low. The senior WWII pilot in the tower, sensing the danger to the young pilot, radioed to him, "You're low, give it more power." This instruction was again repeated with more urgency, "You are low, give it more power!" Seeing that the young pilot was not going to make it to the top of the plateau and the runway, the tower barked an explosive order, "Take Off Power!" The trusting young pilot reached up and pulled back the throttle to turn OFF the power. He didn't make the runway.

In the subsequent investigation of the accident, it was found the differences in their background and experience got in the way of effective communication. More standardized communications procedures were put into place to avoid another incident of this nature. It is a sad fact – aviation has progressed on the blood of its predecessors.

We lost one of our Basic School classmates, Mike James. Mike's education and passion was in aircraft engineering. He flew the Sikorsky CH-53 Echo Sea Stallion. There had been several accidents with this helicopter, but investigations had not uncovered the engineering problem. The decision had been made to continue to fly until enough data could be collected to resolve the issue. Even though Mike knew the risks, he accepted them. He gave his devotion to his duty, his country, and his passion.

OPERATION BEAR HUNT '85

From January to December 1984, I was stationed at Camp Foster in Okinawa, Japan. I was assigned as the commanding officer of Bravo Company, 3rd Landing Support Battalion. This logistics assignment was a departure from my combat engineer specialty, but engineers were sometimes assigned to such units when necessary. It turned out to be an excellent tour for me; company command under an outstanding Battalion Commander; an exciting three-month deployment to South Korea; and I met the woman I would marry fourteen years later (but that's another story).

In August I was ordered to form a Landing Support Detachment (LSD) to serve with the Combat Service Support Battalion (CSSD-37) that would deploy to South Korea in support of Operation Bear Hunt 1985. In late September, we boarded Navy amphibs and steamed across the East China Sea to Inchon, South Korea. I left a detachment at Camp Seattle in Inchon and the rest of us moved to a base camp adjacent to the village of Uncheon, somewhat near the Demilitarized Zone (DMZ). My LSD supported Bear Hunt from October through December.

My main body conducted ship loading/unloading ops, remote airfield ops, railroad embarkation ops, and helicopter support ops across the length and breadth of South Korea. The Camp Seattle Detachment handled Inchon ship operations. Together my LSD moved all Marine ground assets into and out of South Korea, and all significant movements of Marine Corps assets within South Korea for three months.

In November the CSSD commander notified me that three ships would arrive at Pusan in two days. He ordered me to get to Pusan ASAP with the men and material-handling equipment necessary to unload the ships. I formed an offload plan and gathered Marines and most of the equipment we needed to execute. We needed to make a tough 70-mile convoy through Seoul and into Inchon to pick up some additional material-handling equipment. We would rest overnight and convoy roughly 200 miles to Pusan the next day. The convoy consisted of HMMWVs, 5-Ton trucks, and low-boys hauling heavy equipment.

South Korea was especially tense at that time. North and South Korean officials were negotiating how North Korea could carry out an offer to send relief supplies to recent flood victims in the South. The negotiations were intense and, in the end, bore no fruit. The sticking point was North Korea's insistence to carry supplies directly to the South Korean capital of Seoul via Inchon. As it turned out, South Korea wasn't having any of that! During the negotiations all military movements in South Korea – which were carefully controlled and coordinated anyway – were even more strictly controlled.

Normally we would have submitted a convoy request and waited days for the approval, but we had no time for that. CSSB HQ took responsibility for reporting our convoy requirement, explaining the situation, and gaining the necessary approvals. If they did so, they were not effective.

On the day of departure, I climbed aboard the lead HMMWV and we headed south for Inchon. About halfway there we rounded a blind curve to find a South Korean Army Detachment deployed across the road. Their .50 caliber machine guns were trained on us, and they were ready to rock and roll. It was an extremely tense situation. South Korean forces were not to be messed with. With the potent threat poised just miles to the north they took national defense very seriously – as they had to do. And South Korean forces had a reputation for being trigger happy.

I halted the convoy and sat quietly for a minute to let them recognize us as U.S. forces. Then, accompanied by my interpreter, I carefully exited the HMMWV and approached the unit that was ready to blow us off the map. I met their commander and explained the situation. He radioed his headquarters, and we awaited their response. The commander reported that Inchon was closed to all U.S. military vehicles. We could not enter.

There was no time to contact base camp or attempt negotiations. Time was working against me, and there was nothing to do but re-route for Pusan and get the job done with the men and equipment I had at hand. Semper Gumby! Instead of resting over-night at Camp Seattle, we travelled as far as we could toward Pusan and then pulled over for a few hours of shut eye. That night I spent one of the coldest nights I had ever experienced on the floor of my HMMWV. As I rested there, I re-lived that moment of supreme danger when we rounded that curve and came under the South Korean guns. Just one premature order or nervous gunner and my convoy would have been lit up

– with me at the head of the line. But it had turned out well. My troops and I were alive and well – if cold – and we were en route to accomplish our mission. I thanked my lucky stars.

We made it to Pusan in time, adapted to the new situation – as Marines are so good at doing – and unloaded the ships in good order. Upon returning to base camp, I had a few words with the S-3.

OVER MY DEAD BODY

For me, the most interesting thing about being a Marine officer is the level of responsibility handed to us at such a young age. I remember at The Basic School we were taught that events line up, particularly in war, in such a way that a platoon commander or company commander could find himself in a situation wherein he could impact or even change world events. The decisions that young officers make a dozen times a day seem to lack complexity, but they hone the decision-making process so that when, as they say, "The balloon goes up," they can think quickly and be decisive.

The training tests patience and endurance. Bravery is not a learned skill but perverseness, self-awareness, and self-confidence to the point of cockiness, allow for bravery to grow inside of those who are placed in harm's way. Such, I believe, was the case of a young Captain charged with protecting a piece of real estate in southern Lebanon.

In the months prior to February of 1983, there had been several disagreements between the Marines positioned south of the airport, near the university, and the Israelis who held positions nearby. The Multinational Force, in country to help the Lebanese following the Israeli conflict with the PLO who had set up in Lebanon, consisted of the Marines, the British, French and Italian Army units. I recall a frustrated British officer once told me, "The only ones over here more arrogant than you Marines are the Israelis." I suggested that maybe they had a right to be since they had never really lost a war since the formation of the country. But he was right, they were arrogant to the point of being pompous and their swagger, unchecked, grew.

In mid-February, three Israeli tanks approached an area guarded by the men under Captain Charles Johnson. These tanks were seen coming from quite a distance and Captain Johnson called and signaled to them to stop while they were still 300 yards away. Still, the tanks proceeded, driving past a Lebanese checkpoint and to within a foot of Captain Johnson before stopping. He stood his ground and told the Israeli commander that the tanks could not proceed. The commander, a Lieutenant Colonel, said that he would proceed down to some nearby railroad tracks and that he wanted to see the Marine general. The two exchanged niceties for a few moments and the tank commander finally stated that he was going to proceed anyway and then mounted his tank.

Then, in a daring act of bravado, Captain Johnson drew and loaded his .45 pistol and told the Israeli that the tanks would only proceed, "OVER MY DEAD BODY!" The lead tank moved away a bit, but the others moved toward the Marine position. Johnson again drew his pistol and mounted the tank, repeating his order for them to turn around. The Israeli spoke on the radio, Johnson dismounted the tank, and the three tanks drove away.

Each party reported back to their superiors, who reported to their superiors, etc., etc. Soon the Marine spokesman told the story to the press in much the same way as I have related it. They also mentioned the previous clashes, particularly with the tank commander who had been involved in two previous altercations. Then the State Department made a statement, more conciliatory, that the US and Israelis should get together and make sure that the lines separating the two are more clearly defined.

Finally, the secretary of Defense, Caspar Weinberger, made a statement praising Johnson's actions. Johnson himself said that it wasn't really that big a deal. For their part, the Israeli embassy pointed out that the US had not participated in the drawing of the lines of demarcation, that their man was in the right and that there was really no need to draw a pistol.

Everyone was able to save face, but the press had a field day. A political cartoon in one of the major news magazines showed two frames. In the first was a picture of the Marine issue .45. It was labeled: "M1911A1 automatic pistol, .45 caliber, recoil operated, magazine fed, self-loading, hand weapon."

The second cartoon frame had exactly the same picture, except the butt of the pistol was crumpled, demonstrating how Johnson had slammed the butt of his pistol on the hood of the tank to call the Tank commander out. This cartoon was labeled: "M1911A1 automatic pistol, .45 caliber, recoil operated, magazine fed, self-loading, ANTI-TANK WEAPON." Every news agency carried the story and Johnson was an instant hero.

I even picked up an "Over My Dead Body Beirut 1983" t-shirt from one of the local street vendors. It was all we could talk about for a while, but sometimes the conversation would change from the bravado of the act to the more serious question of what might have happened if that tank commander decided to take him up on his "over my dead body" threat? What would have happened if the antagonism between two officers had escalated? Johnson was absolutely our hero, but what if they hadn't backed down? As I mentioned before, sometimes the actions of a single man can change the events of history.

PICKING UP AN ST1

As a Marine comes from his primary MOS school he has to be accepted into his new unit by his peers. Marines think of very interesting ways to initiate the new guy into the platoon by making him the butt of the joke and seeing how he takes it. As a communications platoon commander, my men understood that I was about building camaraderie and accomplishing the mission. If we were able to do that and have a little fun at the same time, all the better.

From time to time, the pressure would build within the unit. Inspections, deadlines, and late hours made for short tempers and a lack of team effort. Just before a big inspection, we were in such a state at my multichannel (MUX) platoon. We had been to the field for several weeks, returned and cleaned up our dirty gear, and were trying to make our radios work again. Lots of trips to maintenance, lots of radios down, lots of frustration and an inspection right around the corner.

The morning of the inspection, we looked pretty good, but things were tense with the CO, and we had less than two hours before inspection. We were laying out displays in perfectly symmetrical lines. We hid the broken bits and the tears in the canvas antenna bags, shined up the mirrors on the jeeps, Armor All'd all the rubber bits to make them shine. Everything was coming together.

There was, however, a general feeling of uneasiness. The Gunny turned to me and said, "Sir, these guys are wrapped too tight. We need to loosen them up before the colonel gets here or they're gonna choke."

I said, "I've got an ST1 in Lt. Estevez's office. Do you think that would work?"

"Probably would. We just got a newbie fresh from comm school. Send him."

With that, we stepped out onto our display area and I began going berserk. "Gunny, where the hell is our ST1? It's supposed to be right here! Who took the ST1?"

The Gunny started shouting at the top of his lungs, "Where's the ST1? Who's got the ST1? We got less than two hours till inspection time and we need that ST1!" Smiles shown on the faces of the more experienced members of the platoon and they began to answer up.

"Gunny, it broke about ten days ago. We took it to maintenance and they shit-canned it and ordered us a new one. It came in yesterday and should be over at supply," replied Corporal Wall. "I can run down and get it if you need me to."

"No, no, we need you here to get us ready for the CO's visit. Let's get our new guy to run down there. He's got the least experience on the gear. Everybody else turn to and let's get this done. PFC Ashton, get over here." Ashton was given directions to supply while I was calling Al Estevez to tell him to get my ST1 ready.

Ashton ran like the wind down to supply and you could see that the men were already more relaxed. The more experienced of the lot were busy working but were explaining the gag to the newer guys. Meanwhile Ashton was at supply and Estevez was having him sign an ECR card to pick up the box. He was instructed that he should hurry back, but he shouldn't jostle the box around too much as it was a pretty fragile piece of comm gear. The box and contents weighed about 23 pounds and looked very official.

We were only about two blocks away and our lookout told us that Ashton was returning up the street. We readied ourselves as he came, walking quickly and holding the box far in front of him, like he was moving nitroglycerin.

The Gunny made a big deal about how we needed this desperately and thanked Ashton for its prompt and safe delivery. I had the crowbar and began to pry open the box. Ashton stared so intently at the box; he didn't notice that all eyes were on him. The Gunny reached carefully into the box to take out the item. It looked like he was delivering a baby as he extracted it.

The ST1 was a 20-pound rock with a flat place on one side. When in the field, communicators have to sink very long grounding rods into the earth. The ST1, or more appropriately spelled "Stone," was often more effective at pounding the rods into the ground than a hammer, so in the field we used rocks more often than hammers. Ashton stood slack jawed as the men began to laugh.

"That's a beauty Gunny. Much better than the last one! The flat spot's gonna be easier to hit. Can I try it out?"

"No way, this one's not gonna have a scratch on it when the CO sees it."

Ashton took the ribbing in good stride and he was slapped on the back and welcomed properly to the platoon. The colonel came and inspected us, and I put Ashton right by the ST1. As the CO approached, I was unaware that he had been clued in by the boys in supply.

"Is that a new ST1? Looks like it's straight out of the box."

"Yes sir," I said, keeping the joke alive, "and this is PFC Ashton who was able to procure it and get it here just in time for this inspection."

"Excellent job, PFC Ashton!"

HUGE grin appeared on Ashton's face and the tension was gone from the whole platoon. The ST1 had done its job.

PMO REVENGE

I entered the officer ranks through the ten-week OCS class in the summer of 1979. I only knew the members of my own platoon, so it's easy to understand why it seemed to me that everyone came through the same portal as me. When I got to The Basic School, which formed up in October, and I began to meet the others in my class, I realized that a large number had come through the PLC program, which was basically the same as ours but took place over the course of two summers. I also learned that many of them had completed PLC the previous summer and had been away from Quantico for well over a year, some even more. We also had a group of over twenty Naval Academy Graduates, who had graduated the previous May. Since the Marine Corps is part of the Naval Service and since the Corps does not have its own Academy like the Army, Air Force and Navy do, those who attend have the option to serve in the Navy or the Marines.

The Naval Academy is difficult to get into and very difficult on attendees. It's a tough and demanding university and that's without all the harassment and BS that was piled on these guys. These guys were smart. You have to be smart to get in and to stay for the whole four years. While those of us with lesser degrees appreciated the chance to train and serve with them, they were not required to attend OCS and had missed bits of training that we had recently had. In the beginning we helped with little things and very soon we were all on the same page. Like I said, these guys were very bright. I had the pleasure of serving with many Naval Academy grads and, for the most part, they were superb.

Every now and then, the system lets loose a cull, one that thinks perhaps he is better than those around him and that those whose rank is below his are there to serve him, not the country, not the Corps, but him. He is a true ring knocker, pompous, arrogant, and self-interested. I'm sure that there are similar men who come from many different institutions of higher learning, but when you run into one from the Academy, he stands out and you wish someone had stopped him back in Annapolis. Such is the case of a young Second Lieutenant I met at Camp Lejeune in 1980.

It had been one of those days and I don't recall if the CO had asked me to come by or if I just stopped off at the battalion office to self-report whatever it was that happened, so that he didn't hear about it second-hand. I was big on self-reporting, and as I was driving home that afternoon, I noticed the CO's car was still there, along with the sergeant major and the S1. There were just three cars in a row and close to fifteen empty spaces. After all, it was almost 1700 and just about everyone had gone home for the day.

I pulled into an empty space and stepped into the building to see if I could have a word with the colonel. He was in a good mood and invited me to sit, and we quickly finished whatever I came in for and slid into how much better my Georgia Bulldogs were than his Texas Longhorns.

Our conversation (lucky for him) was cut short by loud screaming coming from down the passageway: "Does anyone here own a blue 1979 Monte Carlo, License Number *******?" I heard it, but it didn't sink in.

Without even a five second delay for an answer, it came again: "Does anyone here own a Blue 1979 Monte Carlo, License Number *******?"

The Colonel laughed and, realizing the voice was calling me, I jumped from my comfortable chair and stuck my head out the office door. He was coming up the hall. It was the little lieutenant. He was about 5 foot 7 and wore a Naval Academy ring which he constantly touched, as though someone was going to sneak up and steal it. Some might say he exhibited signs of a Napoleonic Complex, but I don't believe in such things.

Before I could answer, he bellowed again, "Does anyone here own a Blue 1979 Monte Carlo, License Number *******?"

The S1 had already left, leaving the CO, the sergeant major and me, and now him, in the building. EVERYONE knew the CO's and the sergeant major's cars. By use of deductive reasoning, he might have walked through the building looking for anyone who was not the CO or the sergeant major and he would have found his man. But our boy thought screaming up and down the passageway was a more efficient way, so I raised my hand as he approached and answered, "That's me. That's my car. Is there a problem?"

"Oh, it's you." The you as it dripped from his mouth was the most condescending word I had ever heard. It said: you are so far beneath me I cannot believe you are not bowing down before me.

I was in the hatch to the CO's office and from where he stood, he could see the colonel laughing behind me.

"You're in my parking space, but don't worry about it."

"Sorry man, I thought everyone had gone home already. I can move it if you like."

He looked straight through me, a smile of contempt on his face, and said, "No, you're fine."

I sat back down and explained to the boss how Georgia was going to ride Hershel Walker all the way to the Championship. I got up to leave in a few minutes and walked outside to my car. What I saw was truly laughable. The young lieutenant had parked his car six inches behind my rear bumper, blocking me in. There were lots of empty spaces, some even closer to the front door, but he wanted to make a point. I looked back toward the building and saw the lights in his office were out. His intention was clearly to trap me until he returned.

The sidewalks in front of the building were extra wide so you could march a platoon of Marines without putting anyone in the grass. I got in my car, bumped it up onto the curb, then turned, drove down the sidewalk and eased it back to the street at the end of the block.

I drove down the hill, went into my office and called the Provost Marshall's office. I reported a vehicle parked in the middle of the street down in the French Creek area. I waited, and in about ten minutes a tow truck arrived, hooked up his car and drove away. I later heard that he had gone to the chow hall and stayed away from the building for over half an hour, so that I would have to wait for him to return. He had to bum a ride down to the impound lot and pay a fine to retrieve his vehicle.

POLICING THE BEQ

One Monday morning I had Command Duty and when I was coming to work, I decided to swing by the Bachelor Enlisted Quarters (BEQ) to do my round of inspections. When I got there, I discovered that there were beer cans all over the place. The trash can was overflowing with beer cans and the ground was littered with them. Knowing that the base commander lived on base and regularly walked around this area, I decided to pick up as many of the beer cans as I could get into my helmet bag, zipped the bag closed and then I proceed on into the Squadron to catch up with the Sergeant Major to let him know that a Police Call was needed to complete the clean-up of the barracks.

As things turned out, the day was busy from the moment I arrived at work. I dropped my helmet bag in the corner of the Ops office and rushed out for a FOD walk and then back for a Squadron meeting in the Ready Room. After the meeting I was tasked with going over to the Group to get some maps for the Squadron and then returned to get swamped by the day's administrative duties.

Sometime later I suddenly checked my watch and realized that it was time to brief for the flight. We met in the Ops Office, got our flight mission, and ran down to check the aircraft logbook and grab our flight gear and head out to the aircraft. I grabbed my helmet bag and headed out to the aircraft – not thinking at that moment about the bag's contents.

I was flying with a colorful Captain and senior pilot whose call sign was Tongo. Tongo and I had flown together several times since I joined the squadron and here we were, once again on a troop lift mission to the Kahuku Mountain Training Area on the north shore of Oahu. As we got ready to start up the CH-46E, I bent over to open my helmet bag. At that moment I remembered I hadn't emptied the beer cans as I had been unable to catch up with the Sergeant Major. Whoops! Discretely I tipped my helmet in the bag hoping that the cans would quietly fall to the bottom of the bag and remain there. I made my motions slowly so as to keep the cans from making a racquet and giving away my secret. I don't know if Tongo saw or heard the cans then, he never said, but I was acutely aware that I had a little issue.

As we were a flight of two CH-46E aircraft and on a schedule that required us to keep our departure time, I let the sleeping beer cans lie. I partially zipped up my helmet bag once I had my helmet out of the bag and in my lap. Zipping the bag up one handed was not easy, and I was only able to partially close the bag. We started the aircraft, did a radio check with our wingman and taxied for takeoff at the 101 pad and off we went over Kaneohe Bay, over the Hammerhead Shark waters and past Chinaman's Hat and on to the Kahuku Training area.

The mission went well, and we picked up a final group of marines at the last LZ and started flying back to Kaneohe. On the way back, unnoticed by me, my helmet bag had started to unzip a bit and open to display its contents. I noticed Tongo looking down in the direction of my helmet bag. Then he looked at me and said those fateful words "What's that in your helmet bag?" I went on to explain the situation at the BEQ. After a moment or two he looked back at me with a little twinkle in his eye. I'd seen that look before with Tongo and it meant that he had just gleaned another non-conformist, slightly off base (perhaps full cowboy off the ranch) crazy idea.

Tongo began to rock the aircraft back and forth. The aircraft movements were not so much aggressive as let's say "free form". But we were all definitely rocking and the aircrew took notice as did the passengers. I was wondering what he was up to. I know the folks in the back were wondering what was going on. Then Tongo reaches over to my helmet bag and grabs an empty beer can. He crushes it in his hand and throws it down the cabin aisle where it would obviously be seen by everyone. He then gives me this good old boy look and a nudge on my shoulder saying, "That will make their day!". Then he repeats the action with a second empty beer can.

I was aghast. Really? WTF etc. The he reached across the cockpit passage, grabbed another beer and now with the empty beer can in hand gives me another shoulder nudge. I knew the beer cans were empty, but I doubt anyone else on the aircraft even considered that for a moment. With the rocking aircraft, the empty cans being thrown down the aisle and beer cans being waved across the cockpit, the picture from the rear must have been terrifying!

Just as Tongo had crushed the third beer can and was about to throw it down the aisle as well, we got a quick intercom warning from our crew chief that simply said, "UH OH!"). The next second we were greeted by one irate, red-faced, and totally livid major who poked his head into the cockpit and start screaming at us. I'm not sure I understood one word of what he said, but we got the picture – he couldn't take a joke! I pondered the idea of trying to explain the situation, but I decided that this was probably not the best time to explain the humorous details of the situation. That explanation would be reserved for the two of us standing locked up on the CO's red carpet.

Fortunately, once the details came out and everyone understood that safety had never been compromised and that our (Tongo's) attempt at levity was intended only to get a laugh or chuckle, we managed to get off with buying the grunts who were aboard pizza and beer and then later a round of beer at the Officers Club on Friday night.

That was one of the three most infamous pranks that I witnessed Tongo pulling in Hawaii in the early 1980's.

POWER OF ATTORNEY

Young Marines fall in love easily and were often married to their high school sweetheart who they brought with them to live in base housing at Camp Lejeune. Just as often, they would simply fall in love and move in with some sweet young girl in town, contributing more than his fair share to the household expenses. Either way, when a deployment was coming up, a young man's fancy turned to thoughts of; What if I don't come back alive? It was during these times they would visit me in the legal office and ask about a will and a power of attorney for the most wonderful woman on planet Earth.

It was our own fault. We gave classes on acting responsibly just before deployments. I told them they should take care of their loved ones; make sure they had a will, make sure the beneficiary(ies) for their government SGLI life insurance was correct. In general, I taught them that their affairs should be in order, because we have a dangerous profession, and you just never know. It wasn't exactly surprising then that some of them showed up to do just that.

I also knew, however, that once the boat pulled out, the young ladies left behind could not all be trusted to do the right thing. That's why I always told them that I would need a few minutes to pull all the papers together for signature and that in the meantime I would like them to step next door to the office of our career planner, Top Baker, and tell him what they just asked me to do.

"But sir, what's Top Baker got to do with it?" they would ask. "He doesn't do a will or power of attorney."

"Just humor me," I'd say. "Step in and tell the top you're waiting for your power of attorney. He'll be happy to chat with you."

What our young Marines didn't know was that Top Baker had left our battalion just three years before, with nineteen years in the Corps. He was to serve what was supposed to be his final year in Okinawa.

A wizened old veteran like Top really knew how to work the system. He had a house, a boat, and two cars, and he set up allotment checks in such a way that upon his departure from Okinawa a year later, all of these would be totally paid off, so he would come back to Jacksonville without any major bills. He also set up an allotment for his wife to have money for household expenses, which left him with almost nothing coming to himself.

He had been married to the same lady for most of his twenty years in the Corps, so she had experienced long separations before and knew how to handle the day to day running of the household without him. He left her an unlimited power of attorney and a copy of his will, leaving his life insurance to her as his only beneficiary.

He got to Okinawa and wrote her a letter. He got one in return. For the entire year, he wrote and received letters a couple times a week. She wrote about the backed-up garbage disposal, the leaky toilet, and the power outage during the big storm. She wrote about the hurricane that was coming and how she was going to Ohio to stay with her mom until it passed. He wrote about the heat and the long days at work.

Finally, he wrote that he was coming home. He told her the date and the flight number and to meet him at the Jacksonville airport. He arrived at the airport at the designated time and date, but she was not there. He laughed because he thought that the International Date Line had messed her up and that she was coming on the wrong day.

He decided to take a cab home and surprise her. He got to the house at about 9:00 p.m. and thought he would unlock the door and slip in and surprise her. He unlocked the door and stepped into his living room, only to find a family of four eating popcorn and watching a movie. The dad jumped up and started toward him. That's when he found out that his wife had sold the house to these folks almost a year ago (about two weeks after he left for Okinawa).

He also found out that she had sold both cars and the boat at about the same time. Then he found out she had cashed in his life insurance policy for its cash value and that she had been living with several lance corporals and not paying any rent for most of the year. She had, just a couple of days before, filed for divorce, which would entitle her to fifty percent of his retirement check for the rest of his life.

Understand, Top had planned on having a house, a boat, a car, etc. all paid for. His retirement check would be fifty percent of his Marine Corps pay. He had calculated that with a part-time job, he and his wife could live comfortably. He now had no place to live, no car to drive, and was about to receive twenty-five percent of his previous pay. The next day he went to his old commanding officer and told him of his plight. They were able to withdraw his retirement papers and under a hardship program, return him to the Marine Corps at full pay.

Top Baker would tell this tale of woe to the young Marines I sent in for a chat. The kid would come back to me, typically white as a sheet, and withdraw his request for power of attorney. At most he might check his beneficiary to make sure she got the $10,000 if he died. Other than that, they seldom needed any further legal counseling. It was great having him next door.

PROPELLER HEAD

Having graduated from OCS in the summer of 1979 I entered The Basic School quite full of myself. I had the world by the tail and was certainly destined for great things. I had a contract with the US Government which said that as soon as I completed the rigorous curriculum at TBS, I would be going to Pensacola, Florida to learn to fly airplanes for the Marine Corps. I was hitting on all eight cylinders and nothing could stop me. I was in step, standing tall and looking good.

I had never before felt so good about myself and what I was doing with my life. I had never before felt so proud of my accomplishments. I had not heard the word "No" in so long I had practically forgotten it was there. Everyone was telling me yes. Opportunity was everywhere and life was exceptionally good. I am so glad that I had this time, and I am so grateful to have had a period where I was so blissfully unaware of life's true nature, that life will reach up when you least expect it and knock you senseless. Then before you can gain your composure and rise again, knock you down repeatedly; that "No" will one day come more frequently than "Yes" and that the real challenges of life lay ahead of me.

I look back at this time with nostalgia; there were none that I was beholden to, none that counted on me for sustenance, few bills, few consequences for my actions; it was like the world sort of expected me to be stupid and forgave me in advance for not knowing much. It wasn't going to get any easier than this.

I remember that, like college, many of the classes at TBS were not very useful. As a future aviator, I was learning the basics of artillery, supply, mapping, history, and engineering. While it was fun to blow stuff up with C4, to throw hand grenades and to watch a Bouncing Betty go BOOM, I didn't see how this was going to be of value to me as I terrorized the skies.

I did understand that aviation only existed to support the troops on the ground, so I really needed to understand fire team, squad and platoon tactics. I would be their support so I would need to recognize what my teammates on the ground were doing. I admit I loved going to the field and rolling around in the dirt, seeing how many expletives I could string together in a single sentence and smoking cigars larger than my penis. As the months drug slowly on, the classes became less interesting, and I began to get antsy to get on with the flying part of my training. My mind wandered from whatever we were studying to aviation as the days passed. I had a "Waiting to Go to Pensacola" sign posted on my door with a cartoon of a WWI-type aviator bedecked with a leather helmet, large goggles and flowing white scarf. I had a mobile hanging in my room with a dozen or so biplanes hanging from my ceiling. There was a biplane statue on my bookcase, and aviation magazines and books piled on my coffee table. The Marines had my body in Quantico, but my mind was already in Pensacola.

I bought a little balsa plane, the kind with the rubber band attached to the propeller so it could be wound up and thrown with the prop spinning for a few seconds to achieve flight. I tried it out once. It crashed and broke into pieces, but I saved the propeller and rubber band and mounted it on my helmet as a joke of sorts; that I was an air guy in a ground school – my touch of individuality.

A few days later, we were going to the field for some tactics practice when Captain Mularkey, the platoon commander for second platoon, saw it. He lit up and RAN to me, pulled me out of formation, took me aside, placed me at the position of attention and chewed me out for the next five minutes. Was this supposed to be funny? Was I some sort of comedian? Didn't I know that enemy soldiers could see my red propeller from a mile away, positioned directly between my eyes? Didn't I know the Marine Corps was trying to protect my life by camouflaging me? What did I mean by ruining the wonderful job they had done by putting a RED PROPELLER right in the middle of my forehead? Did I have some sort of death wish?

Humbled before my peers, I removed the adornment and went on with my training. My comrades in arms were kind enough to only mention the incident about every fifteen minutes over the next few weeks. I was in a Jiffy Store in March of 1980, with only a few weeks left in TBS when a toy plane caught my eye. I bought it and kept it hidden until the final time that we went to the field. We only had a short time left before graduation and my wounds had almost healed from the propeller incident, so I was yet again emboldened.

As we fell out for formation there was much laughing in the ranks at my newest creation. The staff was milling about as we formed up, and I saw Captain Mularkey as he tried to figure out what was so funny. He made eye contact with me and that's when he saw it. I had replaced the red propeller that he had so despised with a GREEN, tactical one, one that would never be detected by enemy combatants wishing to see me dead. I was safely wrapped in green and would be invisible on the battlefield.

He walked toward me and lifted his arms outward and to the side, palms to the sky, in submission. "I give up. You're a lost cause. I appreciate you getting into compliance," he barked.

As he turned away, I said, "I have a brown one for the desert and a white one in case it snows!"

"I'm sure you do, lieutenant. I'm sure you do."

Like I said, it was great to be in a world where they sort of expected me to be stupid and forgave me in advance.

PURRSONAL FRIENDS OF MINE

When I was on deployment with HMM-261 on the USS Guam from October 1983 to May 1984, we spent most of the time off the coast of Beirut, Lebanon, with a nine-day jaunt to Grenada on the way to the eastern Mediterranean. During those seven months, I had brushes with famous people from time to time. Entertainers, high ranking bureaucrats, politicians, and news TV personnel came and went.

My first brush with fame was not from Wayne Newton, who was the first entertainer to come to the Guam and the other ships in the MARG. I didn't want to see his concert on the hangar bay, but I went anyway because, well, it beat that night's wardroom movie, Psychotronic Man; a movie so bad, MST3K refused to mock it during their heyday. As it turns out, it was one of the best concerts I've ever attended. The man is incredibly talented. Glad I went. One of the very decent things Wayne did was gather as many Marines' phone numbers as he could and then he called their wives and girlfriends to personally thank them for what they were going through and also to give them the personal messages written by each husband.

The next big name to come to the Guam was Loretta Lynn, whom I did get a semi-brush with. When her band arrived, her guitar player, Dave Thornhill (he was the guy on stage who helped Sissy Spacek, playing Loretta, remember the lyrics in the movie, Coal Miners Daughter) had the misfortune of getting his guitars lost in transit. No guitar player, no concerts.

I was out flying when Loretta's entourage flew in from Larnaca, Cyprus via one of our CH-53's, so I missed their arrival. However, when I got back that day from flying, one of the other squadron pilots was waiting for me in my room. He said that Loretta's guitar player needed to borrow my Martin D-35 to perform the concerts on all the ships in the MARG since his guitar was lost in transit. I was very tentative about it. It was my first Martin and I'd saved up money for a long time to purchase it. It meant a whole lot to me, and I didn't want it to be left on the USS Manitowoc or some other ship after her concerts, so that some jackass sailor could keep it forever (if you're an acoustic player, I know you feel me). The squadron ops officer and the ship's XO came by and promised I'd get it back immediately after her shows were finished. I relented due to the "Don't be an asshole" pressure.

Lorett-ee played her concerts and I even got to talk to Dave Thornhill and some of the other band members while they were on the Guam; really good guys and bursting with more talent in their clipped fingernails than I would ever have if I lived to be a thousand. The day before Loretta went back to the US, she signed autographs for a few hours. She gave me one of her memorabilia t-shirts and signed it, Thanks for letting me use your guitar, I love you, Loretta. All the other band members signed it as well. Very cool. You're welcome, Mrs. Lynn.

The Bob Hope show came out to entertain us and they even filmed a show, with camera crews and the whole Hollywood production deal, one night on the Guam. It played on national television as well. They were there for about a week during Christmas 1983 and basically base camped on the Guam during their stay. We flew the stars and production crew to all the ships in the MARG. They performed a show on each ship large enough to host them, then we'd pick them up and fly them back to the Guam. Some of the stars included Vic Damone, George Kirby, Ann Gillian, Kathy Lee Crosby, Miss USA 1983 Julie Hayek, and Brooke Shields.

Being a new aircraft commander, I flew every day, several hours a day, during December and really wanted to get Christmas Day off. On Christmas Eve Day, I was scheduled to be the CO's copilot to fly the Bob Hope stars to the USS New Jersey and back so they could perform their show on the battleship. In fact, it was the only time I ever flew with the Commanding Officer. This would be my first big Hollywood break and first brush with the whole Bob Hope fame bubble.

After the flight brief (when you're a young pilot and fly as then LtCol Granville "Granny" R. Amos' copilot, there really isn't a need for a brief), I knew exactly what to do. I got in first and started the aircraft while Granny strapped in and took the controls. He did all the flying and all the talking on the radios while I sat on my hands, did the check list stuff, and switched radio frequencies when necessary. Pretty simple. He definitely earned that right, and I was glad to oblige. Besides, all the Bob Hope stars were onboard.

One of the stars with whom Granny was underwhelmed was Brooke Shields. He had to eat in the captain's mess every night with the stars and got stuck having to sit next to self-absorbed Brooke for each meal. He brought back a few stories of Brooke's idiocy from the captain's mess to the squadron ready room during the Bob Hope deal. She was a spoiled ditz at that time. Maybe she got smarter later on in life, but in 1983, she was a taco short of a combo platter and sadly, Granny had to put up with her "Brooke-ness" three times a day.

As I was going through the checklist, getting the helo started, rotors turning, preflight checklist done, Brooke stepped into the tiny cockpit access tunnel to inflict herself onto her favorite Marine, Granny Amos. The cockpit noise is incredibly loud in a CH-46E when the auxiliary power unit is on and then gets louder from there when the engines start, the transmissions whine and the rotors turn. It's LOUD. As I started the number one engine, I heard this weird, muffled voice sound. I was busy, didn't turn to look, and didn't know it was Brooke.

Granny came up on the intercom and said, "Get her out of the cockpit." Utterly clueless as to what the CO was referring, I kept on with the checklist. Once again the muffled voice that sounded like, "Hi-i-i-i!" broke through the helo noise. I turned to look, and it was Brooke, sporting white hearing protection, looking at Granny and anxiously waiting for his excited response. I said, "Skipper, I think your main squeeze is trying to talk to you." Failing to see the humor, Granny reiterated, "Logger, get her the f*ck out of my cockpit!" I obliged, tapped Ms. Shields on the shoulder, pulled back the left sound protection ear cup and said, "Granny says hi and wants you to go take your seat. He can't wait to talk to you at dinner." Fortunately, Granny couldn't hear what I said but he was glad that Brooke went to sit down. Hopefully Granny won't read this account before the HMM-261 40th reunion because he's not too old to kick my ass.

On Christmas Day, I did get the day off as did most of the pilots and aircrew, since only one or two flights were flown that day. In the morning, Ann Gillian knocked on my room door to wish my roommate, Terry Schmidt, and I a Merry Christmas. She was one of the stars who made it a point to walk around the ship that day and say hello, wish us a Merry Christmas, and ask how we were all doing. It was a real surprise. She and her husband were very gracious and kind people.

The night before the Bob Hope Show left us to return to the States, I was walking through the Guam's passageway enroute to the wardroom. The passageways were always dark and dimly lit after sunset. Out of the darkness came a very lost Bob Hope. I assumed he was looking for the captain's mess. He froze and stared at me with the most terrified look on a face I had ever seen. I thanked him for bringing his show to us Marines and sailors and asked him if he needed directions to the captain's mess. He never spoke a word and continued to stare at me like I was about to brutally murder him. I gave him directions while he maintained a terrified look, slowly backed away from me like he was backing away from certain death, and I went on to the wardroom. Very bizarre.

My last brush with the Bob Hope Show was the day Tony Morales and I got to fly as Granny's wingmen to Larnaca, Cyprus to take the Bob Hope entourage to the waiting, VIP'd C-141. Granny flew all the stars, and I flew the production crew. It was always a treat to go to Larnaca, plus Tony and I had several hundred dollars in booze orders we had to get at the airport's duty-free shop for some of the guys back on the ship.

We landed in Cyprus and there was a delay with the C-141 so several of the stars walked around the tarmac while they waited. Ann Gillian, Kathy Lee Crosby, and Julie Hayek walked over to my aircraft and wanted pictures with the likes of a rag tag CH-46 flight crew. Julie Hayek grabbed Tony's cameras and snapped pictures of us, the stars standing next to the aircrew, and a picture of me standing in front of the 46. It was back when I still had hair. It's hanging in the "I-Love-Me" half bath, the sacred location and only place in the house where my wife Vicky lets me hang all my military memorabilia. (Of course, I'm the king of the castle. Why do you ask?)

Another brush with stardom struck the day I flew as wingman behind one of our Huey's, carrying Charlton Heston as a passenger from the Guam to Larnaca. After we landed, Charlton got out of the Huey and instead of going straight to the Air Force C-9, he walked over to my aircraft. While we were still turning, he shook the crew chief's hand, the left door gunner's hand, walked to the pilot's side and then copilot's side of the aircraft, reached up and shook our hands. He waved at us, gave us a salute, and walked onto the C-9.

A not so memorable brush with fame was when I flew an extremely rude, arrogant, and very stupid reporter for the then three-year-old news broadcast, CNN, from BIA to the USS Snelling. His arrogant and extremely dangerous antics, along with his camera and sound crew, really torqued off my crew chief as well as the entire flight crew. On the way to the Snelling, after launching from the airport and within two miles of the coast, we were required to fly at 50 feet to avoid radar and infra-red guided missiles. At two miles we were then required to climb to 200 feet the rest of the way to the ships. Right after I did a quick climb from 50 feet to 200 feet and leveled off, the crew chief who had been putting up with the CNN jerk, calmly said, "Sir, the CNN guy just puked into his briefcase." I don't believe in Karma but if I did…

My last big brush with fame was with General Al Gray. Before joining HMM-261 and while I was a copilot in HMM-365, I flew General Gray several times from the 2nd MARDIV HQ building to wherever he wanted to go. He wanted the aircraft shut down before he arrived and of course we always did that. The first time I flew the general, he asked me who I was. I found out that he did that with every Marine he'd ever encountered. What I didn't know at the time was that he remembered every Marine's name he'd ever met. Every time I flew him, he always greeted me with his famous slug in the chest and, "Semper Fi, Lieutenant Russell!" He did the same thing with all the crew members. I always responded with, "Semper Fi, sir!"

A few years later at the New River Marine Corps Ball, General Gray was the guest speaker. After his speech and the cake ceremony, he made the rounds, greeting Marines. He caught my eye and walked straight over to me, slugged me in the chest and said, "Semper Fi, Captain Russell!" I was surprised that he still remembered.

Fast forward five years later: I was in Twentynine Palms doing my reserve two weeks of fun at Camp Wilson. On our last day, we went to the hangar at the expeditionary airfield to brief for the flight back to El Toro. Just after the brief and before the preflight, the Commandant of the Marine Corp's G-4 jet landed and taxied over to the hangar. The Commandant, General Al Gray, seeing us all grouped in the hangar, walked over, and gave us a pep talk. When he finished, he made eye contact with me and walked over, gave me the chest slug, and said, "Semper Fi, Captain Russell!" He shook hands with a few more squadron mates and went on to the waiting staff car. My squadron-mates nearly crapped their pants, asking me, "How the hell does the Commandant know you?"

RIB BUSTER, CAREER IN THE CRAPPER

All my life I had wanted to be a Marine Corps officer. It was my dream. The Marines are the best, the toughest, America's finest. Being part of such an honored and revered organization would factor hugely into the sculpting my life's plan.

High school had trundled along. Not exactly a remarkable experience, but when finally, over, I was off to college. Next step, to join the PLC, the Platoon Leaders Class, the Marine Corps' version of college ROTC. In four years, no doubt, I would graduate from college and become a Marine Corps officer.

Not so fast! College! Freedom! Trouble!

Having been raised in an isolated and protected military household, I wasn't ready for the flood gates of freedom to burst open. Disaster awaited. All those parties! Beer! No supervision. I thought I was in heaven but was, in truth, on my way to 'hell.'

Fast forward three years. I found myself with almost two years of class credits, and worse, disillusioned. I had hit rock bottom. Yes, I had received quite an education. But not in the classroom. My command of the obvious shouted it was time to change my major from party to something with a more promising future.

Like so many young men, looking for an anchor in their lives, I looked to the military as a way out of the mess I had found myself in. A mess of my own making.

I informed my family I was going to drop out of college and enlist in the Marine Corps. The announcement was met with incredulity. Hmm. At least I would be out of their way and maybe, If I did make it through Parris Island boot camp, I would be shipped off far, far away. For altogether different reasons, we all desired that happy ending!

Boot camp came and went. Fascinating stories abound. Like the one where the drill sergeant deliberately shot and wounded one of the recruits while the recruit was running sprints between the 100- and 200-yard markers at the firing range. The recruit was slightly injured. Six months after graduating from boot camp I saw the staff sergeant working on the back end of a trash truck at Camp Lejeune.

Then there is the time when several of us NCOs in the presidential helicopter squadron, HMX-1, brought our girlfriends aboard one of the helicopters used to fly the president around. It was New Year's Eve, inside the Quantico hangar. We brought in the new year with a bang!

Five years into my enlisted service, I was now a sergeant. My sights were set on making the jump to Officer of Marines. The ultimate career, in my humble, but accurate opinion.

My time as an enlisted Marine taught me a lot and I felt prepared me for bigger things.

Officers Candidate School (OCS) had a reputation for being one of the toughest programs in all the military services. The attrition rate, the number of candidates that do not make it through the training was at that time about 35 - 40%. That meant one in three to four of us would not make it to graduation. Translating into possibly not getting the gold bars I so coveted.

But I believed in myself. I could do this.

The stakes were high. If I didn't make the grade, I would be sent back to the enlisted ranks. Since joining the Corps, five years earlier, I was getting used to winning. But the mere thought of being sent back resurrected emotions associated with my failed college experience. The thought of failing OCS nauseated me.

I went for it!

Nine weeks into to training, the unimaginable happened. I do not remember exactly how it happened, but something went wrong.

With one week to go, the Confidence Course, a physically challenging obstacle course, then a couple of days later the killer hike in all our gear. Then it would be over. I would definitely graduate. Get over that damn Confidence Course and take plenty of water for the hike. I am a big sweater and never have enough water. I got this!

Okay, I admit climbing is not my thing. The wall of logs that are placed incrementally higher, one after the other was intimidating. But what the hell, it's called the Confidence Course. I have confidence! I Got This!

Off I went. I swung myself onto the first log, about four feet of the ground. Then jumped up to the second higher log, feeling good. One last jump up to the log sitting at least fifteen feet in the air and the hardest part was over!

I leapt up and hit the log sideways with the right side of me chest, my right arm draped over the log. Ah shit, that hurt, my rib cage felt like it had been pummeled by a sledgehammer. I reached up and over and grabbed the log with my left hand and dragged my body over the top. My head felt light, like I was going to pass out. I was in shock. I'd gone blank and was in survival mode. How I finished the course, I do not know.

Back in the barracks I stayed behind in the showers, skipping chow, letting the hot water course across my chest. Eight ibuprofen later, I was able to rejoin the class for afternoon training. But the pain was so severe I could barely concentrate on the classroom training. It didn't really matter; the academics weren't much of a challenge. Would the physical training be my undoing?

I knew I had to survive the next four or five days.

What to do?

That night I snuck into the infirmary not turning on any lights. Fortunately, there was enough ambient light to see my way around. I filled up the huge metal therapy tub with warm water and turned on the jets. After soaking at least thirty minutes, I scrounged around for tape. I'd seen in the movies where people with broken ribs were always taped up. I could do that.

Oh, one problem. When that tape comes off, it would really hurt. Chest hair. Where are the razors? I found them and quickly manscaped. Hm, that looks good. Jeez, I do have abs.

The taping went quickly, but kinda crooked. I have never been able to get the sound out of my head, that of the tape scratching off the roll as I wrapped and wrapped. It's like that scraping sound of 'It's a Small, Small World' at Disney.

It's true, ignorance is bliss. For I didn't know I was probably doing the worst thing that one can do under the circumstances. The possibility of a puncturing a lung with one of my broken ribs never crossed my mind.

And yes, I pilfered a lot of ibuprofen, ingesting 1600mg every three hours for five days. I have asked my liver for forgiveness many times.

The next four night, the same thing. Sneak into the infirmary, unwrap the tape, trying not to cry like a baby, soak, and re-wrap. Sleep deprivation crept it slowly.

The next days were extremely uncomfortable. I moved as carefully and as slowly as possible. All the while hoping I would not be discovered. I do recall being asked if I was okay a couple of times. I shrugged it off and said it was a sinus headache. The tape and accompanying pain restricted movement. My posture was ridiculously prefect! It was impossible not to stand or sit up straight. I think the 'guy' taping me up over did it.

The biggest hurdle loomed large. What was sure to me to be the longest hike in the world in full military gear! It was dreadful. Again, I don't know how I survived it. I sweated like a pig and was internally moaning like a baby. I focused on the guy hiking in front of me and pretty much spent all my energy denying the excruciating pain brought on by endless miles carrying a rifle and a 60 lb. pack strapped on my back, pulling on by ribs.

I kept repeating, "I will get those gold bars!"

I'll will never forget arriving back at the barracks. The platoon was dismissed. I was covered, soaked head to foot in sweat. I looked around, marveling that the hike was over. Too exhausted for euphoria, I just stood there watching my fellow Marines disappear into the barracks. I was alone savoring my victory. I had won.

Days later my dream came true, gold bars were pinned on my shoulders.

SEA BAT

Marines and Sailors are known to have a bit of a rivalry and to take jabs, verbal and physical, at each other whenever in close proximity to one another. Sailing across the Atlantic aboard the USS Pensacola in 1982 was a great experience. I had never felt so welcome aboard a ship, and my men felt the same.

Commander Palen was particularly welcoming, keeping the Marines informed of whatever there was to do aboard his ship. He would hop on the 1MC (ship's intercom) on the bridge and announce, "There's a very large Great White about 15 yards off the port bow! If you have a chance, you might want to come up and have a look at him!" The entire ship would rumble with everyone rushing to get cameras and to see the shark.

As we passed through the Sargasso Sea, he read to us on the 1MC from Columbus's ship's log about his voyage through the exact point where we were. They were in the doldrums with no wind and nearly no movement, with supplies running low, and the captain's reading was inspiring to our entire crew.

It was a little surprising then, when he announced one day that a sea bat had been captured in a net as it flew by the ship and that if anyone wanted to see it, they could view it in a box down in the well of the ship. My cabin mate and I thought a sea bat was a fish and wondered what all this was about. We thought we should check it out.

We went to the rail overlooking the well deck and saw a boatswain's mate standing beside a wooden box. There was a tiny peephole just below waist high, requiring the viewer to bend over to look in the box. A bunch of sailors stood a small distance away and a handful of recon Marines walked up and asked where they could see the sea bat. A couple of sailors had set the gag up well by arriving just before the Marines, peeping, one at a time, in the tiny hole in the box and declaring the bat to be the strangest creature they ever saw; and another commented that he'd seen them before, but this one was much bigger.

Of course, this enticed the Marines. When the first one bent way down to look into the box, out stepped a sturdy young sailor with a cricket bat and put a full swing right across the butt of the unsuspecting bat seeker. It looked like it hurt like hell, but the kid recovered quickly and when he turned around, the sailor held up the weapon and said, "SEE? BAT!"

This was absolutely hilarious to all the sailors in the area. If they had done this to a supply type or maybe a communicator that might have been the end of it, but this boy was recon and those guys stick together. If you hit my brother on the butt with a stick, you hit me. We knew this wasn't finished and it didn't take long for the counterattack.

The Marines, having little to occupy their time on the ride over, were always training. There were small group training classes being taught all over the ship. We would announce each evening at the captain's staff meeting what classes were being taught the next day and if anyone thought the class might be of interest to others, they'd invite them to attend. Permission was always granted.

A couple of nights later the recon commander announced that his staff sergeant would be teaching his men to climb a rope using a Prusik knot. This had recently been seen in the James Bond movie, *For Your Eyes Only*, in which Roger Moore uses his shoelaces attached to a rope to ascend a mountain. This sounded very interesting, and the captain and XO made a note of it.

At the appointed time the next day, the captain made an announcement and twenty or so sailors showed up down in the well deck for the demonstration. The muscle laden staff sergeant showed them how to use boot laces to make a rope climb much easier by allowing yourself to "rest" mid climb. He said it was developed fifty years before by an Austrian mountain climber, but that James Bond had made it famous. It was well received and when he was done, he asked everyone to stick around for a waterproofing class. He lost much of his audience, but a few, mostly campers, stuck around and, of course, so did the recon detachment.

The instructor started out explaining how to keep yourself and your clothes dry while in the field. He showed lots of ideas for small items that could be put into plastic bags and how a garbage bag would fit over the pack. He talked of Scotch Guarding shelter halves and other useful hacks.

By now all but one of the sailors had wandered off, waterproofing not being as sexy as rope climbing. The instructor then said there was a new item about to come into the supply system that would keep your sleeping bag dry. He laid out a sleeping bag on the deck and invited one of the sailors to get into the bag. The unsuspecting innocent climbed into the bag and the instructor zipped it up to his knees. The instructor then showed a large black plastic bag and with help from a couple of assistants, put the sleeping bag into the plastic bag. "This will keep your bag dry in the wettest conditions," he continued.

You need to remember, when putting it into the covering, you always keep both zippers aligned so that you can zip them up from inside. He then asked the sailor in the bag to lay back and zip up his sleeping bag and the plastic cover until both were at the top. The young man did so, leaving about a foot unzipped in both bags. Without another word the staff sergeant zipped the plastic bag all the way to the top, completely sealing the bag. Then silence.

In a few seconds the kid inside said, "Hey there's no air hole!" and started trying to get out. The instructor replied, "After many years of research, the Marine Corps determined that there is no need for an air hole in a BODY BAG!"

With that, all the Marines quickly departed the area leaving the young sailor violently squirming to no avail. The plastic on a body bag is thick and the zipper only works from the outside. The recon commander had positioned himself on the rail above and ran quickly to the bridge, explained the situation to the captain and asked permission to speak on the 1MC. Being an equal opportunity joker, the captain allowed it.

The recon commander spoke slowly, "A couple of days ago, a sea bat was trapped on this vessel. If you were part of that scheme, you may want to go down to the well deck, as we have caught a sailor in a body bag. SEE? Body Bag!"

The rest of the trip was friendly. The crew was yet again, hospitable.

SKIING THE ATLANTIC

While in Beirut in 1982, I had the opportunity to pull liberty in Antalya, Turkey. Antalya was hardly the place for sailors and Marines who had not seen a liberty port in better than six months. It had gorgeous harbor views, full of yachts and mountains in the distance, ancient cobblestone streets, and Hadrian's Gate, built for the Roman emperor in the first century, none of which interested the sailors and Marines in the least.

As I mentioned in a previous story, some ensigns from the Pensacola and I wound up at the women's prison because we had asked to be taken to where the women were. We left considerably disappointed and came back to Antalya to a bar in the center of town. It was a single room about 30 feet by 30 feet with a small bar in one corner and ten or twelve little cafe tables. We sat down and ordered a round of Raki.

Just about every country around the Mediterranean has its own anise flavored drink; ouzo in Greece, sambuca in Italy, but the favorite of Turkey is Raki. It's like liquid licorice and goes down easy and quickly. I believe it's between 80 and a 100 proof and very sweet.

As we entered the bar, I noticed some young sailors from the Pensacola already well ahead of us sitting in the back of the room. I asked if any of them belonged to any of the ensigns with me. One of them spoke up and laid claim to several of them. I told him the bartender was eyeballing them and we should maybe keep an eye on them. They were getting a little boisterous and the owner seemed to be getting nervous.

The ensign got up and went back to talk to his guys. He told them about the looks they were getting and how they should keep it down and not disturb the locals. They thanked him and he returned. After a couple of more Rakis they got louder and began an arm-wrestling contest; loser buys the winner a drink. Arm wrestling doesn't take long so soon, several more drinks had been consumed.

One of them came out of his shirt so that he could more easily flex his impressive biceps and more quickly dispose of his next opponent. The ensign rose again and was about to intervene when the arm-wrestling table turned over and a half dozen glasses hit the floor and shattered. He quickly cut a deal with the proprietor and the glasses were paid for by the partiers. At this time the ensign told the wrestlers that their liberty was secured and that they should immediately return to the ship. The shirtless one lost his Raki fueled mind. He started screaming and saying awful things about the ensign's mother.

As he was leaving the bar, he put his fist through the front window, which was basically the front wall of the bar. About one third of the front wall was shattered in an instant. I grabbed my wallet, pulled my ID card out and gave the wallet to the ensign. "Find out how much money he wants for his window!" I said, then turning to the other officers. "Don't let anyone leave until we have enough money to pay for this! I'm gonna try to get this guy back to the ship before they lock him up!"

The young sailor's arm was bleeding pretty badly, but miraculously, no one else was hurt. I rushed to him and grabbed two fistfuls of shirt. I got right in his face and screamed, "Can you hear me?"

"Yes sir," he said quietly.

Still yelling, "These people have to believe I'm gonna hurt you worse than they're gonna hurt you or they won't let you out of here! Do you understand?"

"Yes sir."

"I'm gonna hit you really hard! When you go down, don't move. Just stay still!"

With that, I jaw jacked him and down he went. I stood over him screaming and then kicked him. He didn't move. I grabbed him by the ankles and started dragging him down the street, his head bobbing up and down as it bumped on the cobblestones. The men in the bar stood stunned, still more shocked from the broken glass than to try to stop us.

When we neared the bottom of the hill, I saw the shuttle boat about 60 yards away. Coming from the opposite direction in a military truck was a carload of soldiers going to the bar because of the disturbance. I kept dragging my man and they drove right past us. I put the sailor on my shoulder in a fireman's carry and ran as fast as I could to the boat. A couple of sailors saw us coming and helped me get him in the boat.

"We need to get him to the ship right away," I told the head honcho.

"Sir, we don't leave for another ten minutes."

"Call Commander Palen. Tell him I have a man who needs to be on the ship or the civilian authorities may get him. This guy's in trouble and we need to move."

I think the blood running down his arm convinced them more than the fear in my voice. We were underway immediately. Still, Commander Palen was standing on the rail when we returned to the ship, and I went to him and explained the situation. He had the young man arrested and had him taken to sick bay to be sewn up.

A little while later the others returned to the ship and brought my wallet back. I think my share was a little over 50 bucks. I enjoyed celebrity status for the next couple of days on the ship as the Marine that pulled Watkins' ass out of the fire. Sailors pointed at me from afar, telling the story as they had heard it. I was even approached by a couple of sailors who wanted to hear it from me. We sailed into Beirut. I went ashore thinking that was the end of that.

We wrapped up our deployment, packed up our gear and headed home. I sailed home aboard the Pensacola. We stopped in Rota, Spain for a few days to de-snail our equipment and then across the Atlantic.

The Navy Relief Drive was in full swing, and 100% participation was expected. Commander Palen loved having recognition for his ship and decided to raise a lot of money for Navy Relief by auctioning off "Captain for a Day." One lucky sailor was going to get to sit in the captain's Chair, sleep in the captain's bed and eat in the captain's stateroom. Everything the captain had was his.

The way it worked was that individual departments would pool their money and then have a drawing for who would actually be captain. The winner, in turn, was allowed to have "guests" (gentlemen from his department) who would be invited to meals, to sit in the captain's seat on the bridge, and to enjoy for a day, the joys of being favored by the captain. The winner was announced, and the plans set in place for a fun day at sea.

Commander Palen announced on the 1MC what the "captain" and his mates were doing from time to time. All in all, it was a pretty successful way to raise money and morale. I was standing on the rail when it was announced that the "captain" would be taking his skiff out for a spin. The skiff is the boat used to shuttle the captain from ship to ship. Basically, it's an oceangoing motorboat.

The sea that day was like glass. I figured they'd drive around the other ships and show off for a while and then come back for steak and lobster. They were lowering the skiff down into the water right in front of me, when a young sailor signaled to stop the winch. He looked directly at me and said, "Lieutenant, aren't you the one that got Watkins out of Turkey?"

I said, "Yes," not knowing what to expect.

"Well Sir, Watkins is in our department, and you really looked after him. So, one of our guys found a pair of water skis down in the hold and would you like to go water skiing with us?"

Seconds later I was over the rail and in the skiff. We cruised by all the other ships with sailors and Marines hanging over the rail yelling at us. I never skied in front of a couple thousand people before, but I knew better than to try anything fancy. I'm the only one I know who has ever skied in the middle of the Atlantic Ocean. I owe it all to a drunken sailor.

SPRING BUTT BINGO

While at the Basic School in Quantico, we attended lots of classes that were introductory to all things Marine Corps. We had classes in the history and traditions of the Corps, land navigation, terrain appreciation, close order drill, basic engineering, artillery, aviation, communications, orienteering, and even etiquette. The etiquette classes were necessary because although we might go to the field and roll in the mud, when we returned we were expected to know which fork to use and which wine class to charge while attending a formal dinner.

I later attended a class on Marine Corps Instruction which all about how to teach the Marine Corps way. At the beginning of each class the learning objectives were explained. Always we heard the phrase: "At the end of this class you will know A, B, and C." The class would begin, and we were always told to hold all questions until the end.

The instructor would tell us what we needed to know, word for word. He would tell us again and then, in slightly different words, tell us one more time, such that we had heard twenty minutes of instruction in an hour. But, on a positive note, we knew the material.

There were some lieutenants who always had a few questions following each class. They would raise their hands, be recognized, stand up, and ask their questions loudly enough for the entire 160-man class to hear. There were some who were not shy in the least about asking questions to demonstrate their firm-grasps-of-the-obvious.

We were told that our jobs were about life and death and so there was no such thing as a stupid question. It soon became obvious to many of us that this was not even remotely true. We were not allowed to leave as long as anyone had questions. We would often sit until we had used up the break time between classes and would have to move directly to the next hour of instruction without benefit of a restroom break.

One instructor tried to throttle back on the questions by telling us that the only reason some lieutenants were asking questions was "to make you look smart, or me look stupid." Nothing seemed to help. We had a group who tried to impress fellow students and instructors with their knowledge by asking the most tedious questions and, in doing so, pissed off both groups.

I'm not sure where it came from, but some comic relief from this tedium came to us in the form of a game called "Spring Butt Bingo." The name came from the fact that we had to stand in order to ask a question, so those who always asked questions were said to have springs in their butts. As I recall, there was a "verifier" who had a list of all the men in the company.

In order to play, you filled out what was similar to a bingo card with a name of a lieutenant in each block. So across the top of your card it might read: "Smith, Jones, Johnson, Williams and Evans." We would fill out the remaining 20 blocks, written in ink so you couldn't change later, have the card verified, and give the verifier a dollar. We all knew who the most frequent spring butts were and would write their names on our cards twice (maximum allowable) and in the center square. We could play multiple cards but had to pay for each, and the verifier had to initial every card that was participating; the verifier's sheet showed who was playing and with how many cards. As the Q&A session began at the end of class, we sat intently, hoping that our favorite spring butt would ask a question.

The pot would regularly be between 20 and 50 dollars, and I believe we flew under the radar until one day an excited Second Lieutenant Russell shouted "BINGO!" in the middle of class and the entire operation was exposed. After months of coming close, it was his first win.

I don't recall if they shut us down because we were possibly inhibiting those who had genuine questions or because we were running an illegal gambling operation (this seems unlikely since we bet on EVERYTHING, even what time a given instructor would say a certain word), but the bingo game was shut down. Those with names on the bingo cards were still clueless, and their questions got even more stupid.

STUCK TANKS AT MCCRES, CAMP RIPLEY, MN

In the mid 1980's I was a tank platoon commander in Company B, 8th Tank Battalion, in Syracuse, New York. One summer our company ATD (Active Duty for Training) was to support reserve infantry battalions going through MCCRES (Marine Corps Combat Readiness Evaluation System) at Camp Ripley National Guard Base near Little Falls, Minnesota. Each of our company's platoons was attached to one of the infantry regiment's battalions with the first week devoted to small unit training and the second week to the evaluation. The company drew its tanks and M88 armored retrievers from the National Guard.

At the time, there was a lot of MOS (Military Occupational Specialty) mismatch among reservists and the units with which they affiliated. The policy was to fill units, then try to school train or on-the-job train the Marines in their new jobs later. In my company, I was the only school-trained tank officer (MOS 1802), and my tank commanders were all on-the-job trained. Even the company I&I (Inspector-Instructor), Captain Malarkey, was an amtrac officer by training. My platoon sergeant, a gunnery sergeant, was a reconnaissance Marine and relatively new to tanks.

Our first week at Camp Ripley was very busy between getting our borrowed tanks in reasonable shape and training in individual, crew, and platoon skills, with emphasis on MCCRES evaluated skills. One afternoon we had a maneuver area all to ourselves to practice coordinated platoon movement tactics and coordination. I knew one of the things the evaluators were likely to do was to kill me off and force my platoon sergeant to run the platoon, something in which he had very little experience.

The training area was long and open with low rolling hills, perfect for maneuver practice. In several areas were woods and brush in swamp land that looked firm and dry but was not. I pointed those areas out to my leaders, but in my haste to get to work and with all the training my Marines were trying to absorb, the message got lost. My fault, but we all paid for it.

I told the gunny that I was dead, that he was in command, and to practice the tactical maneuvers we had gone over across the training area while I watched, and then we'd have a critique. We had a jeep and trailer assigned to us for administrative needs. I had the jeep driver take me to a hill on the far end of the maneuver area where once the platoon came over a ridge in the middle of the range, I could watch them as I ate my MRE. The driver went back to join the platoon to serve as a runner if needed, since there were no man-pack radios available (the infantry battalions had them all).

Boy, did I feel smart sitting there on that hill eating my lunch! I'd set up some great training in a great area and my platoon sergeant and tank commanders could practice their skills without me breathing down their necks. I could hear the diesels roaring and every so often see plumes of black smoke as the tanks maneuvered. Once the gunny felt comfortable with his practice, my five tanks would come roaring over the ridge doing all the tactical maneuvers we'd gone over. Yup, any minute now, as soon as they got organized.... Then I saw my jeep and driver bouncing along the trail headed for my position.

When my driver pulled up, he said, "Sir, you better come with me." I said, "Lance corporal, where are my tanks?" And he replied, "The lance corporal would rather not say. You just better come with me, sir." When we arrived at the other end of the training area, I found the two tanks from gunny's section and my platoon sergeant sitting on his turret with his head in his hand.

I already knew the answer, but I had to ask, "Gunny, where's the rest of the platoon?" He had the most mournful look on his face as he looked at me and pointed into the swamp, where I could now see three sets of antennae sticking up above the brush. Somehow, they'd gone the wrong way. One tank was modestly stuck in mud half-way up its suspension. The next was buried a little deeper and farther into the swamp and the last had hoped to escape by gunning it and was buried so deep I had to step down onto the rear deck!

A radio call for retriever support was met with the response that they were knee-deep in supporting the platoon with the battalion currently undergoing the MCRES and wouldn't be available until tomorrow at the earliest. Tanks can recover another tank with the tow cables they carry. It's slow, muddy, hard work and sometimes dangerous, but it is a necessary skill. We hadn't planned to conduct real recovery training, but there it was.

Soon we were all covered head to toe with thick, smelly mud. We had to dive under the mud to hook up to the tow pintles of the stuck tank, and then link the cables back to a tank on firm ground. We started with the least stuck and closest vehicle. When we were ready to pull, there was a driver and commander in each tank with hatches closed in case something gave way. Both tanks would power in reverse and hopefully the stuck tank could back out the way it came. If not, we would have to cable up another tank behind the towing tank to provide more power.

To pull the last tank out we had to link three tow tanks together. For each pull, I was off to one side at a safe distance, a man shaped pile of mud giving hand and arm signals and hoping everything held together as the well over a 1000 horsepower tried to overcome mass, gravity, and muddy suction.

Sometime in the early evening Capt. Malarkey arrived to check on our progress. I figured I'd get a good ass chewing and some unsolicited advice about whatever we were doing wrong. I'm afraid I was too tired, cold and busy to remember my military manners.

When he walked up to me, I simply said, "What?" He smiled at me, slapped me on the back, getting his clean uniform muddied in the process, and said, "Call me if you need me." Then he walked back to his jeep and left. I never got any blowback from anyone about the situation and I'm sure that was because of his support and willingness to let us solve our own mess. We got all the tanks out without incident well after midnight. My Marines got valuable, though unplanned, training, we became a tighter platoon, and I got to witness some real leadership. It only took three showers to get the mud out of me

SUPPORT FROM "TABASCO MAC"

I had orders for Beirut in the fall of 1982 and, a month or so before departing, took leave to visit my parents for a few days. My Dad was a retired Marine master gunnery sergeant and a veteran of WWII, Korea, and Vietnam, so deployments sort of ran in my family. He and I were out in his barn scrounging through his old footlockers when he gave me a rusty old K Bar and a Marine Corps issue pocketknife along with a couple of swagger sticks that he had been required to carry (and hated). At the bottom of one of the Vietnam lockers I came across a small green pamphlet entitled, "The Charlie Ration Cookbook or No Food is Too Good for the Man Up Front."

I thumbed through it and found that it was a tongue-in-cheek cookbook, published by the McIlhenny Company out of Avery Island, Louisiana. For the under-educated, these are the folks that make Tabasco Pepper Sauce. The book said that the idea had come from Brigadier General Walter McIlhenny ("Tabasco Mac"), who was a WWII Marine veteran of Peleliu, and was a result of letters he had received from GI's serving in Vietnam, asking for recipes that would turn C-rations into something that resembled food.

The recipes (most of which contained Tabasco among the ingredients) were written by gourmet chef, playwright and WWII veteran, Christopher Blake. The recipes often included items that Marines could usually manage to scrounge from the local village and included such delightful fare as "Fox Hole Dinner for Two," "Cease Fire Casserole," and "Combat Zone Burgoo." The cartoon illustrations in the cookbook were drawn by an artist very familiar to Marines, who drew the "Gizmo" and "Eight Ball" series in Leatherneck magazine.

My dad told me that the McIlhenny Company had wrapped these cookbooks around a bottle of Tabasco sauce, slid this into a waterproof container, dropped in a P-38 (John Wayne) can opener or two, and shipped them off to the Soldiers and Marines in Vietnam. He said there were plenty enough to go around. Apparently, the whole thing was funded by the Tabasco folks as their contribution to the war effort, something very rare in America's least favored war. I thought it was pretty cool and stuffed it into my field jacket pocket and closed the footlocker.

On my drive home to North Carolina, I took out the book and began to mull over in my mind how I could use it on my upcoming deployment. The idea occurred to me that a lot had changed since Vietnam, but that Marines were basically the same. We were transitioning from C rations to MREs and we had moved from a full-on war in Vietnam to the peacekeeping mission in Lebanon. But Marines still gotta eat. So, what if instead of Tabasco sending us recipes, we sent them recipes of MREs coupled with what we found in the local village? It might be fun and might take off a little of the edge.

On Monday morning I got a quick audience with Colonel Jim Meade, the 22nd MAU CO, and explained the idea to him. He liked it but suggested I try to get a few more copies of the old cookbook to illustrate what it was we were looking for regarding recipes. We both saw the venture as a potential morale booster and a way to get the Marines' minds off the tedium of the long days away from home.

I went back to my office and called the McIlhenny Company and explained that I'd like to talk to someone about getting a few of the cookbooks sent to me as a template for a new cookbook. The receptionist said, without hesitation, "Oh, you need to talk to the General!"

I had no idea that General McIlhenny was still active in the company. He had taken over its Presidency in 1949 and was still serving in that capacity. He was co-founder of the Marine Military Academy in Harlingen, Texas and truly LOVED the Marine Corps. I was talking to the right man! I explained the idea I had about having the Marines write recipes and publishing a new cookbook like the one he had done for Vietnam. He said, "I understand, and I'm behind it one hundred percent, lieutenant. Now, what can we do to help?"

"Well, sir, we only have the one book, and I was wondering if you all might have a few extra lying around there somewhere that we could have?"

"Sure, we can do that. We got lots of 'em. How many did you have in mind?"

"That sort of depends on what they cost, General."

"I see. Well, for you they're free of charge. Let me help you out Lieutenant. How many men we got on this deployment?"

"About two thousand, sir."

"Fine, there'll be 2,500 cookbooks in the mail to you this afternoon. Now, if you are able to get a collection of recipes, go ahead and mail them here and put them to my attention. We'll get you a new cookbook published, just like our old one. Anything for the Marines!"

I gave him my address and in a few days the cookbooks arrived. I took them over and showed them to Col Meade. He was certainly surprised at the response. There was also a letter from General McIlhenny thanking us for the request and wishing us a safe and fruitful deployment. We both mailed him thank-you letters that afternoon. Colonel Meade told me he would let me know when to hand out the cookbooks and let the men in on the idea.

A couple of weeks after we landed in Beirut, he sent for me and had me travel to all the sites and pitch the idea. We got great initial response. In Vietnam, the local food that Marines ate were bamboo shoots, water chestnuts, breadfruit, plantains, and rice. In Lebanon, the "Hey Joe's" (street vendors) had oranges, pita bread, onions, fish, and chickpeas. Not many Marines were in a position to buy from them since we stayed "inside the wire," but recipes started to trickle in, until one day we had a couple of Marines get pretty sick and it was determined that the oranges they'd gotten from a street vendor were the cause. Colonel Meade put a ban on buying from street vendors and the recipes dried up. We never did get back our momentum and the project just sort of died.

When I got back to the states, I called Tabasco Mac and told him what had happened. I told him how much we appreciated his support and that I was sorry we hadn't been successful. He said he understood and that he appreciated what we were trying to do. We talked about the importance of morale and how the little things mean a lot when you're living in a hole in the ground and eating MREs.

General McIlhenny died two years later, leaving most of his estate to the Marine Military Academy in Harlingen, Texas. I would have loved to have met him in person and to have presented him with a Middle Eastern version of his cookbook.

TAILHOOK '91

Desert Shield/Desert Storm had ended. We were all returning home victorious and somewhat oblivious as to what to expect once we got home. CNN had become the news source of choice for Americans, but we were not aware. No internet in those days or real time news. What we came home to were all the yellow ribbons and support from Americans that service men had not seen since World War II. We were celebrated and seemingly could do no wrong.

I had never attended a Tailhook and had always wanted to. Having completed my tour, I was selected to be a flight instructor at the RAG. Time moved on and in that course of time, cross countries with RAG students were the norm. I was approached by one particular student who wanted to attend a Blue Angel Air Show in Wilmington, NC to which I agreed.

Well, Tailhook was coming up and finally I had a chance to go so I signed up to attend Tailhook '91. As things go, I did not cross check with my commitments and of course the student saw my name on the Tailhook Roster and promptly asked me, "Sir, I thought we were going to Wilmington for the Air Show that weekend?" I acknowledged that I "screwed up" and said that we would indeed go that weekend.

We went to the Air Show and since I was rushing the Blues, I was invited to attend their briefings both Saturday and Sunday.

We were also provided hotel rooms, as we were part of the Air Show, and ended up with an extra room because one of the crew stayed with his family. I invited my parents down and let them use the extra room. Great weekend for all! We returned to Whidbey Island, Washington on Monday following the air show.

As we all know, Tailhook went as planned and then the proverbial feces hit the fan! Investigations, lawsuits and careers ended from the fallout. NIS sent a team to Whidbey Island and interrogated all those who attended.

Sure enough, my name was still on that original roster and I received my first of two phone calls. First call, she asked if I was Stephen Craig Tyson and I responded yes. Then she asked if I attended Tailhook. I said no and that call ended. The next day she called again and asked me to confirm my name and rank to which I did. Once again, I was asked if I attended Tailhook and once again I said no. She then asked if I had proof to which I said, "Are you challenging my integrity?" She stated she needed proof. I then told her, "I was at a Blue Angel Air Show in Wilmington, NC, sat in with the Blue Angels both days, had a flight plan, hotel records, rental car receipts and had invited my parents down for the weekend. Also, if that is not enough, you can call my mother and here is her number. Do not $%&*!@# call me again!"

I never heard another word, and she never called my mother!

THE CAMERA

cam-er-a: an optical instrument using a small hole to allow light in to capture an image on a light sensitive surface, either slide or picture format.

We were closing in on the end of a deployment to Subic Bay Naval Air Station Philippines, where we were participating in a Cope Thunder Exercise. As per our typical daily routine, we were eating breakfast at the O Club before heading out to the squadron spaces and briefing for the day's flying missions. As we finished up, Don "Namu" Ramey said he was going to go up to his room to retrieve some papers that he needed to take into work that day and would meet us over at the squadron later.

When we all rose to get our personal effects together, I noticed that Namu had left his recently purchased 35 mm camera on the table. I gathered up the camera with my other gear and joined the others in a van to go over to the flight line. In the van, the conversation quickly centered on the newly appropriated camera, and what was the best way to let Namu know that it is probably not the best idea to leave a camera in the hands of a bunch of hell-bent fighter pilots who don't necessarily have his best interests in mind.

Upon entering the squadron spaces, our plan was quickly hatched, and we set out to the men's head, to see if we could find any wretched post-breakfast underwater landscapes. Ah, success! As it seems, a lot of fighter pilots take pride in some of their call of nature crusades. We were able to capture the various monstrosities on film, his film anyway.

Next up was a trip to the nefarious ready room. The ready room was not only the center of activity in any squadron, where important pre-flight briefings took place, but also the epicenter of social activity. All sorts of comical relief and sometimes downright debauchery were on display at various times of day. All of this, I'm sure, was just spontaneous. Surely it had nothing to do with the fact that we had a camera available, and not just any camera, but Namu's camera! And, so, yes, this too was all captured for eternity on film.

We were even able to conjure up epic air battles using the model airplanes that we use for briefing purposes. These models had wooden dowels coming out the tail pipes and are held onto to demonstrate various air to air maneuvers. We got everyone involved, running around the ready room holding models, laughing and cutting up, while someone took pictures with "the camera." There was even an attempt to produce a squadron-wide tribute to Namu by dropping flight suits and mooning the camera – all captured on film.

But at some point, all good things must come to an end; it was announced that Namu had entered the squadron area. I quickly grabbed the camera, went into his office and placed it as innocently as I could in the middle of his desk. And that was the end of it. Or so I thought.

About two or three months after we returned to our home base of Kaneohe, Hawaii, squadron life fell into its routine of pre-flight brief, flight, post-flight brief, and then finishing up any administrative duties in the course of the day. Namu was my section head and renowned for his sense of humor. He usually held court at the O'Club with his wit and quick come backs to any verbal challenge; in short, a cool cucumber who very rarely raised his voice. So, when he walked into the office that Monday morning looking like he was ready to bite someone's head off, needless to say, I took notice.

"Butch, how was YOUR weekend?" He asked, obviously annoyed at my very existence at that point.

"It was good Namu. How was yours?"

"Well Butch, let me tell you about my weekend!" He turned and went over to his desk and sat down, gathering his thoughts as something obviously big was brewing. Suddenly he sat up and exclaimed, "My folks were in from the States. They were sitting on the couch with my kids, and everyone was eager to see the slide show of pictures from our recent overseas deployment. Popcorn was popped and everyone was ready as I started the slide show. Ah, what's this? A nasty turd in a toilet bowl – how the heck? Quick, next slide. Oh my, squadron mates lined up, dropped trou and bare-assed to the world? How can this be happening? Maybe this is just an aberration. Next slide is sure to be better, or not. Good grief, that isn't what I think it is. While my parents were in shock, and my kids in tears, the slide show was quickly brought to an abrupt end."

Namu was obviously annoyed when he looked over and I was doubled over in laughter. "Sorry Namu, I forgot all about the camera. But hey, it's your fault for leaving it on the table at the O Club!"

Namu settled back in his chair, reflected for a minute and then concluded, "Yeah, that was pretty good Butch. I would have probably done the same thing.

THE COST OF DOING BUSINESS

In 1982, as we readied ourselves to deploy to Beirut, my staff sergeant, Rick Watson, informed me that he had applied for and received permission to operate a MARS station once we got set up in-country. I thought it was a great idea, providing us with the challenge of getting a comm shot across the Med and the Atlantic so that our Marines could call home, sort of.

MARS was Military Auxillary Radio Station and was basically a radio signal, using "skip," a single wave transmission received stateside by HAM radio operators who would patch the call from a radio transmission to a telephone call. This would allow us to "call home" for the cost of a collect call from the HAM operator to the wife, girlfriend, or mom, back home.

We got back to the preparations and there wasn't much mention of the MARS station until we arrived in Beirut, established all our communications links, and settled in for the duration. Once comm, particularly wire, is in, it only needs day-to-day maintenance to keep it going, and we began to search for things to do. Watson said we should probably get busy on the MARS station or our men would find other ways to entertain themselves, which is never a good thing.

We pulled an AN-MRC vehicle (a large VHF radio bolted down to the back of an M151 Jeep – a radio on wheels) up on the hill behind the MSSG building. The antenna was the key to the whole operation. The idea is to "skip" a radio wave and get it to come down near enough to a HAM station in the US, so they could pick it up.

Calculations were made and it was determined that we needed a 120-foot-long antenna. It was a single wire that would leave the back of our Jeep, go 60 feet into the air and then back down. The wave would then travel 6,000 miles back to the east coast of the US and hopefully turn into a call home for someone. Our problem was the antenna. It weighed practically nothing, but we didn't have a way to get it 60 feet up in the air.

We used antenna mast sections for our "flyswatter antennas," but they were only designed to go up 20 feet. They were four to five feet in length and we just kept adding sections until we were high enough. Unfortunately, a little wind would blow and some joint would break and the whole thing would come crashing down. Duct tape solved the problem (as it always does). We just reinforced all the joints and the thing stayed up.

We began experimenting, found some east coast operators, and started patching calls through for our comm guys first, just to make sure we had the process down. Our call sign was NNN0MBL. We found that the operators were aware of us and who we were already. They were up and waiting for our signal. The "MBL" part of our call sign stood for "Marines Beirut Lebanon" and there were lots of guys in the HAM community ready to help us.

We put the word out that we were open for business and the sign-up sheets filled immediately. We started patching calls through and, depending on the weather, might get 20 or 30 calls through a night. The operator would get our signal, we would give him a phone number, he would place a long distance collect call to that number, the other party would accept the charges, and the call would begin.

There were problems, but we were the only game in town that allowed Marines to hear a voice from home. One issue was the line. A Marine may be first in line, but maybe we just couldn't get the shot to work that night. Then there were the absentees. Since the parties on the other end didn't know when we might be calling, sometimes they weren't home. That made the married guys wonder where she was and who was she with and that was never good. Third, there was a lack of privacy. We had 20 Marines standing in line listening to one guy scream, "I love you honey... Over." It was embarrassing, and left some unfulfilled, not having fully expressed their undying love to their sweetheart so far away.

Finally, and the worst, there was that necessary "Over." Since it was a single wire call with a HAM operator in the middle, each party was instructed to say "Over" when they were finished talking. The operator would flip a switch and the other person could then speak. We only allowed three-minute calls and it took about two minutes for the average couple to get used to that and settle into reasonable conversation about the broken TV set or the baby's new tooth. About that time, the call was over.

Still, we were gathering crowds and morale was pretty high. We had some success with finding operators in New York and in Florida and points in between. We even hit the west coast every now and then. We were on a streak and were the talk of the town.

One night we got extraordinarily lucky. We got picked up by an operator in Kinston, NC. Charges for long distance calls were based on mileage from phone to phone. Kinston is only fifty miles from Camp Lejeune, NC, where we were stationed, so many of the Marines had families there. Calls patched from Kinston might be 25 cents, so word spread quickly, and the crowd got big and excited.

A young lance corporal came up and wanted to place a call to his girlfriend in Jacksonville. The HAM operator called the long-distance operator and requested a collect, person-to-person call to the young lady. It was here that our luck ended. We never even saw it coming. Neither did he.

The "girlfriend" said she would NOT accept the charges and that she didn't want to speak to him. She didn't say it, but she might as well have added "ever again" to her refusal. Our boy did what any nineteen-year-old, 6,000 miles away from home might have done. He began sobbing and was assisted from our site by good and caring comrades.

We called upon the next contestant, but he too had departed, along with the next and the next. We got a couple of takers, guys who had been married a few years and were feeling confident or lucky, but the crowd quickly diminished, and the air had been let out of the thing. The magic of talking to home was suddenly not so magical. We had a good signal but closed down early that night due to lack of interest. It was clear that few wanted to risk getting "Dear John'd" in front of one hundred people. Better not to hear her voice than to risk utter humiliation.

The next morning, I got a call from Colonel Jim "Large James" Meade, the CO of the MAU. He wished to see me. I brought Watson, thinking he might not chew my ass out as roughly in front of my staff NCO. We entered his office. He smiled and asked us to sit. He said that he should have called us earlier to let us know how we had done such a good job of building morale with our nightly phone calls. Then he said he that he'd heard about what had happened the night before and that, despite our best efforts, morale in the whole unit was currently in the shitter and we had to do something about it and quickly. "So, gents, what do you suggest?"

Watson suggested that we could build a phone booth for more privacy and back the line up so that the man on the radio could not be heard by others. "That's about the best we could do sir, short of using existing landline to call home," he said.

"I think that's so similar to the existing system, the Marines will still shy away from it. Tell me about the landlines. How do we do that?"

We could just tap into the lines here at the airport, make 25 calls two minutes in length each night. It would be like a long-distance call back home only a lot more numbers to dial and there wouldn't be any of that "Over" radio talk like we have now. The big problem would be, if we tap a line, we don't know whose line we're tapping, so we can't know who'd get the bill or for how much."

"Any idea how much it would cost?"

Watson shook his head. "Sir, we don't have any idea what long-distance, particularly international, rates are here. Clearly it would be more than your phone bill back home," I offered.

"Okay, gentlemen, let's do it. Limit 20 calls per night, two minutes each. Let me know when you're up and keep me informed as to how it's going."

We left the office laughing. Watson was like a kid in a candy store. We got some materials together and had a phone booth built. We wrote instructions on how to dial out and had them posted in the booth. We sent some wiremen up the road, Watson tapped a random line at a random building at the airport and the wire was strung through the trees, leading back to our compound and into the phone in our booth.

Rules for signups and for how the phone could be used were printed up. We notified Colonel Meade, and he gave us the okay to proceed. Word got out and we were soon open for business again. The phone booth was a great addition and things were even better than before.

Everything was going great and then, one day, I got a call stating Colonel Meade wanted to see me right away. I grabbed Watson and off we went. As we passed the outer office, I noticed two Lebanese gentlemen in ill-fitting polyester suits sitting on a bench looking nervous and agitated. We walked in and the colonel was studying some papers.

"Be seated," he said brusquely. After a few moments he looked up, still serious. "Any idea what this is?" he asked, faintly waving a handful of papers.

"Is it the phone bill, sir?"

"Yes Lieutenant, it is the phone bill. Take a look," he said, handing it across the desk.

Watson and I looked over the bill. It only covered the last three weeks of the previous month, but it was more than $6,000 and had several hundred calls on it.

"Well gents, does that look about right to you?"

"Based on international rates back home sir, I thought it would be more. But you can see, no calls more than two minutes and no more than 20 calls per night were made," I said.

"I understand," he said. "Just didn't think they'd discover it before we headed home. Lieutenant, could you ask those two gentlemen waiting outside to step in please?"

I stepped out and asked the Lebanese chaps to come in. Appropriate introductions were made and once we all knew each other Colonel Meade said, "Gentlemen, these are the guys who tapped into your phone lines and have generated this phone bill that you want me to do something about."

I couldn't believe he had outed us that way. After all, he was the one who told us to do it. We would never have done it without his permission! But he wasn't finished.

He said, "Gentlemen, before we arrived here, your airport wasn't even functioning. Since our arrival, we have protected this sector of the city and allowed air traffic to continue as it did before. You are both family men and I assume you go home in the evenings and kiss your wives and children. My Marines don't get to do that because they're serving you, thousands of miles from their homes. I don't think it's too much to let them hear a voice from home once or twice a month, so I'm going to let this continue. Please tell your superiors that this is the new cost of doing business, so they can charge more for airport services if they need to. The thing for you to decide is, do you want to pay the phone bill or have us pull out and see if you can keep the airport open on your own? This discussion is over. Please take your bill with you and have a nice day."

When they left, Meade broke into a big smile. "That's not where you thought that was going was it, Ken?"

I was stunned. "No sir, it was not."

THE GREATEST OF THESE IS LOYALTY

I went to Officer Candidate School at Quantico in the summer of 1979. As with all Marine Corps training, the classes were not so difficult: The instructor would tell us the information in a longer version than what was in the text; he would then repeat it using slightly different words; and finally he'd review what he'd just repeated; so you would hear it and read it several times. All you had to do was remember it. Thus, the academics weren't all that tough.

The physical training was. I showed up in pretty good shape, but it was more than I had expected. In fact, it kicked my butt. The psychological aspect was very difficult as well. The run, run, run everywhere you went; the constant preparation for the next inspection, which was the one that everyone failed; the knowledge that you could quit at any time and just go home – this lay ever-present in the back of your mind.

We started as a platoon of 60 and graduated about half of that. Some took the DOR (Drop on Request) route, typically not in touch with the speed and intensity of the place, had just had enough and went home. A few failed out, I think. But the bulk of those that didn't make it went home following the three rounds of peer evaluations. In this exercise, each man rated every other man in his squad. The criteria to be used were the 14 leadership traits outlined in our officer candidate guides. We memorized these and attempted to live them during our time in the Corps. We looked at each man as a leader and rated him (not ourselves) against the others in the squad, using the 14 traits as our guide. Those finishing at the bottom usually went home.

The 14 Traits were: Bearing, Endurance, Knowledge, Courage, Enthusiasm, Loyalty, Decisiveness, Initiative, Dependability, Integrity, Unselfishness, Judgment, Tact, and Justice. And a very large part of our overall grade was Leadership. After all, the purpose of OCS was to weed out, then select, the next generation of leaders for the Corps.

We had an overarching leadership grade, which came from our classes and written tests covering the subject; individual billets or temporary leadership jobs mirroring the positions in a regular Marine unit; the day-to-day observations of each candidate by the staff; an obstacle course called the reaction course, which put each candidate in charge and required him to solve a problem with limited resources; and finally, the peer evals.

We were preparing for a "junk on the bunk" inspection in which we presented our equipment: pack, cartridge belt, ammo pouches, suspenders, shelter half, stakes, pins, rope – all presented in a VERY specific and uniform manner on our bunks. The shelter half had to be folded precisely in a certain way and placed in a certain spot. Likewise, the stakes, pins, and belt all had their places. Even the rope, a six-foot length of small rope, had to be free of loose fabric pieces, called Irish Pendants, and wrapped up in a specific way, placed in a specific spot. The name of the game here was precision and attention to detail.

I was all ready and had assisted a couple of men close to me by inspecting their presentations, and they mine. I was feeling pretty good about this one. My gear was spotless, and everything seemed to be properly presented. I even had several minutes to spare.

About this time, directly across the squad bay from me, I saw Knisely losing his mind. His shelter half rope was suddenly missing. He was frantic. People near him rushed to try to help find it. When you looked down the squad bay from one end to the other across 20 bunks, a missing rope stood out like a sore thumb. He would be caught and losing gear was a major no-no. He said he'd had it five minutes ago. Several of us searched but had no luck finding it.

The platoon was called to attention and we all snapped to at the foot of our racks. I stood across the ten-foot aisle from Knisely and watched him suffer, trying to figure out what happened to the rope and knowing the butt chewing he was about to get in front of the whole platoon; not to mention, the negativity that was going to be on him just before the seven-week peer evals spelled disaster. It would be fresh in the minds of those rating him and his ranking would fall. He was writhing right in front of me. We were arranged alphabetically, and the inspectors were looking at the "D's" when, for some unexplained reason, I broke the position of attention, reached back on my rack, grabbed my rope, showed it to Knisely, who smiled from ear to ear, and threw it across the squad bay. He caught it, checked the location of the inspectors, and put it on his rack.

I remember thinking, while the rope was still in the air, that I had just made a huge mistake. All I could think about was the fact that everyone in my squad had just seen me throw that rope. In a couple of days, they were going to rate me on the leadership traits and time and time again we had been told that the number one trait each officer should possess is Integrity. I had just "cheated" on a test and the whole world had seen it. If they missed it the first time, they had a second chance, because as the inspection team passed Knisely, they went to the other end of the squad bay to look at the "L's" before working their way to me. Knisely tossed my rope back and I placed it on my bunk. As, soon as the inspection was over, my bunk mate, Dave Williams, said, "I think you just screwed up."

He knew, like me, how my actions might be perceived. Integrity was king at OCS and I might well be seen by some as a cheater. They might also rate me down on judgment, since I had shown some pretty poor judgment. And then there was bearing. I was always rated low on bearing. This wasn't going to help any in that area. But, on the other hand, there was dependability, loyalty and initiative.

My friends told me if they had the guts, they'd have done the same thing, so maybe someone would give me high marks for courage. That one hardly ever got a mark since it usually wasn't observed. The next two days were torture. I believe some of my friends were politicking for me, letting other squad members know that what I'd done was a good thing. I was being extra nice to everyone and just hoping for the best.

When the seven-week peer evals came out, it was clear that integrity may have been king with the staff, but among the candidates, loyalty to your fellow Marines was boss. I got rated higher than ever and so did Knisely. OCS is a look at what small units in the Marine Corps are like, sort of. When I got to the fleet, it didn't take me long to learn that there is a certain amount of loyalty that you have to the Corps, to the CO, to the platoon and squad leaders. But the real loyalty is for the person who is right beside you, going through the same thing you are going through. If he is willing to help when you really need it, when your back's against the wall, he has earned your loyalty. Integrity is essential, but loyalty holds the whole thing together

THE HOLE STORY

While in the Basic School at Quantico in 1979 we went to field a few times to practice what we had learned in the classroom. I was fortunate enough on one of these occasions to be assigned to carry the .50 caliber machine gun. I'm sure I did something to deserve such an honor, but I can't recall what it was. It was genuinely heavy and awkward to carry. Some of my buddies took some of the gear from my pack and put it in theirs to lighten my load, but the hike out to our bivouac site was pretty miserable. It was cold and spitting ice, rain and snow, making for a slippery trail and an unbalanced load. My partner (can't recall who it was) carried the tripod, which was also no treat.

We made the bivouac area and were told we would be defending a small hilltop. Our student platoon commander told us where to set up our weapon and instructed us as to fields of fire. We began to dig in as the sun began to set. The hole we dug was not a regular fighting hole, but very specific to complement the employment of the machine gun. It needed to be U-shaped with a man seated on either side of the weapon and the "peninsula" in the middle wide enough that the rocking of the machine gun firing on full auto wouldn't cave in the sides. It had to be several feet deep and each man had to have a sort of dug out chair to sit on. We grabbed our small entrenching tools and set to work.

We dug for hours and from time to time our friends would stop by to lend a hand, their holes being long finished. Late that night, we finally got to a point that it looked good enough to make it through the night. We resolved to finish up in the morning, and my partner took first watch, allowing me to get a few hours' sleep.

It was snowing a little and I had on my field jacket and poncho, with my wooly-pully sweater still in my pack in case it got REALLY cold. I curled up in the "chair" on my side of our hole and, exhausted, went straight to sleep. A few hours later my hole mate shook me to let me know it was my watch.

While I had been sleeping, the snow had turned to rain and then it got very cold. The rainwater had collected in our hole and my feet were frozen into three quarters of an inch of ice. I had to break my boots out of the ice and thought I had frostbite. My partner, having been awake, had lifted his own feet out of the water and up into the "chair" with him. He hadn't bothered to tell me of the problem. I limped over to the fire and started to thaw out my boots and feet.

Before the sun came up, I was warm and so were my boots. I had a cup of coffee in me and had promised myself that tonight would not be like last night. I would not sleep in a half-assed hole and have another miserable night. I went to work on the hole and fetched some stones and limbs from nearby and put them in the bottom, like a floor, allowing water to drain away from our feet. I dug a deep sump on both sides to get water away from us and to serve as a grenade hole. I smoothed out the sides, almost like an adobe hut, and cut the angles sharply. I gathered pine boughs and lined the entire hole with them. I had an extra poncho, which I stretched across the back of the hole to give us some cover but still leaving access to the weapon. I cut some sticks and set them out to better define our fields of fire.

After breakfast we started getting visitors and several of my classmates mentioned what a nice hole we had. A little while later, Colonel E.T. Cook, the Commander of the Basic School, walked the area and stopped at our position, looked down at us and said, "I think that's the finest hole I've ever seen!" He had his photographer take a picture of it. I don't know what happened to the pictures; I didn't get deep selected to captain, so I suppose they never left TBS.

Out of all of the lessons I took from the Basic School, digging that hole was my biggest. I have told the story to hundreds of people in leadership and management training classes through the years. Firstly, there were classmates who truly wished they had a hole as nice as mine. They had "hole envy" even though two nights before they slept in comfortable beds. How quickly we adapt to our current surroundings, changing how we view ourselves and others. What we want depends upon what we have and what others around us have.

I've traveled all over the world and I've met some very poor people. But I learned they feel especially poor when others around them have more. We were all accustomed to living in better surroundings, but for a few days we lived in vacated earth and the ones who worked harder lived in style, relatively speaking. Second, I was VERY proud of my hole! Colonel Cook was like a god to me. For him to take note of my work really meant something to me. From then on, I frequently tried to give credit to my Marines when they did something good, because I knew how that recognition felt.

Lastly, I learned that every day the hole that you inherited can be made better, more livable, even enviable. I'd guess everyone who's ever worked for me has heard the "Hole Story," and they all learned that just because we work in a hole today, doesn't mean we can't be in a mansion by nightfall if we hustle.

The Marine Corps always humbled me before it taught me a life lesson.

THE IMMACULATE AUTOROTATION

Back in the mid-eighties there was a Marine A-4 crash in one of the ranges near the Marine Corps air station in Yuma. The rumor was that the guy lost an engine (it's a single engine, single pilot aircraft) and was too low to eject, so he stayed with the jet and was able to do a very flat, controlled crash landing on a slight downhill slope. The aircraft came apart as it traveled along a one-mile path before it came to a rest. The pilot's ejection seat and the pilot were all that was left of the aircraft. The completely unhurt pilot unstrapped himself and was found sitting on a nearby rock, as the extremely surprised crew in the rescue helicopter landed and took him back to Yuma. The crash site and what was left of the A-4 made anyone assume the pilot died in the crash. He didn't. That is known as the Immaculate Ejection.

In the late eighties, two Marine Reserve CH-46E helicopters were flying in one of the ranges near Fallon, Nevada. They performed a now forbidden tactics maneuver and one of the helicopter's aft rotor heads came in contact with the other helicopter's left fuel tank. It's bad when a helicopter in flight hits anything with the rotors. It's bad like when you jump off of a skyscraper without a parachute or when a tractor trailer hits you head on at 70 miles per hour. It's bad.

The helicopter's aft rotors were immediately out of rotational balance, swung down, and cut off the back of the helicopter from the front. Both generators and the battery are in the aft end so there was a complete loss of electrical power to the forward half. When the aft rotors severed itself from the front half, the rotors somehow crimped the number one hydraulic line (the pump located on the forward transmission), allowing the hydraulic-pressure-only powered flight controls to operate perfectly. The aft end continued to chop itself to pieces as it fell, while the forward half, where the crew chief and pilots were located, continued to fly.

All helicopters have the ability to autorotate without any engine power to a safe landing ONCE. Helicopter pilots train all the time to make sure that if an autorotation is ever required, it's second nature to complete one. The aircraft commander, Steve "Tiny" Toth, had no idea over half of his aircraft was missing. He saw the immediate loss of rotor speed and loss of electrical and engine power and at about 1,000 feet above the ground, instinctively entered an autorotation. Since the airspeed indicator, rotor speed, and altitude indicator operated without electrical power, Tiny had all the gauge information he needed to safely land the forward half.

At about what he figured was 100 feet above the ground, Tiny pulled the nose up to slow the aircraft's forward speed and slow the rate of descent. Then at what he figured was about 50 feet above the ground, he pushed the nose level and used the speed of the rotors to slow the vertical rate of descent to a perfect landing.

Once he landed, the forward half rolled over. The crew chief simply unstrapped and stepped onto the ground, then helped Tiny's copilot, Warren Jones, out of his seat and out of the aircraft. Tiny unstrapped and when he looked back to exit the cockpit, he saw and realized for the first time that the aft end was missing. Hence, the Immaculate Autorotation.

THE PōHAKULOA TALE

Well, you don't see this every day, but this is what happened.

We were nearing home - returning from a six-month deployment to the Western Pacific – Pearl Harbor was now just two nights and a wake-up away. Wives and girlfriends would be waiting. The excitement on board the ship was palpable. Then, just two days before we arrived back in Hawaiian waters, we receive word from the Brigade Commander that one of our infantry squads on board one of our Amphibious Ready Group (ARG) ships had to take over range control duties at the Pōhakuloa Training Area on the Big Island of Hawaii for a two-week Range Control Duty. Ugh. This hit hard, but a squad was selected, and they were flown off the ship by helicopter with all their gear to the Big Island training area the day before the ship was to dock in Pearl Harbor. The rest of us proceeded on towards Pearl Harbor with our Squadron flying our aircraft off the ship before the ship came into port.

Two weeks later after all of us had settled back into our Hawaiian lives with families and girlfriends etc. I was called on to go back to the Big Island to bring the squad home – finally! My co-pilot was of course Tongo. The day came and it was to be a straightforward mission – down and back in the day with a stop on the way back to top off fuel at the Maui airport.

Pōhakuloa Training Area (PTA) is located on the island of Hawaii in the high plateau between Mauna Loa, Mauna Kea and the Hualālai volcanic mountains. It includes a small military airstrip known as Bradshaw Army Airfield. When we got to the small Bradshaw Army Airfield, we found the Range Control "survivors" arriving from the barracks and more than anxious to get home. A small old Toyota pickup truck was shuttling the Marines' gear to the edge of the ramp parking area and heading off to get a few more Marines.

Tongo was assessing the situation and once again he got that little gleam in his eyes as he developed his mischievous plan. Standing with myself and the Crew Chief on the airfield ramp next to the aircraft with the squad gathering about 40-50 feet away, he starts doodling on his knee pad and describes a bit of his plan and says watch. He calls to the squad and asks who's in charge, and we are told that the Sergeant in charge is up at the barracks driving the Toyota. Tongo tells the squad that we have a problem and to have the Sergeant see us when he gets back to the airfield.

About 10 minutes later the Toyota pickup truck arrives and the Sergeant talks to his squad for a moment and then heads right over to talk with us. Tongo proceeds to tell the Sergeant that our aircraft is down for mechanical reasons and that we are working on a solution to our problem. The look on the Sergeant's face was clearly one of quite some disappointment. He goes off to talk to the squad members and you can see the frustration with the situation growing. After huddling with us and doodling some more on his knee pad, Tongo calls to the Sergeant and asks who is the biggest and strongest Marine that he has – Tongo said he had a plan.

Seconds later this huge Marine they called "Corporal Rock" came over with the Sergeant. I suspect his real name was something like "Rockford". Tongo described the problem and the plan of attack, and it went like this.

"The aircraft hydraulic starter is down, and we can't get the aircraft started, but we think there might be a way we can work-around the problem." Tongo says. He goes on, "The Crew Chief has opened the main hydraulic lines to connect them to the auxiliary hydraulic lines so that if we spin the aircraft blades we can get the hydraulic pressure we need to start the aircraft engines and we can fly home." Tongo tells the Sergeant to stay on the ramp's edge with his squad while the crew chief sets Corporal Rock in place to do his job. The crew chief climbs up on the aircraft and gets on top where he can grab the rotor blades. He describes how Corporal Rock will have to grab the blades properly so as to not damage the blade, but that he must also really heave the blades forward quickly to get the hydraulic pressure that we need to be successful. Rock is getting anxious to do it and the squad is cheering him on. It's like a football game with cheerleading as the team takes its position.

As Corporal Rock climbs onto the aircraft stub wing and begins to get in position to climb up to the top of the aircraft, Tongo is watching and checking on the progress. The crew chief is now describing how to grab the blades and take a position from which he can spin the aircraft rotor blades. Rock is getting excited, and the "sports fans" are getting louder. Cpl. Rock is in position. Then as we turn around to get back into the aircraft, Tongo kicks the ground and yells "No! I couldn't live with myself."

Tongo turns-a-round and goes back to Corporal Rock and tells him he just remembered that when you directly spin the blades to start the aircraft, the hydraulic resistance is reduced and the engine in this unloaded condition will instantly accelerate and cause either the drive shaft to come apart under the sudden load or take off the head of the person spinning the blade. Clearly Tongo couldn't live with that risk. The guys were dejected, and Rock was saying that he still could do it, but Tongo insisted that he needed to think through this some more.

After we spent another 20-30 minutes doodling on Tongo's knee pad while the last of the squad was being delivered to the airfield, Tongo straightens up, slaps his forehead and says "Yes! Why didn't I think of this before?" He calls the Sergeant back over and explains the situation and "discovery". What Tongo wants is for the squad to split up and half stand behind each stub-wing. He "realizes" that he can crosstie the aircraft brake hydraulic system to the APU start system through the accumulator system. With the wheels brakes developing the hydraulic energy, the process just works in reverse. "That will work." Tongo said. Of course, none of that was true, but he had fun selling it.

The squad dutifully split up, divided half to each stub-wing. We strapped into the cockpit and set up the switches for the coming start sequence. Our crew chief helped by making sure that everyone stayed behind the stub-wing where they would be well away from the aircraft main landing gear wheels. When all was set up, Tongo calls for the squad to start pushing with the crew chief "monitoring" the hydraulic system from inside the aircraft. These thirteen Marines began to push the helicopter forward. At an airfield altitude of over 6000' elevation, the guys were puffing a bit soon after getting the aircraft moving. After about 20 feet of forward movement, Tongo hits the aircraft brakes and yells out that it has to be faster. We take pause to let them catch their breath and begin again. This time we let them go about 50-60 feet and the aircraft was in fact moving faster. After stomping on the brakes again, Tongo yells out the window that they had just about got it, but that they were still a bit slow by a smidge.

The guys are really puffing now, but they are encouraged. In several minutes they let us know that they were ready to try again. This time after 20-30 feet, we are getting close to the end of the ramp and Tongo yells that we need to turn and proceeds to apply the left brake and when the aircraft straightens out it now has several hundred feet of ramp, but the ramp is slightly downhill from our point. The aircraft picks up speed and gets going faster and faster, but the guys are pushing farther and farther. Tongo yells out you almost got it – keep going! Finally, just as the guys are beginning to have a hard time keeping up, Tongo yells "Clear" and hits the brakes and simultaneously flips the switch to bring on the APU which was never a problem. The aircraft comes to a halt and the APU engine comes to life and the guy cheered and high fived each other.

We flew home uneventfully, each of the guys telling the story over and over to themselves and when we finally landed on the 101 pad the families and girlfriends were waiting. We taxied to our ramp positions, pulled the engines back and hit the rotor brakes until the aircraft blades came to a stop. We lowered the ramp, the guys grabbed their seabags and possessions from the six month deployment and they all raced across the flight ramp yelling and pointing back to our aircraft the whole way. We laughed as they all arrived as heroes each telling their stories of how they had gotten the aircraft started by push start.

THE PRICE FOR PEACE

My dad was a Marine and fought in WWII. He was born in southern Oklahoma, somewhere near Ada, in 1926 and grew up in a place called the Twelve Mile Prairie. In 1942, when he was 16 years old, he lied about his age to some Marine Corps recruiters and enlisted in the Corps. At just 16, he entered combat in the Pacific Island campaigns. Thankfully, Tarawa happened about a year before he enlisted, or I probably wouldn't be writing this short story.

I was too stupid to write down his accounts of history, being a snot-nosed, short-haired, pimple-faced hippie, influenced by similar morons with whom I attended high school. I do remember his forced-to-listen-to tales and the pictures he had taken of some of the island campaigns. At the time I thought most of the pictures were barbaric and inhumane since they depicted dead Japanese soldiers with some charred bodies, killed by flame throwers. There were pictures of him standing on an island where the toughest battle in the Marine Corps was fought and I had zero interest in finding out everything about it I could. Yep, I was an idiot.

He pulled other things out of his footlocker, like bayonets, knives, his metal helmet, a pistol, and a silk scarf that he found on Iwo Jima. It was white and faded. He always unfolded it carefully and said that near the end of the battle for Iwo Jima, when the fighting had pretty much ceased, he had been tasked to search through some of the caves on the opposite side of the island from the initial assault. He said he never told the intel guys about the scarf and said he would have gotten in trouble for keeping it from them.

Dad stepped on the island a lance corporal. He was one of three in his platoon who lived during the initial assault on the beaches with the soft, black beach sand. As they say, "Three steps forward, two steps back." He watched both flags being raised on Suribachi and so many men on the beaches, fighting the onslaught of Japanese gunfire, said, "Those guys are nuts up there," as Dad fought his way from the beach toward the enemy.

He told me about Cushman's Pocket. I didn't want to hear it but every time he talked about Cushman's Pocket, he never mentioned the enormous danger nor how they all advanced forward. He talked about them being forced to use a bunch of pallets of food for cover from Japanese gun fire during the skirmish. The pallet he and a few others used to provide cover contained large cans of peaches. He and the others broke into the cans and enjoyed eating sweet peaches at one point during the battle of Cushman's Pocket. No one found out who did it, and Dad was proud that they all got away with it as they went forward to close on the enemy Japanese.

Because of the thousands of Marines who gave their lives on Iwo Jima so that I could be free to be a teenage idiot, Dad left the island a master sergeant. "Three up, three down," he'd say, as he carefully refolded the silk scarf.

He and I were never close. We simply did not have anything close to a father-son relationship and now I think I can understand why. He had to quit elementary school when he was twelve, go to work from "sun-up to sundown," and couldn't fathom the luxury in which children of the 60's and 70's lived. Complaints from kids like me, who had infinitely more than he had when he was young, would send him into hour-long lectures and personal put downs regarding my future of being a failure. I couldn't understand him at the time and the separation between him and me only grew and grew, long after I left home at 18.

Fast forward 31 years to an even more polarized relationship with my dad, and I wanted to do something for him to show appreciation for what he went through, especially what he did for his country during World War II. I was able to get in contact with historian Stephen A. Ambrose when he announced on C-SPAN he was looking for WWII veterans to interview. I told him a few things about Dad and his Marine Corps experiences I could remember, and Ambrose absolutely needed to talk to him. Ambrose explained that he and producer Stephen Spielberg were making a documentary about the Pacific Theater during WWII. After all the interviewing, filming and such, Dad was featured in their documentary, The Price for Peace. Dad was also one of the guests of honor at the opening of the World War II Museum in New Orleans. He deserved that, and I was so glad that happened for him. Having graduated from teenage idiocy, I'm now very proud to have had a small part in recognizing the sacrifices he made for his country.

THE SANDS OF IWO JIMA

In the late winter/early spring of 1982, male recruits entering the Marine Corps underwent ten weeks of basic training at either Parris Island, South Carolina or San Diego, California. At Parris Island, the ten weeks of basic training consisted of three distinct phases for each series. A series had four platoons with three drill instructors per platoon, a series staff of two officers, and a series gunnery sergeant. Phase One was three weeks focused on introductory topics such as close order drill, Marine Corps history, customs, and courtesies, and physical training. Phase Two was two weeks at the rifle range, culminating in qualifying with the M-16 rifle, and one week of "mess and maintenance" spent working in the dining facility. Phase Three was approximately four weeks with individual combat training, more close order drill, and other topics ending with graduation and the earning of the title, "Marine."

There was a requirement that the recruits attend a movie at the base theater during Phase Three. Rather than allow the recruits to see the scheduled movie, the series staff from a series in the Third Recruit Training Battalion utilized their initiative to arrange for the base theater to show the black and white film The Sands of Iwo Jima. The base theater at Parris Island had a copy of The Sands of Iwo Jima, starring the immortal John Wayne as Sergeant Stryker, on hand for requests such as this. This was long before live-streaming, and the base theater utilized projector systems to play movie reels. Base theaters normally showed second rate or B movies during this era as first rate and blockbuster movies went directly to the local commercial theaters. When the time came for their "movie night," the recruits marched to the base theater to see The Sands of Iwo Jima sans popcorn and soft drinks, as the requirement was only that the recruits have the opportunity to see a movie, not that the recruits have the opportunity to have popcorn, candy, or soft drinks.

THE "SHELL" SLIDES DOWNHILL

One of the great things about becoming a 2nd Lieutenant of the United States Marines is the Marines who surround you. They form a bubble around you in a sense. Every officer in the Corps outranks you and most enlisted have been in the Corps longer than you. The smart, young lieutenants realize the precarious nature of this organizational dynamic and adopt a sense of confident humility. The less fortunate among our young brethren officer corps will have humility enforced upon them in undesirable ways.

Harrumph!! Marines running! Japanese press yelling and snapping pictures and making sucking sounds through their teeth that could be heard yards away – even over all the other mayhem. Fire and smoke! Calls for cease fire over the headset! The battalion and regimental COs almost trampled. I step out of the FDC (Fire Direction Center) tent in dismay and confusion. What the hell is going on! This is not normal for a battery firing exercise.

In 1980, I was the FDO (Fire Direction Officer) of a 155 mm Howitzer battery in Okinawa, Japan – the youngest and lowest ranking officer. We were on a "routine" exercise, just firing rounds weighing about 95 pounds with a charge 2 load over an

Okinawan road onto a postage stamp-sized impact zone about two to three miles away. The occasional, and probably very surprised, 110- to 120-pound Okinawan man and his family would drive by on the road below the firing position in shocked dismay as a loud boom, followed by a whistling sound overhead, attracted their attention, just a normal day for Marines, but a bit disturbing to the driver of a rusting Honda or Toyota tiny van. What could possibly be a cause of concern to these Okinawans and the Japanese press? Didn't they realize that we were there to train for war and save their butts should the need arise?

There was a guy named Murphy. He wrote a bunch of laws – not enforceable by any potentate. Just patterns of behavior he had observed that were so predictable they were like laws of nature. One of them reads: "If anything can go wrong, it will."

Take an 18-year-old kid, put him through Marine boot camp. Assign him to the charge of a corporal or perhaps the oversight of a sergeant in charge of a howitzer crew. Corporal or sergeant assigns him to load a 95-pound shell into the breech of a 155 mm howitzer using a ramming rod with sufficient force to seat the soft copper rings into the rifling of the tube so that no gasses from the subsequently loaded powder bags will escape. What can go wrong! The eighteen-year-old Marine is as happy as a pig in slop to be given such an awesome responsibility with such a weapon capable of incredible destruction.

Same eighteen-year-old Marine pushes the ramming rod against the shell. Not hard enough. Rings do not seat. Order to fire the adjusting round is received by the howitzer team from the FDC. FIRE!

Fire happens – out the end of the howitzer tube!

No shell exits said tube. Not normal. Battery CO now concerned if he will ever make major. Concern elevated by the Marines almost running over battalion and regimental COs and the Japanese press recording events for next day's news in Tokyo. Situation not looking good.

"Check fire" command issued – takes on additional meaning. Is the round cooking in the tube? Will it explode? How far up the tube is the round? Did it execute enough spins in the tube to activate the VT (Variable Time) fuse? Do we call EOD? Do we evacuate the area?

A few minutes elapse and no explosion. God bless the battery CO! He makes the decision to have the young Marine who rammed the round to open the breech block. Everyone watches, including the Japanese press who have now determined that this is definitely not normal. Breech is opened. Japanese press corps makes giant sucking sound through teeth as the blackened round drops to the ground at the feet of the young Marine and his howitzer team chief. Stares of consternation and amazement momentarily dominate the faces of all Marines. Japanese now bantering loudly and taking pictures.

I reenter the picture here. The round must be exited from the firing site. The shell has now been assigned to the protective domain of the 2nd Lieutenant in the battery – me.

The shell has slid downhill – all the way into my custody. Why? Well, of course, if I gave the order to "Fire" and I am the lowest ranking officer, what happens to that shell is my responsibility. That is how it was explained to me.

Go get driver, pick up a blackened 155 mm howitzer round. Drive to the munitions depot, park in front of munitions headquarters. Enter the building. Approach the front desk and start my sales pitch to convince the munitions NCO to accept blackened round.

However, enter first sergeant in charge of the munitions depot having just seen the round in the pickup and having only seen my back. His verbal reaction still rings in my ears and brings a smile as I reflect upon that bonding moment of decades past. Fortunately, battalion and regimental COs are Vietnam-era vets. They know Murphy's law. Battery CO lives to see a deserved promotion to major. The young 2nd Lieutenant learns how the shell slides downhill that day in a new way and confident humility was built.

THE STREETS OF BEIRUT

I served with MSSG 22 under MAU 22 near the Beirut airport in 1982-83. The MAU shower unit was often not working and when it was, it was hardly worth the effort. We had it better than many of the ground units positioned farther from the flagpole, but we weren't comfortable by any means. We had showers available a couple of days a week.

We walked down the dusty dirt street toward the showers wearing PT gear and shower shoes. The showers were in a GP tent with plumbing, in a rectangle just inside the tent wall. The deck was asphalt with wooden pallets laid out like the parquet floors in the Boston Garden. There were gaps between the boards and when they got wet, which was all the time, they were slippery. It was easy to lose a flip flop, twist an ankle or just fall and bust your ass.

There was hot water, which was nice, but the unit that heated and pumped the water sat right beside the shower tent and was powered by a diesel motor. This motor pumped fumes into the tent at approximately the same rate as it pumped water. It was not uncommon to see men gagging, running from the tent to escape the fumes. It made for short showers.

When they first opened, I showered and walked the 200 yards back up the dirt street to my hootch. My wet flip flops picked up the dirt and sand from the street and by the time I got back home I was dirtier than when I left. On days that it rained, there was really no point in going. The mud on the streets was like glue.

I was a liaison serving two days a week at President Bachir Gemayel's residence alongside liaison officers from all of the other Multinational Forces. On my first day, I was given general directions on how to get to the palace, and it was shown to me on a map. We left the American sector and soon realized that our map wasn't to scale and didn't have half of the streets marked. They were also written in Arabic, which none of us could read. I had with me a driver and two riflemen situated in the back seat watching for dangerous situations.

We turned off the main road into a residential area, hoping it would lead up the mountain to the palace. All the safe areas had huge pictures of President Gemayel, so you could tell when you were around friendlies.

We got into a congested area with huge posters of the Ayatollah Khomeini on the sides of the buildings. We were not among friends. Beirut was a large city and the Israelis had bombed it pretty well, knocking out all the traffic lights, so there were police officers at major intersections directing traffic. As it always seems to happen, they only created longer lines of traffic.

One of my riflemen pointed to the bombed-out rooftops all around us where there were lots of hostile looking men with AK 47s looking down on us. I suggested that we couldn't just sit still, and my young driver took the initiative, laid on the little horn of our M151 and jumped the vehicle up on the sidewalk. People cleared out of the way and when we reached the end of the block, the shocked policeman waved us through. We got back on the street and laughed all the way to the palace.

When we arrived, there were spike strips in the road that slowed us down to about five miles per hour. A guard approached me and asked my name. I told him, "Lt Wilcox." He didn't speak English, so he consulted his friend who was in the same predicament. Finally, they showed me the security list and I found that my name was not on it. I had replaced Johnson who was on a ship headed home, so I pointed to his name and said, "Here I am, Wilcox!"

Having cleared security, we entered the compound. When I returned to the MAU two days later, I briefed the staff on our adventure and showed them the location of the hostile area. Colonel Meade made it policy that if we got stopped in hostile areas, honking the horn and driving on the sidewalk was the way to go. In a short time, the police knew the sound of the M151 horn and let us through regularly.

I was able to go on patrol with the recon detachment on a couple of occasions since my work was done as were my collateral duties. On patrol, I could see the city up close. I remember walking past a dirty field where really poor looking kids were kicking something that was supposed to represent a soccer ball. There were about 12 of them running up and down the dust pit.

One little boy, who looked to be about six or seven, sat drawing in the dirt with a stick near the road where we were walking. We each had two MREs in our cargo pockets, which was at least one more MRE than I cared to eat in a day. I reached into my pocket and pulled out one of my MREs and tossed it about five feet away from that little boy. He knew exactly what it was and pounced on it, holding it close like he didn't want it to get away. He had a huge smile on his face. He started to laugh.

The other boys had noticed and came running across the field. Without a word, MREs came flying out from behind me and soon there was plenty for everyone. We never missed a step, just kept walking. No one said thank you. They really didn't need to. The smiles and the laughter were more than enough thanks. It changed the way I thought of an entire country.

When "the people of Lebanon" were spoken of in my presence, all I could see was that little boy and the joy that was on his face. It made it a lot easier to go to work in the morning in a country and culture that were not my own. After all these years, I can still see that kid in my mind. I have seldom seen such joy on the face of a child and over such a simple gift. When I think of him, I think about my opportunities and how if I had grown up somewhere else my life could have been very different.

THE VOICE OF PEACE

I was a CH46E helicopter pilot, flying missions off the coast of Beirut and also missions inside Lebanon, in and around Beirut, in 1983 and 1984. I was a member of Marine Medium Helicopter Squadron 261, or HMM-261 or just 261.

Between noon and 1600 each day, there was an AM station somewhere around Beirut that played rock and roll music. They identified their show as "The Voice of Peace." Someone in the squadron happened upon it while flying, tuning into the ADF (automatic direction finding) navigation radio, curious to see if there were any AM radio stations playing music around Beirut. There were a few, but it wasn't the kind of music anyone in the squadron could endure. However, those of us fortunate enough to be flying during that four-hour window could tune in and listen to the Police, Tears for Fears, Eagles, Big Country, Van Halen and other rock bands in that era.

It was a quirky, yet wonderful little thing that just happened somehow, but was greatly enjoyed by many of us pilots and aircrewmen while we flew missions around Beirut. For weeks, we had no idea where the radio station was located, because the ADF directional needle would never lock on any one location like it did for airports, the other Beirut radio stations, and other fixed locations. It was a mystery, but a welcomed mystery, nonetheless.

One day, I was flying a mission, minding my own business, when the USS Guam air boss (the ship's flight operations director) called me up and asked if I'd fly over to a sailboat that was coming a little uncomfortably close to the big helicopter ship. I was the closest aircraft to the contact, so I flew about three miles over to what looked like a tiny freighter or large sailboat and told the aircrew to aim their .50 caliber machine guns at the small vessel and, if they saw any fire from it, to open up.

Two guys came up on deck, hands and arms waving, obviously unarmed, with big smiles, just sort of saying, "Hello, nice to see you." They looked Middle Eastern to me, and when I told the air boss there were two unarmed men on their deck, the boss asked me to identify the two men's nationality. "Their nationality?" I asked.

The boss said, "Yeah, intel needs to know their nationality." That was a ridiculous ask but like many occasions in the military, ridiculous is sometimes the norm.

Not to come off too disrespectful to the Navy commander, I answered, "They're both of rag-head descent." There were no further anthropological type queries from the USS Guam. I had let them know my cultural expertise is always ready to play, especially when that sort of priority knowledge is paramount to the command intelligence structure instead of something inconsequential like: "Are they armed and are they on a course heading to the big Navy ship?"

I flew for a few more hours and had the ADF radio up as loud as I could, tuned to the great rock and roll music from "The Voice of Peace." At about 1600, I knew their broadcast would end soon.

They always started and ended their show with John Lennon's "Give Peace a Chance." On this particular day however, instead of the John Lennon song, a voice came on the air and said, "We'd like to end our broadcast and thank the helicopter flown by US Marines today who circled us and showed no harm to "The Voice of Peace."

TURKISH PRISON

While serving with the 22nd MAU in Beirut, I had a chance to pull liberty for a couple of days in Antalya, Turkey. I think I was the only Marine officer aboard the USS Pensacola when she pulled out of Beirut, since just about all my Marine friends had made previous runs to Naples. I had sailed over on the Pensacola, so I knew all of the officers on board and figured I'd just join them.

When we landed in Turkey, I hopped in a cab with a bunch of ensigns, pulled out my English/Turkish dictionary and asked him to "take us where the women are." We drove outside of town a short distance and we arrived at a fairly large concrete structure surrounded by a high fence with concertina at the top. We were expecting an area with bars or hotels and music; this plain, dilapidated, ugly building didn't fit the bill. Since we were well outside of town, I asked the cab to wait while we checked the place out.

When we got to the gate, there were armed guards and I quickly found one who spoke English. He explained that this was the women's prison, and the state did not provide meals. If the women here were to eat, either their families could bring them food, or they could sell themselves in order to eat. The guards collected and kept the money, and meals were brought to those who had money in their accounts.

We inquired further into the crimes committed by most of the women. He said some of them had done nothing at all. The government had found their husbands guilty of a crime and the husband, being the breadwinner, had exercised his option to allow his wife to serve his sentence for him. After all, few women had jobs and could not be expected to provide for a family. He said that often, after a husband had his wife incarcerated for his crime, he would abandon her, and she would have to fend for herself. So, the state had come up with the unusual government-operated cat house to keep the ladies from starving.

He gave us a tour and we walked through the foul smelling, dimly lit, dingy rooms. The doors were mostly open, except for those of the ladies who were cared for by families or were currently entertaining. One young girl appeared to be about eight months pregnant. The guard said the state provided no contraception and the ladies often got pregnant. This attracts less customers and, without funds in their accounts, they could starve. Also, if a woman returned home with a new child, the husband was within his rights to divorce her since the child was not his offspring. We took up a collection and put up enough money to feed the girl until she had the baby. It was too depressing for words.

Whenever I saw something like this in my travels it always made me thankful to be an American. We have our own strange customs, but I am still grateful for where I'm from and how I grew up. It also made me think of the old adage: "Tell it to the Marines." Over the years, I've told this story a number of times and always with the same result— jaw-dropping silence. People just can't believe such places exist. The places we went as Marines allowed us to see a side of the world most Americans know nothing about.

As I mentioned before, we were on liberty and had only a few hours to blow off six-months' worth of steam and pay. I had failed the young ensigns miserably with my first request for the cabbie to take us to "where the women are." I adjusted fire, went back to the cab and asked him, in Turkish, to take us to a bar. Just to be sure, I followed up with the word "raki," a Turkish alcoholic beverage. He smiled knowingly, chuckled, and drove back to town.

TRACK GUARDS REPORT

In the summer of 1979, I was summering on the Potomac with my friends at the Officer Candidate School at Brown Field on Marine Corps Base Quantico, Virginia. It was a ten-week program designed to measure fitness to lead as a Marine Officer. It is by far the most grueling and challenging training I ever endured. We lived in constant fear of failing the next inspection, of failing the next run, of being injured on one of the many obstacle courses, of breaking some long-revered rule we knew nothing about.

Academically, the course wasn't particularly challenging. The lecturer told us what would be on each test and we quickly knew what to expect. The physical part was very hard. We exercised in the wet grass before the sun came up, had an obstacle course or two, ran three miles and returned for an exercise session with the infamous Warrant Officer Brown, on loan, specifically to torture us, from the British Royal Marines.

If we weren't in the classroom or physically training, we were marching. We marched every day and everywhere. At first the instructors called basic cadence and commands for us. We learned the difference between our left and our right, column left and right, to the rear, and a few other basics. Soon though, we were assigned billets to demonstrate our abilities as leaders. One of the more difficult billets was that of platoon sergeant, since he marched the platoon everywhere. We were constantly on the move. The more senior billet holders, like company commander or company first sergeant, were more high-profile positions, but I always felt for the platoon sergeant and tried my best to hear the commands and execute with precision – one misstep could screw everybody up.

Our barracks sat on a steep bluff overlooking the Potomac River. Immediately behind the barracks was a road that curved, crossed the railroad tracks and then opened up onto the parade deck, a huge, paved lot where candidates could perform left shoulder arms, right oblique, to the rear march, and column of files to their hearts' content. An afternoon in the hot sun on the grinder was no picnic.

One morning we had returned from our run, showered, put on our uniforms, and formed up to march over to a classroom. We marched around the building and came upon the area most dreaded by anyone responsible for marching candidates. The next 20 seconds would be the most harrowing for the platoon sergeant, as so many commands needed to be given at precisely the correct instant. The sidewalk made a 90-degree turn, running parallel to the road.

"COLUMN LEFT....MARCH!"

"LEFT, RIGHT, LEFT."

So far, so good. The preparatory command and the command of execution were given on the correct foot. The platoon made a left-hand turn and managed to stay on the sidewalk and in step. Knowing that we were about to cross the road, the platoon sergeant needed road guards to block it so that some errant vehicle didn't mow us down.

"ROAD GUARDS OUT!"

"RIGHTLL, LEFT."

The first man in the first and third squads took off running, stopping in the street, standing at parade rest, and creating a path through which we would march unimpeded. We were nearing the end of the sidewalk which turned right. 30 yards up the road were the railroad tracks. At precisely the right moment:

"COLUMN RIGHT....MARCH!"

"TRACK GUARDS OUT!"

"LEFT, RIGHT, LEFT."

As soon as the platoon began making the right turn, the man at the front of the first and third squads took off running to the left and right sides of the road, looking down the tracks. Unlike the road guards who were human shields against oncoming traffic, the track guards would, when given the command, report on whether a train might be coming. Nothing looks worse in your Officer Qualification Record than an annotation that you marched a platoon to a classroom, only to have half of them run over by a train.

"RIGHTLL, LEFT."

We were all in the road and apparently no longer needed the protection of our human shields, so:

"ROAD GUARDS IN!"

This command returned the road guards to the last places in the first and third squads. Automobiles were to yield to pedestrians, particularly groups of 50 or more. We were now about 25 yards from the tracks. On the right-hand side of the road, you could see for some distance, but trains could pass our area rather quickly. Out went the command:

"TRACK GUARDS REPORT!"

Instantly:

"ALL CLEAR ON THE RIGHT!"

No report came from the left. You could almost hear the wheels turning in the platoon sergeant's head. His job is to call out commands and there is no "WHAT ABOUT THE LEFT" command.

So, he tried again:

"TRACK GUARDS REPORT!!!"

"ALL CLEAR ON RIGHT!!!"

Still nothing came from the left, and another plaintive scream from the platoon sergeant:

"TRACK GUARDS REEEEPORT!!!"

"ALL CLEAR ON THE RIGHT!!!"

Then a timid, nervous, questioning reply from the left: "I THINK we can make it."

"PLATOON HALT!!!" screamed the platoon sergeant.

We felt the rush of the wind a couple of seconds before the train actually appeared, doing about 40 miles an hour, passing no more than 20 feet in front of the platoon. In an instant the platoon sergeant was our hero, and the left track guard was known to be a complete idiot. We were all shaken but were soon laughing and mocking his "I THINK we can make it" reply.

The left track guard went home that very day. It was decided that his judgment was not in keeping with the highest traditions of our Corps. I wish I could remember the platoon sergeant's name. I would love to buy him a beer, just to hear him say what was going through his brain in those 20 seconds.

TWO WEDDINGS AND A FUNERAL

Marines are, by their nature, more adventurous than their civilian counterparts, so when it comes to weddings, their celebratory functions are typically well planned but on the edge. I was in a group of groomsmen who were to execute a sword arch and perform ushering duties at a wedding in Parkersburg, West Virginia.

Someone in our group discovered that there was a train which we could catch in Fayetteville, NC that would take us all the way to Charleston, WV, where the groom's people would pick us up. The ride was circuitous, traveling through Raleigh, Greensboro, north to Charlottesville, and west to Charleston. We piled into a couple of vehicles and drove over to Fayetteville, boarded and headed directly to the bar car. The groom, a fellow Marine, was to meet us in West Virginia, but we saw no reason the party shouldn't get started as long as we had a quorum.

We were doing shots, and beers, and more shots, and were most nearly wasted when the train pulled into Raleigh. We were soon joined, and delighted to be so, by a girls' softball team out of western North Carolina. They were an outgoing, gregarious lot, from some little college and seemed to have no one in charge of them. They were corn fed girls with some girth and substance and outnumbered us two to one, but we were Marine officers and accustomed to facing difficult odds. We fed them drinks and we all became better acquainted in the hours of travel that followed.

It turned out they were going to a tournament in Parkersburg, were staying in the same hotel as us, and enjoyed the company of drunken Marines. We were, in fact, drunken Marines, so it couldn't have worked out better. It was destiny. We invited them, not only to the wedding, but to the rehearsal dinner as well.

We arrived in Charleston and the parents of the bride were a bit taken aback, but the father of the groom (a Korea and Vietnam veteran Marine) applauded our initiative and welcomed the young ladies to the party. We had obviously crossed the line of decorum and had to help out with the bill for the rehearsal dinner, making the father of the bride happy. I don't think the bride ever got over the large, muscular girls who showed up at every event for the whole weekend wearing sweatpants. No lasting relationships were forged from our shenanigans, but when any of us gathered in the years that followed, the story was told and retold as a tale of classic Marine misbehavior.

*

At another wedding in Jacksonville, NC we had hoped to get the groom in such a state that we could fly him, as we had done his friend, to some exotic destination on the night before his wedding. He, being one of the smartest among us, had already checked on when the last plane would depart that night so he could make sure to only be a bit tipsy and wide awake at that hour.

We had gone down to Court Street and procured the services of two rambunctious ladies who were trusting enough (for the right price) to dance for the groom in a private residence. We had deliberately not sought the loveliest of the maidens, but rather the least desirable and covered in tattoos. They may well have looked cheap, but they cost us a pretty penny. They stayed late and helped us get our groom totally inebriated and, when he finally passed out, helped us load him into the car.

One member of our group had secured LZ Bluebird over on Camp Lejeune as a training area, so that we were sure he would not be disturbed. We placed some ponchos around the base of a tall, lone pine tree so he wouldn't be bothered by ants. We put a ten-foot chain around the base of the tree and padlocked the ends together. Being a Legal Officer, I had handcuffs, so we handcuffed him around the chain. We gingerly placed him in a sleeping bag and drove away. The next day, we went to pick him up about two hours before his wedding. I asked him, "Did you have any idea where you were?"

He replied, "When I woke up this morning, I looked around and noted that the trees were almost all long-leaf pines, so I knew I was still in the southeast and figured you'd get me to the wedding on time." And so, we did. This speaks highly of the training of a Marine officer, able to see through the fog of what must have been a horrendous hangover and still calmly and objectively assess his situation under the most dire of circumstances.

*

Since our Corps has long been the "first to fight," it draws a unique brand of individual who lives near the edge and is constantly aware that duty can take him to unsafe places. These long absences often do not make the heart grow fonder, but rather quite the opposite. I had a young Marine who did a terrific job for me in Beirut back in '83. He was promoted to sergeant at the end of our deployment and returned home to find that his wife had moved two lance corporals into their house and was sharing his bed with both.

She had a job delivering pizzas at night. Because of her special skills at delivering pizzas, she was requested by name by many of the young Marines living in barracks all over Camp Lejeune. Her tips were reputed to be substantial, such that she didn't mind when my man filed for divorce. They had two small children and he had no chance of gaining custody. His heart was broken, and he fell deeply into the bottle.

The Marines around him tried to steady him and to cover for him, but he quickly grew worse and worse. I was serving as legal officer, so he no longer worked for me, but some of my men from Beirut brought him to me and we talked. I tried to be encouraging and to perk him up, but he was deep down the rabbit hole.

A couple of weeks later, on a long straightaway between Swansboro and Jacksonville, his car went off the road at a very high speed and he died in the wreck. He was alone and no one could remember him going out alone before. He didn't hit the brakes. The car went airborne and then went end over end several times. He wasn't wearing a seat belt.

The next morning the woman who had driven him to this appeared in my office to ask when she could expect the Serviceman's Life Insurance (SGLI) payment. His body was not yet cold, and she wanted his life insurance! I told her there would be an investigation, but that SGLI payment was not contingent upon cause of death. I suggested that we might want to get him buried before we worry about his insurance money. I asked if she needed a chaplain to help with informing his children. She said she already told them, but I gave her the chaplain's number anyway.

Later that day, the Marines who were inventorying his gear called me and asked me to come down to the barracks. I came down and they showed me his will, which they had found in his desk. The will specifically left nothing to his ex-wife. He specified that she was to get nothing, that everything was to go to his children. All he really had was SGLI ($35,000) and a small savings account. I knew that if we sent the will with the personal effects to his home, the wife would find it and throw it away, then take the money. I was not legally allowed to hold it out of the inventory items, so I was at a loss for how to get the money to the kids.

I called base legal with my idea, and they blessed it. He was from upstate North Carolina and was to be buried back home in a few days. I got Staff Sergeant Rick Watson placed on the funeral detail to carry out the plan. I called the Marine's father and told him of our dilemma. I told him to have his grandkids and his lawyer present in his home before the funeral.

As expected, his ex-wife dropped the kids off with their grandparents and left with her boyfriend. Watson arrived with the honor detail and brought his personal effects into the house and presented them to the children. Grandpa helped them open the boxes. They "discovered" the will and he suggested that the paper was very important, that they should give it to the nice man (his attorney), and that he would take care of it for them. In front of 20 witnesses, they agreed. The lawyer took the will and as far as I know, the money was placed in a trust for the children to have when they became of age.

At the funeral, Watson presented the flag to his mother and his kids. His Mom kissed Watson and thanked him for looking after her son's children. Even in death, Marines will look out for each other.

UNARMED PEACEFUL CUBANS

I was a member of the 22nd MAU and a squadron pilot in HMM-261 during Operation Urgent Fury in Grenada. Castro and his Cuban communist thugs invaded the island, murdered the president and installed a puppet leader in October 1983. What was never reported by the American press is that there was a very good reason the Marines invaded and gave the island back to the Grenadians, freeing them from the communist oppression.

The reason you probably read and heard about from the American press was that Reagan was a cowboy and wanted to inject unjust American imperialism throughout the Caribbean. That was not and still is not true. The Marines with whom I served, including myself, couldn't care less if you believe the American press or not. We know the truth. We saw the truth and it wasn't simply "our truth." Sorry that you didn't get it from Time, Newsweek, U.S. News & World Report, the Washington Post, the LA Times, or the New York Times. President Reagan would not allow any press on the island during the first few days of the invasion. I don't know why but I'm glad he did that.

One of the missions I flew was to take the theater commander, Admiral Metcalf from the USS Independence, to Salines Airfield on Grenada, where he would meet the press on the first day they were allowed on the island: October 28, 1983, five days after Urgent Fury began. I was Bob Turner's copilot that day. Metcalf wanted to arrive at Salines twenty minutes before the Air Force C-130, loaded with American press personnel, arrived.

We landed at Salines, taxied to a spot where we had parked a few days earlier, and shut down. The admiral told us he wanted to leave in about two hours, so Bob and I gave ourselves a tour of the surprisingly large airport terminal building that was under construction, being built by Chinese, Cuban, East German, and Russian contractors. These contractors had been kicked out and sent back to Cuba after they were all rounded up by the Marines a day or so earlier. Surprisingly, instead of wearing civilian clothing, they all wore military uniforms...with ranks.

The Salines runway is a little over 9,000 feet long. That's surprisingly long for such a small island. Bob and I noticed that when we began our self-guided tour. The terminal building had two very distinct areas. One area was quite huge and was designed apart from the much smaller passenger terminal area. The walls of the larger portion were all made of about one-foot-thick reinforced concrete walls, probably to protect the building in case Grenada's ancient volcano decided to blow.

The control tower was imbedded into the top of the closest ridge line from the terminal building. It was also built of extremely thick-walled, steel-reinforced concrete. It looked very similar to the WWII German pill boxes that were imbedded into the tops of the ridge lines at Normandy Beach. Apparently, dormant volcanoes tend to strike airports.

Before Bob and I went into the terminal building, the American press arrived and ran quickly to where Admiral Metcalf held the first press conference. Bob and I were nearby and watched as about three dozen of the rudest, most arrogant, self-centered, spoiled rotten adult brats forced themselves onto Admiral Metcalf, a few of them screaming accusations into his face instead of questions.

He and his aide pushed them back and his aide held his arm out between the angry brats and the admiral, letting them know he wasn't afraid to let them have it. When a sound crew person with a ten-foot boom mike started to purposely knock his microphone into the admiral's forehead, I came unglued and started towards the boom operator. Bob grabbed me and said quietly and forcefully, "No, Ken. We don't want you to be on the front page of every newspaper beating the crap out of a poor civilian." He was right and we headed up the hill to check out the airport control tower.

On our way up the hill, a hysterical and sobbing Grenadian woman ran up to us and began telling us what had happened to her just after the Cubans took over the island. She told us that the Cubans forced her and her neighbors into the streets and asked for volunteers to join the new People's Revolutionary Army. When no one responded, they pulled a little girl out of the crowd and shot her in the head. Her distraught father ran out to his dead daughter, screaming in anguish. He was then shot in the head and the Cuban recruiters turned to the crowd and asked them if there was anyone else who refused to volunteer.

Bob and I were more than shocked and of course felt desperately sad for this sobbing woman, and at the same time, we were glad there would be no more events like that occurring on the island. Bob and I pointed to the crowd of American journalists and told her to go down the hill and tell them her story. The world had to know just how terrible these Marxist-communists were to these innocent people, and we assumed some national magazine or newspaper would tell her story. A few months later when we finally received all the national magazines covering Urgent Fury, Bob and I searched for the coverage of that sad woman's horrendous experience. To this day, it has never been reported.

Bob and I went back down the hill and went into the terminal building. The small passenger area was nice, and we followed the large staircase up to the second floor and into a very long room. The doorway was not framed for a door because we had to step over a ten-inch-high wall base to enter the room. There was rebar sticking up from the base so it was apparent that the doorway would be framed in and separate from the passenger side of the terminal building.

Another room, about 20 by 20 feet was open to the long room. It had a few drains in the floor and was rough plumbed with a dozen or so shower heads and shower faucets. Bob and I had been to a lot of airports, both military and civilian but had never seen a long barracks-like room with a large shower room next to it. At the end of the room was a doorway which led into a thirty or forty foot long by six-foot-wide room adjacent to the larger room. It was plumbed to be a men's head for about ten urinals and five or six toilets along one wall and 20 or so sinks along the opposite wall. It was only accessible through the large barracks-like room and from an outside door, which opened up onto concrete stairs down the non-runway side of the building.

Bob and I walked outside and down the stairs and found a door leading into the large ground floor portion of the main terminal building. It was definitely not accessible to the passenger area. Its walls were the thickest of all and the concrete floors had lots of construction debris strewn about. It looked all-the-world to Bob, and I, like a concrete fortified tactical air control center. The large area upstairs looked like a very large barracks facility, something neither of us had ever seen at a civilian airport. Keep in mind, neither of us had degrees in architecture, airport design, nor journalism, so it was just our best guess based on what we saw and deduced. We figured the American journalists would tour the building and objectively report their findings in the national publications.

When the admiral was ready to go, we launched to fly him around parts of the island where Bob and I believed there were no Cuban strongholds. We ended up flying for about seven hours that day. We both talked a little about what the press would report regarding our operation and felt confident the American public would find out and be proud of the president and of the Marines because we gave Grenada back its freedom. When we finally got the American publications about a month later, we were flabbergasted that all of the publications called the cruel communist military invaders, "unarmed and peaceful" Cuban construction workers. There wasn't one word written about how the Cubans terrorized the innocent people of Grenada, nor about the future tactical air center the Soviet, Chinese, and Cuban communists were constructing.

UNLUCKY HOG BOARD

Marines are young, energetic, fun-loving, virile stallions and they attract adventurous, voluptuous, fertile, sexy young women. Well, sometimes anyway. Marines are proud but protective of their girlfriends. When you live on a base with 20,000 male Marines and a fraction of that many women, you become protective. They are proud of their women and there is something in them that wants everyone to know, "This is MY girl!" It is likely that this is the reason they carry and show off pictures of their girlfriends and sometimes wives.

Someone long before my time decided that it would be a good idea to make a proper display of the women of their unit. Each man put a picture of his woman on a piece of plywood, and they would hang this homage collage somewhere appropriate so that all could admire the conquests of the unit, sort of like battle streamers on the unit's flag. This is what passes for art in the Marine Corps. We don't get to see a lot of beauty in the places we are sent, so we make our own.

You may not think a bunch of wallet-sized senior portraits of eighteen-year-old honeys from Nowheresville, Arkansas, mounted on a three-foot by four-foot piece of half-inch exterior plywood is art, but to us it is. The further you are from home, the prettier it gets. She may be a zit-faced heifer, but to a Marine in love, she is the most gorgeous creature on the planet. Such is love.

Sometime after this type of wall covering became popular, someone else decided that it needed a name. This made sense. Everything should have a name. The one they chose made it necessary for the women being displayed never to know that they were on display. The chosen name was "Hog Board." I don't believe General Lejeune ever officially sanctioned either the name or the practice, but even without official recognition, it became, throughout the Corps, a Hog Board. They were everywhere. Some might well have been named, "She walks in beauty, like the night," but, to be fair, most were appropriately named, Hog Board.

While serving in Beirut in 1982, my men asked if it would be okay for them to hang a Hog Board over the switchboard in the Comm Shack. I had no objections as long as they kept it mostly clean. We frequently had Congress members stop by to check on us and to get briefed on how and what we were doing. These were mostly boondoggles that would put them on the ground. They'd borrow my helmet and flak jacket to have their picture taken so their constituents would see the picture and think they had elected John Wayne. They usually stayed about 20 minutes and flew off to some awful destination in Switzerland to recover.

We couldn't have these Congressmen stepping into our Shack and seeing photos of some nubile, unclad princess cavorting above our switchboard. They might get the wrong idea as to the morality of the young warriors protecting our nation. The men said they'd keep it clean and so it was hung. It stayed up for about a month and got quite a bit of conversation.

One of my collateral duties was to pay the Marines sitting on the ships, anchored off Beirut. I had to hop ship to ship with a briefcase full of money and hold pay call somewhere on each ship, then fly to the next. I always tried to finish on the Pensacola because I sailed over on her and had some gear there. I would do a load of laundry, have a hot meal, sleep in a bed and fly back the next morning.

One night, I was in the wardroom and the ship's Communication Officer, and I began talking about the similarities and differences in green (land) and blue (ocean) communications. He was lamenting the sorry state of morale among his men. They had not touched dirt in months and were tired of the day-in, day-out tedium of sitting at anchor. I told him my men would love to take advantage of beds, laundry, and meals that were available on-board ship. We discussed some cross training and soon found ourselves in the Captain's stateroom. We agreed that I would take two of his men back with me and cross train them on green gear. In return, I would send him two of my men and he would train them on blue gear on the ship.

At night, from atop my building, his men would train mine on the use of signal lamps or flashing light. You could see the ship from my building, so this gave us an opportunity to train and to practice Morse code. This was very well received by both units, and I had a line of volunteers who wanted to spend time on the ship.

For the first two weeks, everything worked great. The Marines loved their time on the ship, and the rust-pickers (Navy guys) were enjoying their time ashore. The Pensacola's Captain had called Stars and Stripes to get them to do a story on the Navy-Marine Team working together in perfect harmony. All was going great and then we brought the third Navy pair ashore.

They ate their MREs, toured the area, and got in their cots for some rest. They were going to train on the graveyard shift, coming on at 2300 and being relieved at 0700. One of the pair, Seaman Fleetwood out of Vandalia, Ohio, was assigned to train on the switchboard. This was the quietest time of the day, so we set up some practice calls for him to patch through and soon he got the hang of it. At around 0130 Fleetwood was looking around the room at all the radios, antennae, wire spools and what not, when he spied the Hog Board. As he perused the pulchritude he stopped and made an ominous gasp. Corporal Rodriguez inquired as to the problem.

"What's my girlfriend's picture doing on your wall?"

"Your girlfriend? Which one?"

"This one! We were dating for six months before I shipped out!"

"Oh wow! That's Vesey's girl." One of the Marines ran back to the sleeping quarters, woke poor LCpl Vessey, and summoned him to the comm shack.

It turned out that Vesey was from Xenia, Ohio and the sweet young thing in question was from Dayton, about halfway between Vandalia and Xenia. The sailor produced the exact same picture as the one Vesey had so proudly posted. She not only dated both of them before they left for military service but had continued corresponding with weekly letters to each of them. Both men were crushed and of course blamed her and each other for the love triangle.

There was some cursing, and each challenged the other's masculinity, lineage, and maternal relationship. Coarse language led to fisticuffs and my staff sergeant was called to separate the two. Regrettably, the next day I was forced to send the young sailors back to the ship, Fleetwood with a few bumps and a black eye. Whatever story he told when he returned doesn't matter. Other sailors now viewed us as inhospitable hosts and no longer wanted to play cowboy.

Likewise, my Marines were not so excited to go to the ship. The Hog Board was empty by 0730. The men declared that they would rather not know that their girl was unfaithful than to find out 6,000 miles from home. The Hog Board had become a symbol that made them all question whether their lass could be trusted.

Such is love. Ignorance is bliss.

URGENT FURY

On Tuesday, October 25, 1983, two days after the Marine barracks in Beirut was blown up, the Marines in the 22nd MAU invaded the small island of Grenada. Grenada is part of the Lesser Antilles island chain in the southern Caribbean Sea. I was a copilot and a member of HMM-261. In addition to being a squadron pilot, I was the classified material control coordinator and handled all of the classified message boards for the squadron in addition to classified documents. Our MAU was supposed to relieve the battle-tested Marines of the 24th MAU in Beirut, Lebanon, who had experienced the new surge of hostile fire from the Lebanese terrorists, culminating with the barracks bombing on Sunday, October 23, 1983.

We left Norfolk on Monday, October 17, 1983, headed east and on October 20, we passed Bermuda on our way to the Mediterranean. The next morning, I got up early, went down to the wardroom to grab a bite and then to the ship's message center to pick up the messages and get the message boards ready for the squadron command staff. At breakfast, several Navy officers told us that the ship's heading was 210 and had been all night. Yeah, okay, I thought, let's go on the snipe hunt with the squids so they can have their first laugh. It turns out, they weren't kidding.

We were headed for some small island in the southern Caribbean to remove Cubans who had taken over the island. Cubans were communists. We didn't like communists. In fact, in 1983, we were several years into a long and expensive Cold War against the communists of Cuba, the Soviet Union, and their satellites. And they definitely didn't like the United States. We were going to assault this small island and remove the Cubans who had violently taken over Grenada. The name of the operation was Urgent Fury and the Marines of the 22nd MAU were tasked to eliminate the Cuban threat.

Every pilot in the squadron had a flying assignment on the first day of the assault. Mine was to fly as copilot in the squadron search and rescue aircraft. Scott Forrest was the aircraft commander and both of us were disappointed we were not involved in the initial airborne assault with the infantry. It was what we trained for and what all Marines hoped to get a chance to experience at least once in their lives. However, our planned mission of two hours of flying in circles on the starboard side of the USS Guam, while the rest of the squadron performed their assault mission and then returned, didn't quite turn out as planned.

The main assault brief began at 0230 in the morning. The squadron ready room was not big enough to handle the number of pilots and aircrew who attended the brief, so it was held in the ship's wardroom. Since none of us slept the night before, we milled around the wardroom about a half hour or so before the brief, trying not to be worried that some of us might not be coming back.

Before the brief, I sat in the small anteroom off of the wardroom and played acey-deucey with Jeb Seagle. We tried to take our minds off what was to come and made the typical braggadocious comments, trying to intimidate each other into losing the game. It was one of those silly things that we all did at the time when we played acey-deucy. It was a way to make each other laugh as well. Jeb and I drank coffee, tried to take our minds off reality, laughed a bit and hoped we would soon put into practice all of our years of training. Jeb was an AH-1 Cobra pilot, and he would soon be firing his weapons at what Newsweek, Time and U.S. News & World Report called peaceful and unarmed Cuban construction workers. Jeb didn't return that day. I'm so grateful I got to spend that time with him before the brief. I cherish those few minutes and think about him, his ear-to-ear smile, and his good sense of humor often. Jeb was shot down by the peaceful and unarmed Cuban construction workers.

Later on, that morning, while Scotty and I were boring circles on the starboard side of the USS Guam, we monitored both the UHF and FM radios and heard what the rest of the squadron was involved in as they dropped marine infantry onto Pearls Airfield on the east side of the island. Sometime later, we heard Pat Guigerre call that Jeb and his pilot, Tim Howard, had been shot down.

Jeb was knocked out by the anti-aircraft fire while Tim's right wrist and right hand was blown off. Tim's legs were also badly wounded. Losing power and the aircraft falling from the sky, Tim used what was left of his legs to hold the cyclic steady and used his left hand to lower the collective and then raise it for landing. He had to use his knees to try to flare the nose up to lose airspeed and to lower the nose to land. His hard landing of the now powerless aircraft woke up Jeb. Tim wasn't able to fully egress from his burning aircraft. Jeb helped him get out, pulled him away from the aircraft, and hoped to find Marines in the vicinity to come to their aid.

Under extreme small arms fire, Major Mel DeMars, copilot Captain Larry King, and Staff Sergeant Kelley Neidigh landed their CH-46 nearby where Kelley, in the face of small arms fire, ran to Tim, picked him up and carried him into the back of the aircraft, rescuing Tim and taking him safely back to the USS Guam. Before then, Jeb had been captured and subsequently beaten, tortured to death, and left face down on a nearby beach. Time magazine took a picture of Jeb's brutalized body and placed the photograph within the article that lauded and praised the peaceful and unarmed Cuban construction workers.

During the time the two were on the ground after they had been shot down, the other Cobra, flown by Captain Pat Giguere and Lieutenant Jeff Scharver, was firing weapons to keep the Cubans from reaching Tim and Jeb. Scotty and I heard Pat declare that he was out of bullets and couldn't provide close air support for Mel's CH-46 and for Tim and Jeb, so the only thing he was able to do was try to draw fire to his aircraft and hopefully occupy the enemy long enough for Tim's rescue. It worked but it cost Pat and Jeff their lives. They were both killed instantly by the same anti-aircraft weapon that shot down Tim and Jeb.

Scott and I did partake in some minor operations on the first day and we flew off and on for nearly seven hours, finally landing just after 2300. One of our missions was to fly a few wounded special operations soldiers from a smaller Navy ship to the USS Guam and its small hospital. They were all dressed in civilian clothes with long hair and facial hair and were all badly wounded with bloody bandages over their wounds. One of them was missing his right shoulder and arm. Another died on the short flight to the Guam. Horrific scenes to be sure but there was no time to be shocked. The missions and flying kept on throughout the day.

Huey pilot, Captain Robin Sides, remained in the cockpit and flew for over 24 hours the first day because the only other qualified Huey aircraft commander, Captain Mike Jinnett, was on the other side of the island supporting Marines still operating at Pearls Airfield. Robin was the busiest one that day. This is what I remember about the first day of Operation Urgent Fury.

After we left Grenada, word about Tim Howard's condition trickled in slowly. There was no email, cell phones, or any other modern electronic communications back then. We had radio message traffic and snail mail, period, to communicate. A letter often took two to three weeks to get from the USS Guam to a loved one and then two or three weeks to get a loved one's reply.

We had heard rumors about who visited Tim while he was recovering at Bethesda; what Tim did after he was shot down; and also heard that Tim wanted to remain in the Marine Corps sans right hand from his wrist down and without the ability to perform a PFT due to his wounded leg. Since none of us were there with Tim nor actually saw what Tim did just before he was rescued, we had to rely on what someone back in the States was telling us and that information was several weeks old.

We had heard that President Reagan visited Tim at Bethesda, but it turns out that it was actually the Secretary of the Navy, and Navy reserve A-6 BN, John Lehman. I do believe the rumor that while Tim was waiting for Kelley to pick him up and carry him into Mel's CH-46, as the Cubans were approaching, Tim gave the Cubans an international sign of peace with his left hand, except without using his index finger. Some know the gesture as flipping the bird but since they were all unarmed Cuban construction workers, the American press would have been delighted to know Tim's intention was only meant to be positive and uplifting for the peaceful Cubans. That would have fit Tim's personality after what they had just done to him, and we most certainly wanted it to be true.

Tim did in fact receive a medical waiver and stayed in the Marine Corps. He was an inspiration to all of us in HMM-261 and the 22nd MAU before and after he was shot down. He was also an inspiration to anyone who met him after that because of his success after being so severely wounded.

No surprise though, Tim is a Marine.

WRONG WAY JOSE!

Early in my second WestPac cruise and new as a Helicopter Aircraft Commander (HAC) I discovered how much you had to keep questioning everything to stay ahead of the curve as we used to call it. At first you think you're the new guy out there in the fleet, but you soon learn that you are not alone – there are others who are new, too, and you are often putting great trust in these folks who you may never know, but with whom you have to deal with every day you fly.

One example: We were in the middle of the Pacific Ocean doing flight operations of various kinds. There were troop movements between ships for planning work. There were mail runs between ships to deliver the mail that had arrived on the LHA. There were food and other supply runs to help with this or that shortage etc.

On this particular day it was clear, ceiling and visibility were unrestricted (we called it "CAVU"). It was a great day to be flying. We typically carried enough fuel for a little over 2 hours of flight time. Anything over 2.0 hours and you were in your final reserve – no problem if you were arriving in the pattern and the decks were clear and you were being cleared for landing. On a clear day, no problem - a comfortable landing on the LHA for refueling was pretty much a certain thing.

I had completed several short missions during my first hour, then had done an approach back to the LHA for practice that took us about 15 minutes more. So, at that moment, I had about 0 + 45 minutes of fuel remaining to get back on the deck with an additional 20 minutes of Reserve to spare. Reserve equated to about 110 lbs. of fuel per side in each tank. Our Naval Air Training and Operating Procedures Standardization (NATOPS) manual told us we had to be on deck by 200 lbs. Due to gauge variance and fuel condition, concerns of low fuel air ingestion and a number of other potentialities, the aircraft could flameout anytime below 200 lbs. / side.

Some details for those curious. The CH-46E in the mid-1980's had a range of about 160 nautical miles (nm) or a radius of 80 nm. We typically burned JP-5/8 fuel and carried about 330 gallons per sponson fuel tank for a total of 660 gallons. JP-8 weighs in at 6.7 pounds per gallon, so when full, we were carrying about 4,422 lbs. of fuel total or about 2,200 lbs. / side in each sponson tank. All but 200 lbs. were usable. We burned about 2200 lbs. fuel per hour total for the aircraft or 1100 lbs. per engine / side. This equates to a burn rate of 19-20 lbs./minute, or 330 gallons per hour or 5.5 gallons per minute. Our cockpit gauges read fuel state in lbs. per side starting with a full tank on each side reading between 2200 (2400lbs was the theoretical max.). So, at 75 minutes into the flight, I had burned about 1500lbs of the 2200lbs I had started with. I had 700 lbs. per side remaining. So far so good.

So, at this moment, I was called to take on a new mission to another ship, an LST. I gave my fuel status, and they confirmed the mission as "suitable" and gave me directions or "Pigeons" with a bearing of 1200 the heading being away from the ship's formation. As we were flying away from the LHA – our primary fuel station – I kept a watch on our fuel. On a CAVU day like this I could probably see a ship at about 15-20 miles depending on the ocean haze. I saw nothing. 20 miles would only cost me about 110 lbs. of fuel. No problem. I had 700, but that 700 lbs. had to get be there and back home. I droned on. Still no ship, no wake trail. Nothing. I was out bound now for just over 25 minutes. Not a crisis, but If I didn't see this ship soon, I'd be getting deep into my reserve when I returned. At this point I called to question the Pigeons – Negative on the ship. Request check Pigeons. I continued on, away from the LHA as I waited. Silence. Then another voice came on the radio asking for my bearing. I replied that the directions had been given as bearing 120 degrees from the ship. I was then commanded to reverse directions 180 degrees and continue on to my destination ship. I then gave my fuel state and again there we silence. At that point the Ship's Captain, call sign "Fox Black" came on the radio and requested my state again.

What had happened was that a junior radarman had given us directions 180 degrees backwards and was running us out to sea with no ship ahead at all and no place for us to get emergency fuel. The ship had to divert its course to steam toward me and I towards it. I entered the pattern with about 250 lbs. per side and landed uneventfully, but it had been close. Another 2 or 3 minutes further on the wrong bearing and I wouldn't have made it home without going under 200 lbs. per side.

I was lucky that the Ship's Captain was as good as he was. He regularly monitored all the ship frequencies as well as all the squadron frequencies. He knew where each of his aircraft were located. He regularly would come on the air and over-ride another ship's Captain (usually a Lt Cmdr on the smaller ships) to ensure that the ship gave us safe winds for landing or safe pitch and roll.

I learned from that experience to never trust anything that didn't feel right. This time it was on a CAVU day. The next time it was going to be different.

VIP VISIT

In the mid 80's I was stationed at MCAS Cherry Point. I was assigned to fly "Pedro" as a search and rescue pilot. My collateral duty was the assistant aircraft maintenance officer. The squadron was a mix of two C9B aircraft, four T39's, and four CH46's. Everyday operations ranged from launching the C9's for extended trips overseas, to routine training flights for both T39's and the CH46's.

I was summoned into the CO's office early one morning and was informed that our "routine week" had just ended. I was informed that within the next three days a delegation of all the new senators and congressmen, accompanied by the Commandant of the Marine Corps would be guests in our area. I was also told to find alternate parking for all of our aircraft and to basically make all our workspaces look brand new. Oh, and make sure no Marines are in the area while they are here.

The day prior to the arrival, we managed to clear our entire ramp area so that one of every type of aircraft the Marine Corps owned could be put on static display. All of our maintenance spaces were subjected to complete field days, virtual rehabs, and were inspected by every officer from the Commanding General on down.

The day of the big show arrived. We had placed the on-duty SAR helicopter in the hangar, attached to a tug, just in case there was an actual SAR mission. The only personnel left in our spaces were the CO/XO and the crew for the SAR aircraft.

The two C9's taxied in, shut down, and started discharging the VIP's. Those of us in the SAR crew were observing the melee out of the window by maintenance control when suddenly the door was violently jerked open. After a startling moment, I found myself staring face to face with General Gray, Commandant of the Marine Corps. A little startled also, General Gray stepped back and proceeded to inspect me from head to toe.

I guess he was a little taken aback by our orange flight suits because his first words were, "What the hell are you, the Great Pumpkin?" I proceeded to tell him that we were the on-duty crew for Pedro, the search and rescue helicopters. He chuckled a little bit and asked what exactly was an SAR helicopter. I relayed to him a brief description of the difference between a fleet CH46 and the SAR version and offered to show him. He quickly agreed to a tour of Pedro.

We walked to the hangar, and I escorted the general aboard the aircraft. We both entered the cockpit and sat down. I (very professionally, I might add) began to explain all the differences between the SAR bird and those in the fleet. I took time to explain the added navigational and other systems that were unique to the SAR aircraft.

About ten or 15 minutes into the lesson, the general glared over at me and stated, "Well, I can tell you, there's one thing wrong with this helicopter!" When I asked what that was, General Gray responded, "There's nowhere to spit while you're flying!" Nonplussed, I opened the map case and handed the general a Pepsi can with the lid already removed with a John Wayne. He immediately stuffed his jaw with chewing tobacco and replied, "I guess I was mistaken. This SOB has everything."

The general and I remained in the cockpit for quite a while, each of us enjoying our tobacco vice. After some time, the general inquired if there was a back way out of the hangar. I showed him the rear doors and, turning back to me, smiling, he said thanks and left. Several minutes later a pair of personal armed security guard Marines rushed up to me in the hangar. They breathlessly asked me if I had seen General Gray. I told them nope, hadn't seen him. They then rushed off.

The following day at a meeting, the base CO relayed that General Gray had somehow "showed up" in one of the Harrier squadron workspaces and was livid about what he saw going on there. He was also upset about this, about that, but apparently, he was very pleased with his visit to the SAR helicopter. My CO looked right at me and said, "I probably don't want to know."

VISUAL AIDS

I learned early on that Marines respond well to visual aids. It helps them understand and learn better, so I always had plenty of hands-on, visual aids to help my young Marines grasp the material. Several of my Staff NCOs also used this technique, so we were pretty consistent in our approach to teaching.

In the early 80's, when a new man came on board, we felt it best to get him on the right path right away. Young Marines leave recruit training with Eagles, Globes and Anchors gleaming in their eyes ready to defeat the enemies of America single handedly if necessary. After a few months at their primary MOS training, some of them have fallen into some of their old civilian habits; or worse, they have been exposed to the rotten apples of the Corps and are moving, or have already moved, to the dark side.

My Gunny and I thought it best to let them know on day one how our platoon ran and to point them to those who could help them stay on the straight and narrow. I should say that we met with limited success in this regard, but our cause was just.

When a new man came to me, I would put him at ease, have him sit down and talk about where he was from, where was his family, if he had a girlfriend and where she might be, why the Marine Corps and what were his goals while serving in the Corps. Mostly, it was a get-to-know-you session and I'd give him resources inside and outside the platoon that could help him achieve those goals.

I told him that there were troublemakers who were going nowhere and that he should stay clear of them. I gave him the names in his chain of command so that he always had someone to call for help. I told him to stay off Court Street in Jacksonville, because the people, particularly the women, were not interested in his future, only his money and they would leave him drunk, broke and, too often, in jail.

I even told him that the Marine who was standing duty had my personal number and that I was usually good for bail money. In fact, I made it a point to cash my paycheck and take the money home on payday, so that I'd have bail money over the weekend. I'd deposit whatever I had the next banking day. We would walk through his sparse SRB (Service Record Book) and talk of his opportunities if he could keep his nose clean and apply himself.

Then I would get a little more philosophical. I would reach into my desk drawer and pull out a small green plastic soldier and a little radio. "Look, this is you. You came to work this morning and you're working on the radios, keeping them clean, identifying those that don't work and ordering new parts. You're doing a great job!" This always brought a smile.

Then I pulled out a GI Joe (Marine version, about ten inches high) and said, "This is me. I'm sitting at my desk doing all kinds of paperwork. Here are some reports that the Colonel wants. Here are some fitness reports and proficiency and conduct marks that need to be turned in to admin so that the men in the platoon will qualify for promotion. Here is a report with their rifle scores and here are their PFT scores that all have to be entered into their SRBs. Here I am signing them up for additional schools that will teach them skills they will need to make them competitive. Please note that you are still over here working on the radios and particularly notice that I am not paying close attention to you because I have these other things keeping me busy. As a matter of fact, I am facing the other way. Why do you suppose I'm not watching you? After all, you work for me."

"I don't know, sir." Always the same response.

"Well, it's because THIS GUY lives near our village!" I said, as I pulled out a 16-inch-high Godzilla and slammed him on the desk. "This is the commanding officer, Lt Col Lynch! He is waiting for the reports on how many radios are working and how everybody did on the PFT, and how many haven't been to the rifle range. I am always looking out to make sure he's happy. Unlike the real Godzilla this one thrives on paperwork. So, every day, I fill out the paperwork to keep him away from our village. I can only do that if you are doing your job, making all the comm gear work. Do you know what would happen if I spent all of my time watching you to be sure that you are doing your job?"

"No sir."

"Well, Godzilla here would bring his giant self-down to our village and kick the lieutenant's ass!"

Here I would slam Godzilla into the GI Joe, making him fly across the desk towards the young PFC.

"Now, this is a most unpleasant experience for me, but I have survived. What do you suppose happens next?"

"The lieutenant kicks my ass, sir."

"Not at all. I have the Gunny and several corporals kick your ass, because I don't want Godzilla here to see all that PFC blood all over my neatly pressed cammies, but I think you get the general idea. So, in order to avoid all of this bloodshed, what can we count on you to do?"

"To do my job to the best of my ability, sir!"

"Outstanding, Marine! Please step over to the Gunny's desk so that you can learn about the way Jacksonville works."

The Gunny would go into his pitch: "Welcome to Camp Lejeune and Jacksonville, NC. You probably have already noticed that there are a great deal more men here than women. You have arrived here without a woman of your own, so you, like the tens of thousands of other young Marines, will be looking for one to satisfy your many needs. Let me explain. Here we have two saltshakers and one pepper shaker. The saltshakers represent the Marines, and the pepper shaker represents the women, age 18 to 40, residing in the area. At any given time, about half of the Marines are deployed somewhere on the planet."

Readjusting in his seat, the Gunny continued, "Here goes a saltshaker now. It's going to the Med for the next six months. Look what happens when the boat leaves. The pepper shaker has moved in with the other saltshaker. This is likely to create conflict when the first saltshaker returns. It always does. Please don't get too attached to your pepper shaker while living here at Camp Lejeune and try not to tap into another Marine's pepper supply, unless you are prepared to do battle. Always remember son, if she left him, she'll leave you and she probably ain't worth getting all cut up over. Welcome to Camp Lejeune!"
With that, we'd cut him loose and bail him out of jail the following payday.
You saved our lives. Thanks Tony
On the sixth of January 1984, the Marines in Lebanon were preparing to leave Beirut International Airport and return to the ships located off the coast of Lebanon. Enemy attacks were increasing daily, and threats of another bombing were getting more frequent and the "peace" mission just wasn't working and it wasn't worth losing more Marines. The Marines would finally be flown back to the ships in early February.
Flights from Lebanon's Ministry of Defense to Larnaca, Cyprus and back again were increasing daily with US state department officials. They were there to end the "peace" mission the Marines implemented for them for several years.

Tony and I briefed at 4:30 am, the typical time for all our flights that would be working out of the airport all day (the duty CH-46) with the hope of returning to the ship around 4 pm (1700), have an illegal beer or stiff drink, smoke a few cigarettes, and watch the evening movie in the wardroom after chow. Late afternoon, around 4:30 each day was the time the shooting started, and it lasted each evening until 10 to 11 pm. This day would be a little different.

Tony and I were tasked to work for Major Sublette (Spanky) all day. Spanky was the aviation coordinator and controller at the airport. He was a good guy but expected his aircrew to accomplish their missions and make the Marines proud with no compromises. Failure was never an option for him and none of us were ever interested in failure so we all got along swimmingly.

Tony and I flew several tasks around Beirut with lots of flights from the airport to the Ministry of Defense (MOD) located up in the mountains overlooking Beirut. We also flew from the airport to various ships during the day as well. As the afternoon got closer to its end, Spanky told Tony and I plus Mike Jinnet and Frank McKinney, the duty Huey pilots would have to stay until members of the state department and several Marines were finished at the MOD. Mike and Frank would fly the state folks to Larnaca and we would return the Marines back to the USS Guam.

Our aircraft encountered a problem earlier that had we shut down, we would not be able to restart the aircraft. So, we sat in the aircraft for several hours. Begging Spanky to

replace us with another aircraft and crew proved pointless. He said our mission was mandatory and that he didn't have time to brief another crew with an "up" aircraft. He flew 46's and knew that as long as our APU kept running in flight, we could accomplish the mission, even though our aircraft was not officially considered mission capable. I tried to argue with him that as the aircraft commander, I knew the aircraft wasn't mission capable. He let me know under no uncertain terms, there would be severe consequences if I made that decision...so we waited and waited.
At about 2200 that night, Tony, and I, flew up to the MOD ahead of Mike and Frank so we could land and pick up the Marine entourage first. Tony and I flew back to the airport and landed, waiting for Mike and Frank who were several minutes behind us.
It was overcast that evening in the eastern Med making it pitch black over the water on the way back to the ship. Mike arrived with his passengers, and we were cleared to return to the Guam. Mike flew lead with only his night rotor tip lights and I took off with no lights on, both of us doing so to avoid visual detection from small arms fire, rocket propelled grenades, shoulder launched SAM's. Flying formation at night behind the same kind of aircraft is difficult enough but behind a dissimilar aircraft after a very long day with only rotor tip lights that were hard to see without being two or three rotor widths away close, was extremely difficult and dangerous. I lost sight of Mike, started a turn away and then I got severe vertigo.

I was so bad that I put the aircraft in a nose down, right turn, but my body just knew I was straight and level. I was about to kill nine Marine passengers and four aircrewmen, including myself. There is that terror that begins when your inner compass is telling you one thing and the gauges are telling you the opposite. I had no idea why the vertical speed indicator was pegged down and why the attitude indicator showed is in a forty-five-degree right hand turn. It didn't make sense but for a split second I began to realize I'd never see Vicky again.

Tony grabbed the controls. I still fought his efforts to save us because of my intense vertigo. Thankfully he was a weightlifter extraordinaire at the time and was able to over-power my continued attempts to kill us all. When he got us straight and level, my head slammed into the pilot's side window due to the severity of my vertigo and not because of lateral g-forces. My MRE turkey loaf meal came right up from my stomach, and I was able to keep it down long enough not to throw up all over the cockpit gauges.

Tony flew us back to the ship and made a beautiful left seat night landing much to the air boss' chagrin and strong words to me over the radio. I didn't care. Tony was going to do one more dangerous thing and land us safely no matter what the air boss wanted. The boss had chewed me out a few times before and I knew all he could do to me was make me cut my hair, make me fly 46's, and send me to Beirut.

That night, our Alpha 1-80 classmate, Tony Morales saved my life and the life of twelve other Marines. I am forever grateful to him. So is Vicky by the way. Thanks!

ABOUT THE AUTHORS

The Basic School Class Alpha 1-80 is comprised of men from many racially and culturally diverse backgrounds. Yet they came together to serve their nation forming a bond that has lasted for more than four decades. Every man among them grew into a better person through Marine Corps training and ensuing careers. The stories are true, a reflection of their times; written by men committed to their families, the Marine Corps and country.

The authors chose to remain anonymous. Why? Each had their own reasons. Maybe because their solidarity with one another would be further strengthened. They are, and have always been, one for all. Ultimately the transparency in the stories was made possible by this decision.

ADZ PRESS BOOKS

ADZ PRESS is honored to be a part of bringing this excellent memoir to the attention of our fellow veterans, their families and friends, and the reading public. We encourage you to leave reviews wherever you purchased this book. Books published by ADZ Press are available on Amazon and through your favorite bookstores.

OTHER BOOKS FROM ADZ PRESS:

BROKEN PROMISES: Marine Combat Veteran Turns Whistleblower Exposing Compromised Mental Health Care For Veterans At VA – LTCOL Ted Blickwedel and Jerome Strayve, JR

Whistleblower, LTCOL Ted Blickwedel chronicles horrific events perpetuated by a callous and uncompassionate VA management. This book is a call to action to never allow such behavior to be visited on our veterans or those who care for them again!

AMAZON: https://www.amazon.com/dp/B0B3YY2ZT3

FIRST SPOUSE OF THE UNITED STATES – JR Strayve JR

In a story that parallels today's political and social unrest, there are no taboo subjects. Follow the sexual and political evolution of a gay activist and his husband's quest for the White House. Washington shenanigans, rabid politicians, relentless media, social change, and the remedy for today's non-functioning legislature are fair game.

Amazon: https://www.amazon.com/dp/B07PNS1FD6

BRAXTON'S CENTURY VOL 1 & 2 – JR Strayve JR

This first two volumes of a four-part saga, spanning from 1860 to 1884. The entire saga features a century of world wars and engineering marvels that one might recognize with requited and unrequited love, romances that defy social morays, death, revolutions, and espionage that creates a world that could have been had Prince Braxton been real heir to the English throne.

AMAZON VOL. 1: https://www.amazon.com/dp/1735546763
AMAZONVOL. 2: https://www.amazon.com/dp/B08YNH7KWX

THE LIEUTENANT & THE VINTNER – JR Strayve JR

A story of forbidden love. When SS Lt. Georg von Reichenau is assigned to the French Burgundy under German occupation in WWII, he is reunited with Andre Beaulieu, a gold-medal-winning Olympian downhill racer. But memory can be fickle. Can there be more to this recollection than either man realizes?

AMAZON: https://www.amazon.com/dp/B08F9N7GW7

VAINGLORIOUS – JR Strayve JR

In this alternative history novella, the life of Grand Duchess Ekaterina is more gilded cage than glitz. She has no choice but to follow her father, the czar's, every command or become "forever indisposed" like her mother. Ekaterina must go to great lengths to try and save herself from the powerful men who control her life. A prequel to Braxton's Century Volume I, set at the glittering Russian court of the early 1880s.

AMAZON: https://www.amazon.com/dp/B096KXS5RW

www.ingramcontent.com/pod-product-compliance
Lightning Source LLC
Chambersburg PA
CBHW020134130526
44590CB00039B/160